Everyday

diabetic LIVING

COOKING

VOLUME 5

DIABETIC LIVING® EVERYDAY COOKING
IS PART OF A BOOK SERIES PUBLISHED BY
BETTER HOMES AND GARDENS SPECIAL
INTEREST MEDIA, DES MOINES, IOWA

Country-Style Peach-Plum Tart,
recipe on page 148

Preparing foods that fit
a diabetes meal plan

requires starting with nutritious ingredients. And knowing how many carbohydrates each food choice contains is necessary for helping to control weight and to balance medications. That's why this collection of good-for-you, lightened-up recipes, each with nutritional analysis and diabetic exchanges, is perfect for you and your family.

These recipes, all crafted by registered dietitians, deliver healthful amounts of calories, carbs, fats, and sodium. And each has been given the Better Homes and Gardens® Test Kitchen seal of approval, which means the recipe has been tested for accuracy and ease of preparation and tastes great. Throughout the book you'll also find tips for health-smart cooking, suggestions for simple serve-alongs, and ideas for tasty recipe variations.

If you're looking for fresh morning dishes (page 104), family-style dinners (page 6), any-time snacks (page 120), sweet treats (page 132), and everything that accompanies them, you'll find delicious menu choices that keep you on track with your meal plan. So page through this mouthwatering assortment of healthful recipes and get ready to create nourishing, balanced meals your family will love.

ON THE COVER:
Sweet Asian Beef Stir-Fry
recipe on page 8

Photographer: Jason Donnelly
Food Stylist: Jill Lust

Everyday COOKING
VOLUME 5

CONSUMER MARKETING

Vice President, Consumer Marketing	DAVID BALL
Consumer Product Marketing Director	STEVE SWANSON
Consumer Product Marketing Manager	WENDY MERICAL
Business Director	RON CLINGMAN
Production Manager	AL RODRUCK
Contributing Editorial Director	SHELLI McCONNELL, PURPLE PEAR PUBLISHING, INC.
Contributing Design Director	JILL BUDDEN
Contributing Photographers	JASON DONNELLY, JASON WALSMITH
Contributing Food Stylist	JILL LUST
Contributing Copy Editor	GRETCHEN KAUFFMAN
Contributing Proofreader	CARRIE SCHMITZ
Test Kitchen Director	LYNN BLANCHARD
Test Kitchen Product Supervisor	ELIZABETH BURT, MPH, R.D., L.D.
Editorial Assistant	LORI EGGERS

SPECIAL INTEREST MEDIA

Editorial Director	GREGORY H. KAYKO
Art Director	TIM ALEXANDER
Managing Editor	DOUG KOUMA

DIABETIC LIVING® MAGAZINE

Art Director, Health	MICHELLE BILYEU
Assistant Art Director, Health	ALEXIS WEST-HUNTOON
Food & Nutrition Editor	JESSIE SHAFER

MEREDITH NATIONAL MEDIA GROUP

President TOM HARTY

Vice President, Production BRUCE HESTON

Chairman and Chief Executive Officer STEPHEN M. LACY

Vice Chairman MELL MEREDITH FRAZIER

In Memoriam — E.T. MEREDITH III (1933-2003)

Diabetic Living® *Everyday Cooking* is part of a series published by Meredith Corp., 1716 Locust St., Des Moines, IA 50309-3023.

If you have comments or questions about the editorial material in *Diabetic Living*® *Everyday Cooking*, write to the editor of *Diabetic Living* magazine, Meredith Corp., 1716 Locust St., Des Moines, IA 50309-3023. Send an e-mail to diabeticlivingmeredith.com or call 800/678-2651. *Diabetic Living* magazine is available by subscription or on the newsstand. To order a subscription to *Diabetic Living* magazine, go to *DiabeticLivingOnline.com.*

contents

3 introduction

6 family-pleasing dinners

40 fresh salad meals

58 comforting soups and stews

76 sensational sandwiches

90 simple sides and salads

104 eye-opening breakfasts

120 good-for-you snacks

132 delightful desserts

154 recipe index

160 metric information

BLT Cups
recipe on page 122

family-pleasing dinners

The pleasure of eating together begins with a meal the entire family will enjoy. From pan-seared steak and roasted pork to stir-fried chicken and grilled fish, here's a collection of recipes that all will savor. And the best part— each entrée is just as healthful as it is delicious.

Beef with Mushrooms and Pearl Onions in Red Wine Reduction

Elegant, easy, and diabetes-friendly— that perfectly describes this flavorful entrée.

SERVINGS 4 (½ steak and ⅔ cup sauce each)
CARB. PER SERVING 11 g

- 2 8-ounce boneless beef top loin steaks, cut ¾ to 1 inch thick
- ½ teaspoon cracked black pepper
- ¼ teaspoon salt
- 1 teaspoon olive oil
- 8 ounces fresh mushrooms, quartered
- 1 cup frozen pearl onions
- 4 cloves garlic, minced
- ¾ cup dry red wine
- 1 cup lower-sodium beef broth
- 2 tablespoons whole wheat flour
- 1 tablespoon snipped fresh parsley

1. Trim fat from steaks. Sprinkle steaks with the pepper and salt. Preheat a large skillet over medium-high heat. Add oil; swirl to lightly coat skillet. Reduce heat to medium. Add steaks; cook for 8 to 10 minutes or until medium rare (145°F), turning once. Transfer steaks to a tray or plate; cover with foil and let stand while preparing sauce.

2. For sauce, in the same skillet cook mushrooms and onions over medium-high heat about 5 minutes or until tender, stirring frequently. Add garlic. Cook for 1 minute more. Remove skillet from heat; add wine. Return skillet to heat. Boil gently, uncovered, for 5 minutes, stirring occasionally. Whisk together broth and flour; add to skillet. Cook and stir until sauce is thickened and bubbly; cook and stir for 1 minute more.

3. Return steaks to skillet; heat through, turning to coat steaks evenly with sauce. Transfer steaks and sauce to serving plates. Sprinkle with parsley.

PER SERVING: 287 cal., 11 g total fat (4 g sat. fat), 64 mg chol., 330 mg sodium, 11 g carb. (2 g fiber, 3 g sugars), 28 g pro. Exchanges: 1 vegetable, 0.5 starch, 3.5 lean meat, 1 fat. Carb choices: 1.

Sweet Asian Beef Stir-Fry

For a change of pace, this slimmed-down stir-fry is served over multigrain pasta instead of rice.

SERVINGS 4 (½ cup cooked spaghetti and 1 cup beef stir-fry each)

CARB. PER SERVING 30 g

- **3** tablespoons low-sugar orange marmalade
- **2** tablespoons light teriyaki sauce
- **2** tablespoons water
- **1** tablespoon grated fresh ginger
- **¼** to ½ teaspoon crushed red pepper
- **3** ounces dried multigrain spaghetti or soba (buckwheat noodles)

- Nonstick cooking spray
- **2** cups small broccoli florets
- **½** of a small red onion, cut into thin wedges
- **1** cup packaged julienned carrots or 2 carrots, cut into thin bite-size strips
- **2** teaspoons canola oil
- **12** ounces boneless beef top sirloin steak, cut into thin bite-size strips*
- **3** cups shredded napa cabbage
- **1** teaspoon sesame seeds, toasted (optional)

1. For sauce, in a small bowl combine marmalade, teriyaki sauce, the water, ginger, and crushed red pepper; set aside. Cook spaghetti according to package directions.

2. Meanwhile, coat an unheated large nonstick skillet or wok with cooking spray. Preheat over medium-high heat. Add broccoli and red onion to hot skillet. Cover and cook for 3 minutes, stirring occasionally. Add carrots; cover and cook for 3 to 4 minutes more or until vegetables are crisp-tender, stirring occasionally. Remove vegetables from skillet.

3. Add oil to the same skillet. Add beef strips. Stir-fry over medium-high heat for 3 to 5 minutes or until beef is slightly pink in center. Return vegetables to skillet along with sauce and cabbage. Cook and stir for 1 to 2 minutes or until heated through and cabbage is just wilted. Serve immediately over the hot cooked spaghetti. If desired, sprinkle with sesame seeds.

*TEST KITCHEN TIP: For easier slicing, partially freeze the steak before cutting it.

PER SERVING: 279 cal., 6 g total fat (2 g sat. fat), 36 mg chol., 259 mg sodium, 30 g carb. (5 g fiber, 8 g sugars), 25 g pro. Exchanges: 2 vegetable, 1 starch, 2.5 lean meat, 1 fat. Carb choices: 2.

Jerk-Seasoned Beef Skewers

Jerk-Seasoned Beef Skewers

If using wooden skewers, soak them in enough water to cover for at least 30 minutes before threading on the beef and vegetables.

SERVINGS 4 (2 skewers each)
CARB. PER SERVING 14 g

¼ cup snipped fresh cilantro
¼ cup rice vinegar
¼ cup orange juice
2 tablespoons canola oil
2 cloves garlic, minced
2 teaspoons Jamaican jerk seasoning
1 pound boneless beef sirloin steak
2 small green sweet peppers, cut into 2-inch pieces
1 medium onion, cut into thin wedges
2 medium oranges, cut into 8 wedges each

1. For marinade, in a medium bowl whisk together cilantro, vinegar, orange juice, oil, garlic, and jerk seasoning. Pour mixture into a large resealable plastic bag set in a deep bowl. Trim fat from beef; cut beef into 1-inch cubes. Add beef, pepper pieces, and onion wedges. Seal bag; turn to coat meat. Marinate in the refrigerator for 4 to 6 hours, turning occasionally.

2. Drain meat and vegetables, discarding marinade. On eight 10- to 12-inch skewers alternately thread beef, pepper pieces, onion wedges, and orange wedges, leaving a ¼-inch space between pieces.

3. For a charcoal grill, place kabobs on the grill rack directly over medium coals. Grill, uncovered, for 8 to 10 minutes or until beef pieces are slightly pink in the centers, turning occasionally. (For a gas grill, preheat grill. Reduce heat to medium. Place kabobs on grill rack over heat. Cover and grill as above.)

PER SERVING: 242 cal., 9 g total fat (2 g sat. fat), 53 mg chol., 144 mg sodium, 14 g carb. (3 g fiber, 9 g sugars), 26 g pro. Exchanges: 1 vegetable, 0.5 fruit, 3.5 lean meat, 1 fat. Carb choices: 1.

Chicken-Fried Steak

The key to ensuring that the coating gets crispy
is to use a very large nonstick skillet
so all the steak pieces fit in a single layer.

SERVINGS 4 (1 steak and about 3 tablespoons gravy each)

CARB. PER SERVING 22 g

- 4 4- to 5-ounce boneless beef chuck top blade (flat iron) steaks or cube steaks, cut ½ inch thick
- ⅓ cup flour
- ½ teaspoon Montreal or Kansas City steak seasoning
- ¼ teaspoon salt
- ¼ cup refrigerated or frozen egg product, thawed
- 2 tablespoons fat-free milk
- 1 cup crushed cornflakes (2 cups whole flakes)
   Nonstick cooking spray
- 1 teaspoon butter
- ¼ cup finely chopped onion
- 1 clove garlic, minced
- 1 tablespoon bourbon (optional)
- ¾ cup fat-free milk
- 1 tablespoon flour
- ¼ teaspoon Montreal or Kansas City steak seasoning
   Freshly ground black pepper (optional)

1. Trim fat from steaks. If necessary, place each steak between two pieces of plastic wrap and pound lightly with the flat side of a meat mallet until ½ inch thick; remove plastic wrap.

2. In a shallow dish combine the ⅓ cup flour, the ½ teaspoon steak seasoning, and the salt. In another shallow dish combine egg and the 2 tablespoons milk. Place crushed cornflakes in a third shallow dish. Dip steaks into flour mixture, turning to coat evenly. Dip into egg mixture, then into cornflakes, turning to coat evenly.

3. Coat an unheated very large nonstick skillet with cooking spray; heat skillet over medium-high heat. Add steaks to skillet. Cook for 10 to 12 minutes for medium rare (145°F) to medium (160°F), turning once halfway through cooking. If steaks brown too quickly, reduce heat to medium. Remove steaks from skillet; cover to keep warm.

4. For gravy, in the same skillet melt butter over medium heat. Add onion and garlic to skillet; cook for 3 to 5 minutes or until onion is tender, stirring occasionally. If desired, add bourbon, stirring to scrape up any crusty browned bits. In a small bowl whisk together the ¾ cup milk, 1 tablespoon flour, and

¼ teaspoon steak seasoning until smooth. Add milk mixture all at once to onion mixture. Cook and stir until thickened and bubbly. Cook and stir for 1 minute more.

5. Serve steaks with gravy. If desired, sprinkle with pepper.

PER SERVING: 317 cal., 13 g total fat (5 g sat. fat), 78 mg chol., 400 mg sodium, 22 g carb. (1 g fiber, 4 g sugars), 27 g pro. Exchanges: 1.5 starch, 3.5 lean meat, 1 fat. Carb choices: 1.5.

Spiced Bulgur with Beef and Mango

Maximize prep time by cutting up the beef, mango,
and vegetables while the bulgur is standing.

SERVINGS 4 (scant ½ cup bulgur and ⅔ cup toppers each)

CARB. PER SERVING 25 g

- 1 cup reduced-sodium chicken broth
- ⅔ cup bulgur
- 1 clove garlic, minced
- ½ teaspoon ground cumin
- ¼ teaspoon ground coriander
- ⅛ teaspoon ground cinnamon
- ⅛ teaspoon cayenne pepper
- 6 ounces lower-sodium deli roast beef, cut into thin strips
- ½ of a medium mango, peeled and coarsely chopped
- ½ cup fresh pea pods, halved crosswise
- 2 green onions, sliced
- ¼ cup snipped fresh cilantro
- ¼ cup unsalted peanuts, chopped (optional)

1. In a 1½-quart microwave-safe casserole combine broth, uncooked bulgur, garlic, cumin, coriander, cinnamon, and cayenne pepper. Microwave, covered, on 100 percent power (high) about 4 minutes or until mixture is boiling. Remove from microwave. Let stand about 20 minutes or until bulgur is tender. Drain if necessary.

2. Divide bulgur mixture among four serving bowls. Top with beef, mango, pea pods, green onions, cilantro, and, if desired, peanuts.

PER SERVING: 164 cal., 2 g total fat (1 g sat. fat), 26 mg chol., 421 mg sodium, 25 g carb. (5 g fiber, 5 g sugars), 13 g pro. Exchanges: 1.5 starch, 1.5 lean meat. Carb choices: 1.5.

QUICK TIP ◖
For a little zing, squeeze a wedge of lime over this saladlike entrée and then toss the mixture.

Spiced Bulgur with
Beef and Mango

Italian Beef and Polenta

*For lump-free polenta, use a wire whisk to
stir the mixture in the saucepan.*

SERVINGS 4 (3 ounces cooked steak, 1 cup vegetables,
and ⅓ cup polenta each)
CARB. PER SERVING 29 g

- 1 **pound boneless beef tri-tip steak, 1 to 1½ inches thick**
- ¼ **teaspoon salt**
- ¼ **teaspoon black pepper**
- 1 **tablespoon olive oil**
- 2 **cups red sweet pepper strips**
- 2 **cups trimmed fresh green beans**
- ¾ **cup instant polenta**
- 2 **tablespoons finely shredded Parmesan cheese**
- 2 **teaspoons snipped fresh oregano**

1. Preheat broiler. Trim fat from steak. Cut steak into four portions; sprinkle with salt and black pepper. Place steak portions on the unheated rack of a broiler pan. Broil 3 to 4 inches from the heat for 9 to 15 minutes or to desired doneness, turning once halfway through broiling. Cover and let stand for 5 minutes.

2. Meanwhile, in a large skillet heat olive oil over medium-high heat. Add sweet pepper strips and green beans; reduce heat to medium. Cook and stir for 8 to 10 minutes or until vegetables are tender.

3. Prepare polenta according to package directions. Stir in Parmesan cheese and 1 teaspoon of the oregano.

4. To serve, stir the remaining 1 teaspoon oregano into the vegetables. Divide polenta and vegetable mixture among four dinner plates; top with sliced steak.

PER SERVING: 328 cal., 11 g total fat (3 g sat. fat), 48 mg chol., 254 mg sodium, 29 g carb. (5 g fiber, 4 g sugars), 27 g pro. Exchanges: 1 vegetable, 1.5 starch, 3 lean meat, 1 fat. Carb choices: 2.

Italian Beef
and Polenta

Classic Diner
Meat Loaf

Classic Diner Meat Loaf

Buy the leanest ground beef you can find
for this comfort-food favorite.

SERVINGS 8 (1 slice each)
CARB. PER SERVING 8 g

⅔ cup fat-free milk
½ cup refrigerated or frozen egg product, thawed, or
   3 egg whites
2 cups soft whole wheat bread crumbs
2 green onions, thinly sliced
1 tablespoon Worcestershire sauce
1 teaspoon dried thyme or oregano, crushed
¼ teaspoon salt
⅛ teaspoon black pepper
1½ pounds 90% or higher lean ground beef
¼ cup ketchup
1 tablespoon balsamic vinegar
1 clove garlic, minced

1. Preheat oven to 350°F. Line a 2-quart rectangular baking dish with foil; set aside. In a large bowl combine milk and egg. Stir in bread crumbs, green onions, Worcestershire sauce, thyme, salt, and pepper. Add ground beef; mix well. Shape meat mixture into an 8×5-inch rectangle in the prepared baking dish.
2. Bake for 50 minutes. Spoon off fat. In a small bowl combine ketchup, vinegar, and garlic. Spread over meat loaf. Bake about 10 minutes more or until meat is done (160°F).
3. Let stand for 10 minutes before serving. Spoon off any fat. Cut into slices.
PER SERVING: 197 cal., 9 g total fat (4 g sat. fat), 56 mg chol., 308 mg sodium, 8 g carb. (1 g fiber, 4 g sugars), 20 g pro. Exchanges: 0.5 starch, 2.5 lean meat, 1 fat. Carb choices: 0.5.

Baked Corn Dogs

Believe it! These corn dogs do fit into a diabetes meal plan.
Using reduced-fat franks and baking rather than
frying are the keys.

SERVINGS 6 (1 corn dog each)
CARB. PER SERVING 29 g or 27 g

Nonstick cooking spray
¾ cup flour
⅓ cup yellow cornmeal
1 tablespoon sugar*

1 teaspoon baking powder
¼ teaspoon dry mustard
⅛ teaspoon salt
⅓ cup fat-fee milk
1 egg, lightly beaten
1 teaspoon canola oil
6 wooden skewers
6 reduced-fat frankfurters
Yellow mustard (optional)

1. Preheat oven to 400°F. Lightly coat a baking sheet with cooking spray; set aside. For batter, in a medium bowl stir together flour, cornmeal, sugar, baking powder, dry mustard, and salt. In a small bowl combine milk, egg, and oil. Add milk mixture to flour mixture; mix just until combined (mixture will be thick).
2. Pat frankfurters dry with paper towels. Insert wooden skewers into ends of the frankfurters. Holding on to skewer, rotate each frankfurter over bowl and spread batter to coat frankfurter evenly. Place on prepared baking sheet. Bake for 14 to 16 minutes or until golden brown. If desired, serve with yellow mustard.
*SUGAR SUBSTITUTES: Choose from Splenda Granular, Equal Spoonful or packets, or Sweet'N Low bulk or packets. Follow package directions to use product amount equivalent to 1 tablespoon sugar.
PER SERVING: 189 cal., 4 g total fat (1 g sat. fat), 56 mg chol., 567 mg sodium, 29 g carb. (1 g fiber, 5 g sugars), 10 g pro. Exchanges: 2 starch, 0.5 medium-fat meat. Carb choices: 2.
PER SERVING WITH SUBSTITUTE: Same as above, except 181 cal., 27 g carb. (3 g sugars).

Pork Scaloppini in White Wine Sauce

Use cooked baby carrots as a bed for serving these tender pork slices and perfectly seasoned wine sauce.

SERVINGS 4 (about 3 ounces cooked meat and ¼ cup sauce each)

CARB. PER SERVING 8 g

- 1 1-pound pork tenderloin
- ¼ teaspoon black pepper
- 3 tablespoons whole wheat flour
- 4 teaspoons olive oil
- 2 cloves garlic, minced
- ½ cup dry white wine or reduced-sodium chicken broth
- 2 teaspoons snipped fresh sage or ½ teaspoon dried sage, crushed
- 1 teaspoon snipped fresh rosemary or ¼ teaspoon dried rosemary, crushed
- 1 cup reduced-sodium chicken broth
- 2 tablespoons cold water
- 1 tablespoon cornstarch
- 2 tablespoons snipped fresh parsley (optional)

1. Trim fat from meat. Cut meat into ½-inch slices. Place each slice between two pieces of plastic wrap. Using the flat side of a meat mallet, pound meat lightly until ¼ inch thick. Remove plastic wrap. Sprinkle meat with pepper. Place flour in a shallow dish. Dip meat into flour, turning to coat evenly.

2. In a very large skillet heat 2 teaspoons of the oil over medium-high heat. Add half of the meat to skillet. Cook about 4 minutes or until meat is browned, turning once halfway through cooking. Remove meat from skillet; cover to keep warm.

3. Add the remaining 2 teaspoons oil to skillet; cook the remaining meat as directed above. Remove from skillet; cover to keep warm.

4. For sauce, add garlic to the same skillet; cook and stir for 30 seconds. Add wine, sage, and rosemary; cook and stir for 2 minutes. Add broth; return meat to skillet. Bring just to boiling. Cook, uncovered, for 2 minutes. In a small bowl stir together the water and cornstarch; stir into broth mixture. Cook and stir for 2 minutes more.

5. Transfer meat to four serving plates; top with sauce. If desired, sprinkle with parsley.

PER SERVING: 220 cal., 7 g total fat (1 g sat. fat), 73 mg chol., 199 mg sodium, 8 g carb. (1 g fiber, 1 g sugars), 25 g pro. Exchanges: 0.5 starch, 3.5 lean meat, 0.5 fat. Carb choices: 0.5.

Mole-Style Pork and Tamale Pie

Cocoa powder, chipotle chile pepper, cumin, and cinnamon team up to give this corn bread-topped pork pie rich Tex-Mex flavor without adding a lot of carbs, calories, or fat.

SERVINGS 6 (1 cup each)

CARB. PER SERVING 26 g

Nonstick cooking spray
- 1 large onion, chopped (1 cup)
- 1 small red sweet pepper, chopped (½ cup)
- 4 cloves garlic, minced
- 1 8-ounce can tomato sauce
- 1 tablespoon unsweetened cocoa powder
- 1 to 2 teaspoons chopped canned chipotle pepper in adobo sauce*
- ½ teaspoon ground cumin
- ¼ teaspoon ground cinnamon
- 4 teaspoons canola oil
- 1 pound boneless pork loin roast, cut into ½-inch cubes
- 2 medium zucchini, chopped (about 3 cups)
- ¾ cup fat-free milk
- ½ cup refrigerated or frozen egg product, thawed, or 2 eggs
- ½ cup flour
- ½ cup yellow cornmeal
- ¼ teaspoon salt

Pork Scaloppini
in White Wine Sauce

Mole-Style Pork
and Tamale Pie

1. Preheat oven to 400°F. Coat an unheated oven-going large skillet with cooking spray. Preheat skillet over medium heat. Add onion, sweet pepper, and garlic; cook about 5 minutes or until just tender, stirring occasionally. Transfer half of the onion mixture to a blender or food processor. Add tomato sauce, cocoa powder, chipotle pepper, cumin, and cinnamon. Cover and blend or process until smooth. Set aside.

2. Add 2 teaspoons of the oil to the remaining onion mixture in skillet. Add pork and zucchini; cook over medium heat for 4 to 6 minutes or until pork is no longer pink and zucchini is just tender, stirring occasionally. Drain off liquid if necessary. Stir in blended sauce; heat to boiling. Spread in an even layer.

3. Meanwhile, in a medium bowl whisk together milk, egg, and the remaining 2 teaspoons oil. Whisk in flour,

cornmeal, and salt until smooth. Pour flour mixture evenly over pork mixture in skillet, covering completely.

4. Bake, uncovered, for 30 to 35 minutes or until topping is set and filling bubbles at the edges. Serve immediately.

*TEST KITCHEN TIP: Because chile peppers contain volatile oils that can burn your skin and eyes, avoid direct contact with them as much as possible. When working with chile peppers, wear plastic or rubber gloves. If your bare hands do touch the peppers, wash your hands and nails well with soap and warm water.

PER SERVING: 262 cal., 7 g total fat (1 g sat. fat), 48 mg chol., 371 mg sodium, 26 g carb. (3 g fiber, 5 g sugars), 24 g pro. Exchanges: 1 vegetable, 1.5 starch, 2.5 lean meat, 0.5 fat. Carb choices: 2.

Mushroom-Tomato-Stuffed Pork Loin

Round out the meal by serving the savory pork with a simple salad. Fresh spinach studded with cherry tomato wedges and drizzled with a bottled vinaigrette dressing fills the bill.

SERVINGS 6 (⅙ of roast each)

CARB. PER SERVING 10 g

- 1 large portobello mushroom (about 6 ounces) or 2 cups button mushrooms
- ½ of a medium fresh poblano chile pepper, seeded and chopped* (about ½ cup)
- 1 medium onion, chopped (½ cup)
- 3 cloves garlic, minced
- 2 teaspoons olive oil
- ¾ cup reduced-sodium chicken broth
- ¼ cup quick-cooking (hominy) grits
- 2 tablespoons snipped dried tomatoes (not oil-pack)
- 1 1½- to 2-pound boneless pork loin roast
- ¼ teaspoon black pepper

Mushroom-Tomato-Stuffed Pork Loin

1. Remove stem from portobello mushroom if using; if desired, scrape out scales. Chop mushroom. (Or if using button mushrooms, chop mushrooms.) In a large nonstick skillet cook chopped mushrooms, chile pepper, onion, and garlic in hot oil over medium heat for 5 to 8 minutes or until tender, stirring occasionally. Remove mixture from skillet; set aside.

2. In the same skillet bring broth to boiling. Gradually stir in grits; stir in tomatoes. Reduce heat to low. Cook, uncovered, for 2 to 3 minutes or until thick, stirring frequently. Remove from heat and stir in mushroom mixture. Set aside.

3. Preheat oven to 350°F. Trim fat from roast. Place roast on cutting board with one end toward you. Using a long sharp knife, make a lengthwise cut 1 inch in from the left side of the roast, cutting down to about 1 inch from the bottom of the roast. Turn the knife and cut to the right, as if forming the letter L; stop when you get to about 1 inch from the right side of the roast.

4. Open up the roast so it lies nearly flat on the cutting board. Place a large piece of plastic wrap over the roast. Using the flat side of a meat mallet, pound meat to ¼- to ½-inch thickness. Discard plastic wrap. Spread mushroom mixture over meat, leaving a 1-inch border around the edge. Starting from one of the long sides, roll meat around filling. Using 100-percent-cotton kitchen string, tie securely at 1½-inch intervals. Sprinkle meat with black pepper. Place on a rack in a shallow roasting pan.

5. Insert an oven-going meat thermometer into center of meat. Roast, uncovered, for 40 to 45 minutes or until thermometer registers 145°F. Let meat stand for 3 minutes before serving.

*****TEST KITCHEN TIP:** Because chile peppers contain volatile oils that can burn your skin and eyes, avoid direct contact with them as much as possible. When working with chile peppers, wear plastic or rubber gloves. If your bare hands do touch the peppers, wash your hands and nails well with soap and warm water.

PER SERVING: 209 cal., 6 g total fat (2 g sat. fat), 71 mg chol., 153 mg sodium, 10 g carb. (1 g fiber, 2 g sugars), 28 g pro. Exchanges: 0.5 vegetable, 0.5 starch, 3.5 lean meat. Carb choices: 0.5.

Chicken Cacciatore

Chicken Cacciatore

The red wine and white wine vinegar give this chicken-and-veggie combo a tantalizing tang. Besides great flavor, one serving delivers 242 percent of the vitamin A you need in a day.

SERVINGS 4 (2 pieces chicken and 1⅔ cups vegetable sauce each)

CARB. PER SERVING 30 g

⅓ **cup flour**
2 **pounds chicken thighs and/or drumsticks, skinned (8 pieces)**
¼ **teaspoon kosher salt or sea salt**
⅛ **teaspoon freshly ground black pepper**
2 **tablespoons olive oil**
4 **small carrots, peeled and cut crosswise into thirds**
3 **stalks celery, cut crosswise into quarters**
1 **medium onion, coarsely chopped (½ cup)**
8 **cloves garlic, peeled and thinly sliced**
¼ **cup tomato paste**
1 **cup reduced-sodium chicken broth**
1 **cup dry red wine or cranberry juice**
2 **tablespoons white wine vinegar**
6 **medium roma tomatoes, coarsely chopped**
1 **tablespoon snipped fresh thyme or 1 teaspoon dried thyme, crushed**
2 **tablespoons freshly grated Parmesan cheese**
2 **tablespoons snipped fresh Italian (flat-leaf) parsley**

1. Spread flour in a shallow dish. Season chicken pieces with the salt and pepper. Dip chicken in the flour, turning to coat evenly and gently shaking off excess.
2. In a 5-quart Dutch oven heat oil over medium-high heat. Add chicken pieces; cook about 6 minutes or until browned, turning occasionally.
3. Remove chicken from Dutch oven; set aside. Drain off fat, reserving 2 tablespoons in the Dutch oven. Add carrots, celery, onion, and garlic. Cook about 5 minutes or just until onion is tender, stirring occasionally.
4. Stir in tomato paste. Add broth, wine, and vinegar; bring to boiling. Add tomatoes and thyme. Return chicken to Dutch oven. Bring to boiling; reduce heat. Simmer, covered, for 60 to 70 minutes or until chicken and vegetables are tender.
5. To serve, place chicken, vegetables, and cooking juices on a serving platter. Sprinkle with Parmesan cheese and parsley.

PER SERVING: 407 cal., 13 g total fat (3 g sat. fat), 109 mg chol., 600 mg sodium, 30 g carb. (6 g fiber, 11 g sugars), 32 g pro. Exchanges: 2.5 vegetable, 1 carb., 4 lean meat, 2 fat. Carb choices: 2.

Sautéed Chicken Breasts
with Simple Chive Sauce

Jerk Braised Chicken Thighs
with Sweet Potatoes

Mediterranean
Stuffed Chicken

recipe on page 20

Heat 'n' Eat

Although meals cooked from scratch are generally the most nutritious, it's OK to eat carefully chosen frozen meals a couple of times a week. Avoid frosty fingertips in the freezer section by taking a look at these tips before leaving home.

1. **Scope out** frozen dinners' nutrition information online so you don't have to comparison shop in the chilly freezer section.

2. **Don't toss** the brands known for better nutrition in your cart without checking the nutrition label.

3. **Check the amount** of sodium in the dinner first; some entrées contain 1,500 milligrams or more. Find meals with 600 milligrams of sodium or less.

4. **Pick meals** with up to 45–60 grams of carbohydrate (based on your meal plan) and 3 grams of fiber or more.

5. **Choose frozen dinners** with 400 calories or less and 10 grams of total fat or less.

Jerk Braised Chicken Thighs with Sweet Potatoes

Jerk seasoning—a bodacious blend of chile peppers, herbs, and sweet spices—infuses chicken thighs and sweet potatoes with an intriguing, sweet-hot kick.

SERVINGS 4 (2 chicken thighs and ½ cup potatoes each)

CARB. PER SERVING 20 g

- 8 chicken thighs, skinned
- ¼ teaspoon salt
- ¼ teaspoon black pepper
- 1 tablespoon olive oil
- 1 medium onion, halved and thinly sliced
- 1 tablespoon grated fresh ginger
- 2 cloves garlic, minced
- 1 cup reduced-sodium chicken broth
- 2 teaspoons Jamaican jerk seasoning
- 2 small sweet potatoes, peeled, halved lengthwise, and sliced ½ inch thick (about 1 pound)
  Snipped fresh cilantro

1. Sprinkle chicken thighs with salt and pepper. In a very large skillet heat oil over medium-high heat. Add chicken; cook until browned on both sides. Remove chicken from skillet. Drain fat; reserving 1 tablespoon in the skillet.
2. In the same skillet cook onion, ginger, and garlic in the reserved fat. Cook and stir about 4 minutes or until tender. Add broth, stirring to scrape up any browned bits from bottom of skillet. Bring to boiling.
3. Return chicken to skillet. Sprinkle chicken with jerk seasoning. Return to boiling; reduce heat. Simmer, covered, for 20 minutes. Add sweet potatoes to skillet. Simmer, covered, about 15 minutes more or until chicken is done (180°F) and sweet potatoes are tender. Sprinkle with cilantro.

PER SERVING: 283 cal., 9 g total fat (2 g sat. fat), 115 mg chol., 604 mg sodium, 20 g carb. (3 g fiber, 5 g sugars), 30 g pro. Exchanges: 1 starch, 4 lean meat, 0.5 fat. Carb choices: 1.

Sautéed Chicken Breasts with Simple Chive Sauce

For a quick and colorful side dish, cut up some garden-fresh vegetables to stir-fry.

SERVINGS 4 (1 chicken breast and 3 tablespoons sauce each)

CARB. PER SERVING 9 g

- 4 4-ounce skinless, boneless chicken breast halves
- ¼ teaspoon salt
- ¼ teaspoon black pepper
- 3 tablespoons whole wheat flour
- 1 tablespoon olive oil
- ½ cup finely chopped shallots
- ½ cup dry white wine or reduced-sodium chicken broth
- 1 cup reduced-sodium chicken broth
- 1 tablespoon snipped fresh chives

1. Sprinkle chicken breasts with salt and pepper. Place flour in a shallow dish; dip chicken in flour, turning to coat all sides.
2. Preheat a large skillet over medium-high heat. Add oil to skillet; swirl to lightly coat skillet. Add chicken breast halves, smooth sides down; cook about 5 minutes or until the chicken is golden brown.
3. Turn chicken; cook for 4 to 5 minutes more or until chicken is no longer pink (170°F). Transfer chicken to a warm serving platter; set aside.
4. For sauce, add shallots to hot skillet; cook for 2 minutes, stirring frequently. Carefully add wine; cook about 1 minute more or until the liquid is reduced by half, stirring to scrape up any browned bits from bottom of skillet.
5. Add the 1 cup chicken broth to skillet; cook for 3 to 4 minutes or until liquid is reduced by half. Stir in chives. Return chicken to skillet; heat about 30 seconds. Serve immediately.

PER SERVING: 217 cal., 5 g total fat (1 g sat. fat), 66 mg chol., 366 mg sodium, 9 g carb. (1 g fiber, 1 g sugars), 28 g pro. Exchanges: 0.5 starch, 3.5 lean meat. Carb choices: 0.5.

Mediterranean Stuffed Chicken

Rich in vitamin C and antioxidants, artichoke hearts lend a touch of sophistication and wonderful flavor to this veggie- and cheese-stuffed chicken. Pictured on page 18.

SERVINGS 4 (1 breast half each)
CARB. PER SERVING 2 g

- 4 skinless, boneless chicken breast halves (1 to 1½ pounds total)
- ¼ cup crumbled reduced-fat feta cheese (1 ounce)
- ¼ cup finely chopped, drained bottled marinated artichoke hearts
- 2 tablespoons finely chopped, drained bottled roasted red sweet peppers
- 2 tablespoons thinly sliced green onion (1)
- 2 teaspoons snipped fresh oregano or ½ teaspoon dried oregano, crushed
- ⅛ teaspoon black pepper
  Nonstick cooking spray

1. Using a sharp knife, cut a pocket in each chicken breast half by cutting horizontally through the thickest portion to, but not through, the opposite side. Set aside.
2. In a small bowl combine feta, artichoke hearts, roasted peppers, green onion, and oregano. Spoon evenly into pockets in chicken breasts. If necessary, secure openings with wooden toothpicks. Sprinkle chicken with black pepper.
3. Coat an unheated large nonstick skillet with cooking spray. Preheat skillet over medium heat. Add chicken. Cook for 12 to 14 minutes or until no longer pink (170°F), turning once.
GRILLING DIRECTIONS: For a charcoal grill, grill chicken on the rack of an uncovered grill directly over medium coals for 12 to 15 minutes or until chicken is no longer pink (170°F), turning once halfway through grilling. (For a gas grill, preheat grill. Reduce heat to medium. Place chicken on grill rack over heat. Cover and grill as above.)
PER SERVING: 171 cal., 5 g total fat (2 g sat. fat), 68 mg chol., 226 mg sodium, 2 g carb. (0 g fiber, 3 g sugars), 28 g pro. Exchanges: 4 lean meat, 1 fat. Carb choices: 0.

Pumpkin, Bean, and Chicken Enchiladas

You'll find pico de gallo or fresh salsa in the produce section at the supermarket.

SERVINGS 4 (2 enchiladas each)
CARB. PER SERVING 44 g

  Nonstick cooking spray
- 1 medium onion, chopped (½ cup)
- 1 fresh jalapeño chile pepper, seeded and finely chopped*
- 2 teaspoons olive oil
- 1 15-ounce can pumpkin
- 1½ to 1¾ cups water
- 1 teaspoon chili powder
- ½ teaspoon salt
- ½ teaspoon ground cumin
- 1 cup no-salt-added red kidney beans, rinsed and drained
- 1½ cups shredded cooked chicken breast
- ½ cup shredded part-skim mozzarella cheese (2 ounces)
- 8 6-inch white corn tortillas, softened
  Pico de gallo or salsa (optional)

1. Preheat oven to 400°F. Lightly coat a 2-quart rectangular baking dish with cooking spray; set aside. In a medium saucepan cook and stir onion and chile pepper in hot oil over medium-high heat about 5 minutes or until onion is tender. Stir in pumpkin, 1½ cups of the water, the chili powder, salt, and cumin. Cook and stir until heated through. If necessary, stir in enough of the remaining ¼ cup water to reach desired consistency.
2. In a large bowl slightly mash beans. Stir in half of the pumpkin mixture, the cooked chicken, and ¼ cup of the cheese.
3. Spoon a generous ⅓ cup of the bean mixture onto each tortilla. Roll up tortillas; place, seam sides down, in the prepared baking dish. Pour the remaining pumpkin mixture over tortilla roll-ups.
4. Bake, covered, for 15 minutes. Sprinkle with the remaining ¼ cup cheese. Bake, uncovered, about 10 minutes more or until heated through. If desired, serve with pico de gallo.
*TEST KITCHEN TIP: Because chile peppers contain volatile oils that can burn your skin and eyes, avoid direct contact with them as much as possible. When working with chile peppers, wear plastic or rubber gloves. If your bare hands do touch the peppers, wash your hands and nails well with soap and warm water.
PER SERVING: 357 cal., 8 g total fat (3 g sat. fat), 54 mg chol., 465 mg sodium, 44 g carb. (12 g fiber, 5 g sugars), 28 g pro. Exchanges: 1 vegetable, 2.5 starch, 2.5 lean meat, 0.5 fat. Carb choices: 3.

QUICK TIP

Corn tortillas are easier to work with if they are soft and pliable. To soften, place tortillas between paper towels. Microwave on 100 percent power (high) for 30 to 40 seconds.

Pumpkin, Bean, and Chicken Enchiladas

Red Beans and
Rice with Chicken

Chicken-Peanut Stir-Fry

When stir-frying, use a wooden spoon to gently toss ingredients to keep them moving and cooking evenly.

SERVINGS 4 (1¼ cups each)
CARB. PER SERVING 34 g

- 4 ounces banh pho (Vietnamese wide rice noodles)
- ½ teaspoon finely shredded lime peel
- 3 tablespoons lime juice
- 2 tablespoons peanut butter
- 1 tablespoon fish sauce
- 1 tablespoon water
- 4 cloves garlic, minced
- 2 teaspoons Asian chile bean sauce or ½ teaspoon crushed red pepper
- 3 teaspoons canola oil
- 1 pound skinless, boneless chicken breast, cut into bite-size strips
- 1 medium red sweet pepper, cut into thin bite-size strips (1 cup)
- 3 green onions, thinly sliced, with green tops separated from white bottoms
- 2 cups packaged shredded broccoli (broccoli slaw mix)
- 2 tablespoons unsalted peanuts, finely chopped

1. Fill a large saucepan half-full with water; bring to boiling. Remove saucepan from heat. Add noodles; let stand for 8 minutes. Drain well in a colander.

2. For sauce, in a small bowl combine lime peel, lime juice, peanut butter, fish sauce, the 1 tablespoon water, the garlic, and bean sauce. Whisk together well until smooth; set aside.

3. In a very large nonstick skillet or large nonstick wok heat 2 teaspoons of the oil over medium-high heat. Add chicken; stir-fry for 4 to 6 minutes or until chicken is no longer pink. Transfer chicken to a bowl.

4. Add the remaining 1 teaspoon oil to the skillet. Add sweet pepper and stir-fry for 2 minutes. Add drained noodles and white bottoms of green onions. Stir-fry for 2 minutes. Add broccoli, sauce, and chicken. Cook and stir until heated through. Sprinkle with green onion tops and peanuts. Divide mixture among four serving plates.

PER SERVING: 368 cal., 11 g total fat (2 g sat. fat), 66 mg chol., 556 mg sodium, 34 g carb. (3 g fiber, 4 g sugars), 32 g pro. Exchanges: 1 vegetable, 2 starch, 3.5 lean meat, 1 fat. Carb choices: 2.

Red Beans and Rice with Chicken

You need only 20 minutes to get this Mexican-style one-dish dinner from the stove top to the table.

SERVINGS 4 (1 cup each)
CARB. PER SERVING 30 g

- 10 ounces skinless, boneless chicken breast, cut into 1-inch pieces
- ¼ teaspoon salt
- ¼ teaspoon black pepper
- 1 medium green sweet pepper, coarsely chopped (¾ cup)
- 1 medium onion, chopped (½ cup)
- 2 cloves garlic, minced
- 1 tablespoon olive oil
- 1 15-ounce can no-salt-added red beans, rinsed and drained
- 1 1-cup container ready-to-serve cooked brown rice
- ¼ cup reduced-sodium chicken broth
- ½ teaspoon ground cumin
- ¼ teaspoon cayenne pepper
  Lime wedges
  Cayenne pepper (optional)

1. Sprinkle chicken with salt and black pepper. In a large skillet cook and stir chicken, sweet pepper, onion, and garlic in hot oil over medium-high heat for 8 to 10 minutes or until chicken is no longer pink and vegetables are tender.

2. Stir beans, rice, broth, cumin, and the ¼ teaspoon cayenne pepper into chicken mixture in skillet. Heat through. Serve with lime wedges. If desired, sprinkle with additional cayenne pepper.

PER SERVING: 272 cal., 5 g total fat (1 g sat. fat), 41 mg chol., 311 mg sodium, 30 g carb. (10 g fiber, 2 g sugars), 25 g pro. Exchanges: 0.5 vegetable, 2 starch, 2.5 lean meat. Carb choices: 2.

Mushroom and Chicken Stroganoff

Mushroom and Chicken Stroganoff

Looking for ways to use up leftover rotisserie chicken?
Try it in this family-favorite dish.

SERVINGS 6 (½ cup noodles and ⅔ cup chicken mixture each)
CARB. PER SERVING 29 g

- 1 8-ounce carton light sour cream
- 2 tablespoons flour
- 1 tablespoon Worcestershire-style marinade for chicken
- ½ teaspoon dried thyme, crushed
- ½ teaspoon instant chicken bouillon granules
- ¼ teaspoon black pepper
- ½ cup water
- 1 8-ounce package fresh mushrooms, sliced
- 1 medium onion, chopped (½ cup)
- 2 cloves garlic, minced
- 1 tablespoon canola oil or olive oil
- 2½ cups coarsely shredded cooked chicken
- 3 cups hot cooked egg noodles
- 1 tomato, chopped

1. In a small bowl combine ⅔ cup of the sour cream, the flour, Worcestershire-style marinade, thyme, bouillon granules, and pepper. Gradually stir in the water until combined. Set aside.
2. In very large skillet cook mushrooms, onion, and garlic in hot oil over medium-high heat until tender, stirring occasionally. Stir in chicken.
3. Add sour cream mixture to skillet; cook and stir until thickened and bubbly. Reduce heat; cook and stir for 2 minutes more.
4. Serve chicken mixture over noodles; top with remaining sour cream and chopped tomato.
PER SERVING: 322 cal., 12 g total fat (4 g sat. fat), 88 mg chol., 191 mg sodium, 29 g carb. (2 g fiber, 3 g sugars), 24 g pro. Exchanges: 0.5 vegetable, 1.5 starch, 2.5 lean meat, 1.5 fat. Carb choices: 2.

Tandoori-Style Turkey Kabobs

Turn the bag of turkey in marinade a few times
to keep the cubes coated with the creamy mixture.

SERVINGS 4 (5 ounces cooked turkey and ⅔ cup salad each)
CARB. PER SERVING 34 g

- ¾ cup plain low-fat yogurt
- 2 teaspoons finely shredded lime peel
- 3 tablespoons lime juice
- 1 tablespoon bottled minced garlic
- 1 tablespoon bottled minced ginger
- ½ of a fresh serrano chile pepper, seeded and finely chopped*
- 2 teaspoons paprika
- 1 teaspoon ground cumin
- ½ teaspoon ground coriander
- ½ teaspoon ground cardamom
- ¼ teaspoon cayenne pepper
- 1½ pounds turkey tenderloins, cut into 1½-inch cubes
- 1 recipe Carrot-Radish Salad
- Lime wedges (optional)
- Green onion strips (optional)

1. For marinade, in a small bowl combine yogurt, lime peel, lime juice, garlic, ginger, serrano pepper, paprika, cumin, coriander, cardamom, and cayenne pepper.
2. Place turkey cubes in a large resealable plastic bag set in a shallow dish. Add marinade. Seal bag and turn to coat cubes well. Marinate in the refrigerator for at least 4 hours or up to 24 hours. Prepare Carrot-Radish Salad; cover and chill.
3. Remove turkey from marinade, discarding marinade. Thread cubes onto 6- to 8-inch skewers,** leaving a ¼-inch space between cubes.
4. For a charcoal grill, place kabobs on the grill rack directly over medium coals. Grill, uncovered, for 14 to 16 minutes or until turkey is no longer pink (170°F). (For a gas grill, preheat grill. Reduce heat to medium. Place kabobs on grill rack over heat. Cover and grill as above.) Serve immediately with Carrot-Radish Salad and, if desired, lime wedges and onion strips.
CARROT-RADISH SALAD: In a medium bowl stir together 1½ cups shredded carrots; ½ cup shredded radishes; ½ cup golden raisins; and 2 green onions, bias-sliced. In a small bowl stir together ⅓ cup plain low-fat yogurt, ¼ teaspoon finely shredded lime peel, 1 tablespoon lime juice, 1 tablespoon honey, and ¼ teaspoon ground coriander. Stir into carrot mixture until well combined. Cover and chill 1 to 4 hours. Stir well before serving.

*TEST KITCHEN TIP: Because chile peppers contain volatile oils that can burn your skin and eyes, avoid direct contact with them as much as possible. When working with chile peppers, wear plastic or rubber gloves. If your bare hands do touch the peppers, wash your hands and nails well with soap and warm water.

**TEST KITCHEN TIP: If using wooden skewers, soak them in enough water to cover for at least 30 minutes before using.

PER SERVING: 346 cal., 3 g total fat (1 g sat. fat), 109 mg chol., 170 mg sodium, 34 g carb. (4 g fiber, 24 g sugars), 47 g pro. Exchanges: 1 vegetable, 2 carb., 6.5 lean meat. Carb choices: 2.

Tandoori-Style
Turkey Kabobs

Homemade Walking Tacos

Suit your taste by varying the amount of crushed red pepper that spices up the meat mixture.

SERVINGS 5 (1 package chips, 1½ ounces cooked meat, about ½ cup vegetables, and 1 tablespoon cheese each)

CARB. PER SERVING 16 g

- 8 ounces uncooked lean ground turkey breast or chicken breast
- ¼ cup chopped onion
- ¼ cup chopped red sweet pepper
- 2 teaspoons olive oil or canola oil
- 1 tablespoon reduced-sodium taco seasoning
- 1 tablespoon water
- ⅛ to ¼ teaspoon crushed red pepper
  Black pepper
- 5 100-calorie packages nacho cheese-flavor tortilla chips
- 1 cup shredded romaine lettuce
- ⅔ cup diced tomato
- ⅓ cup shredded reduced-fat cheddar cheese
- 5 teaspoons light sour cream (optional)

1. In a large skillet cook turkey, onion, and sweet pepper in hot oil over medium heat until turkey is no longer pink, using a wooden spoon to break up meat as it cooks. Stir in taco seasoning, the water, crushed red pepper, and black pepper. Cook and stir for 1 minute more.

2. Meanwhile, open the bags of tortilla chips; if desired, gently crush chips. Divide lettuce among the bags. Divide cooked turkey mixture, tomato, and cheese among the bags. If desired, top each with a teaspoon of the sour cream. Use a fork to mix together and eat from the bag.

PER SERVING: 207 cal., 10 g total fat (2 g sat. fat), 28 mg chol., 327 mg sodium, 16 g carb. (1 g fiber, 2 g sugars), 15 g pro. Exchanges: 0.5 vegetable, 1 starch, 1.5 lean meat, 1.5 fat. Carb choices: 1.

Barbecue Glazed Turkey

If chicken is your bird of choice, use four skinless, boneless chicken breast halves in place of the turkey tenderloin.

SERVINGS 4 (3 ounces cooked turkey and about 1 tablespoon sauce each)

CARB. PER SERVING 10 g

- ⅔ cup reduced-sugar ketchup
- ¼ cup orange juice
- 3 tablespoons snipped fresh cilantro
- 1 clove garlic, minced
- ¼ teaspoon ground cumin
- ¼ teaspoon black pepper
- 1 large turkey breast tenderloin (about 1 pound), split in half horizontally

1. For sauce, in a small saucepan combine ketchup, orange juice, 2 tablespoons of the cilantro, the garlic, cumin, and pepper. Bring to boiling over medium heat, stirring constantly. Reduce heat. Simmer, uncovered, for 5 minutes. Transfer ⅓ cup of the sauce to a small bowl for brushing the turkey; keep remaining sauce warm.

2. For a charcoal grill, place turkey pieces on the grill rack directly over medium coals. Grill, uncovered, for 12 to 16 minutes or until no longer pink, turning once halfway through grilling and brushing with the ⅓ cup sauce for the last 2 minutes of grilling. (For a gas grill, preheat grill. Reduce heat to medium. Place turkey pieces on grill rack over heat. Cover and grill as above.)

3. Slice turkey and serve with remaining sauce. Sprinkle with remaining 1 tablespoon cilantro.

PER SERVING: 163 cal., 1 g total fat (0 g sat. fat), 70 mg chol., 298 mg sodium, 10 g carb. (0 g fiber, 7 g sugars), 28 g pro. Exchanges: 0.5 carb., 3.5 lean meat. Carb choices: 0.5.

Barbecue
Glazed Turkey

Fish and Sugar Snap Peas en Papillote

Cooking the fish and vegetables en papillote (in an envelope) allows them to bake in their own wine-enhanced juices for a wonderful melding of flavors. When the parchment is opened, the aroma is amazing.

SERVINGS 6 (1 packet each)
CARB. PER SERVING 7 g

- 2 tablespoons butter, cut into 6 slices
- 6 8-ounce red snapper or white fish fillets
- ½ teaspoon sea salt
- ¼ teaspoon freshly ground black pepper
- 1 cup sugar snap peas, halved diagonally
- 12 baby carrots with tops, trimmed and quartered lengthwise
- 6 slices lemon
- ¼ cup finely chopped shallots
- 12 sprigs fresh thyme or lemon thyme
- 6 tablespoons dry white wine
  Lemon wedges (optional)

1. Position oven racks in the top third and center of the oven. Preheat oven to 400°F.

2. Cut six 18×12-inch pieces of parchment paper. Place sheets of parchment on a work surface with the short ends facing you. Fold each sheet of parchment crosswise in half to crease, then unfold. Place one slice of butter on the lower half of each sheet of parchment. Place snapper fillets on the butter; sprinkle with the salt and pepper. Top each fillet with sugar snap peas, carrots, a lemon slice, shallots, and two thyme sprigs. Drizzle each with 1 tablespoon wine.

3. Fold each sheet of parchment over to enclose the fish and vegetables. To seal, turn up a corner of the cut edges of the paper and fold, then fold again, forming the second fold on top of the first fold. Continue folding to enclose all the way around the packet. When you reach the end, twist the last fold to seal. Repeat with remaining packets. Place the packets on two large baking sheets.

4. Bake both sheets at once about 12 minutes or until the paper is well browned and fish begins to flake when tested with a fork, switching the position of the baking sheets halfway through baking for even cooking. Transfer packets to plates and serve, allowing each diner to cut open the packet at the table. If desired, pass lemon wedges with the fish.

PER SERVING: 301 cal., 7 g total fat (3 g sat. fat), 94 mg chol., 324 mg sodium, 7 g carb. (2 g fiber, 3 g sugars), 48 g pro. Exchanges: 0.5 vegetable, 6 lean meat. Carb choices: 0.5.

Fish and Sugar Snap Peas en Papillote

❯ QUICK TIP

If baby carrots with tops are not available at your supermarket, make an easy swap of 1 cup julienned carrots.

Fish and Chips-Style Cod

If restaurant-style fish and chips is a favorite you're afraid won't fit into your diabetes meal plan, here's a happy surprise. This recipe gives you crispy fish for only 177 calories and 8 grams of fat a serving. It's yummy with a splash of malt vinegar.

SERVINGS 4 (2 fish pieces each)

CARB. PER SERVING 4 g

1 **pound fresh or frozen cod or halibut fillets**
½ **cup flour**
⅓ **cup fat-free milk**
⅓ **cup ale or nonalcoholic beer**
1 **egg or ¼ cup refrigerated or frozen egg product, thawed**
¼ **teaspoon kosher salt**
   Freshly ground black pepper
½ **cup canola oil**
   Malt vinegar
   Fried Parsley (optional)

1. Thaw fish, if frozen. Set aside. In a medium bowl whisk together flour, milk, ale, egg, salt, and pepper until combined. Cover and chill batter for 30 minutes.
2. Preheat oven to 250°F. Rinse fish under cold running water; pat dry with paper towels. Cut fish crosswise into eight pieces total.

3. In a medium skillet heat oil over medium-high heat for 2 minutes. Dip four pieces of the fish in the batter, turning to coat and letting excess batter drip off. Fry the fish pieces in the hot oil about 4 minutes or until golden brown and fish flakes easily when tested with a fork, turning once. Transfer fried fish to paper towels; let stand to drain. Place fish on a baking sheet; keep warm in the oven. Repeat with remaining fish pieces.

4. Serve fish with malt vinegar and, if desired, garnish with Fried Parsley.

FRIED PARSLEY: After cooking fish in the oil, add several sprigs of fresh Italian (flat-leaf) parsley to the hot oil. Cook until parsley is no longer bubbly. Using a slotted spoon, remove parsley from oil. Drain on paper towels.

PER SERVING: 177 cal., 8 g total fat (1 g sat. fat), 55 mg chol., 118 mg sodium, 4 g carb. (0 g fiber, 0 g sugars), 21 g pro. Exchanges: 3 lean meat, 1 fat. Carb choices: 0.

Grilled Salmon with Apple-Onion Relish

One mixture plays two roles—part is used as a marinade for the salmon and the remaining is stirred into the relish.

SERVINGS 4 (1 fillet and ½ cup relish each)
CARB. PER SERVING 15 g

- 1 cup apple or hickory wood chips (optional)
- 4 4- to 5-ounce fresh or frozen salmon fillets with skin, cut 1 inch thick
- ¼ cup finely chopped red sweet pepper
- ¼ cup cider vinegar
- ¼ cup apple juice
- 1 tablespoon toasted sesame oil
- ⅛ teaspoon salt
- ⅛ teaspoon black pepper
- 2 medium red-skin cooking apples
  Nonstick cooking spray
- ¼ teaspoon ground allspice
- ⅛ teaspoon ground cardamom
- 2 ½-inch-thick slices red onion
  Fresh salad greens (optional)

1. If using wood chips, soak wood chips in enough water to cover for at least 1 hour before grilling. Drain before using. Thaw fish, if frozen. Rinse fish; pat dry with paper towels.

2. For marinade, in a small bowl combine sweet pepper, vinegar, apple juice, and oil. Reserve ¼ cup of the marinade. Place salmon in a large resealable plastic bag. Pour remaining marinade over salmon in bag. Seal bag;

turn to coat salmon. Place in a shallow dish; marinate in the refrigerator for 2 to 4 hours, turning bag occasionally.

3. Remove salmon from marinade, discarding used marinade. Sprinkle tops of salmon fillets with the salt and black pepper. Core apples. Trim tops and bottoms off apples and discard. Cut apples horizontally into ¼-inch-thick slices. Lightly coat both sides of apple slices with cooking spray. In a small bowl combine allspice and cardamom. Sprinkle over apple slices.

4. For a charcoal grill, sprinkle wood chips (if using) directly over medium coals. Place fish, meaty sides down, on the greased grill rack directly over the medium coals. Grill, uncovered, for 3 minutes. Turn skin sides down. Grill, uncovered, for 5 to 7 minutes more or until fish flakes easily when tested with a fork. Grill onion slices for 8 to 10 minutes or until tender, turning once. Grill apple slices for 4 to 6 minutes or until warmed through and just tender, turning once. (For a gas grill, preheat grill. Reduce heat to medium. Add wood chips [if using] according to manufacturer's directions. Place fish, onions, and apple slices on greased grill rack over heat. Cover and grill as above.)

5. Coarsely chop the apples and onions. Toss with reserved marinade mixture. Serve on top of salmon. If desired, serve with salad greens.

PER SERVING: 308 cal., 17 g total fat (4 g sat. fat), 62 mg chol., 142 mg sodium, 15 g carb. (2 g fiber, 11 g sugars), 24 g pro. Exchanges: 0.5 vegetable, 0.5 fruit, 3 medium-fat meat, 0.5 fat. Carb choices: 1.

Grilled Salmon with Apple-Onion Relish

Asian-Style Tuna Kabobs

If you have sesame seeds on hand,
sprinkle a few over the kabobs before serving.

SERVINGS 8 (1 kabob each)
CARB. PER SERVING 10 g

1½ pounds fresh or frozen tuna steaks
⅓ cup rice vinegar
¼ cup grated fresh ginger
¼ cup peanut oil
¼ cup toasted sesame oil
¼ cup soy sauce
¼ cup honey
2 tablespoons tahini (sesame seed paste) (optional)
2 tablespoons snipped fresh cilantro
1 fresh serrano chile pepper, stemmed, seeded, and finely chopped*
1 medium yellow sweet pepper, cut into 1-inch pieces
8 green onions, trimmed and each cut into 4 pieces

1. Thaw fish, if frozen. Rinse fish; pat dry with paper towels. Cut fish into 1¼-inch cubes.

2. For marinade, in a medium bowl combine rice vinegar, ginger, peanut oil, sesame oil, soy sauce, honey, tahini (if desired), cilantro, and chile pepper. Divide the marinade in half and reserve half for dipping. Add fish cubes to remaining marinade; mix gently to coat. Cover and marinate in the refrigerator for 45 minutes (do not marinate any longer).

3. Drain fish, reserving marinade for brushing. On eight long skewers** alternately thread fish cubes, sweet pepper pieces, and green onion pieces.

4. For a charcoal grill, place skewers on the grill rack directly over medium coals. Grill, uncovered, for 6 to 8 minutes or until fish is pink in the center but flakes easily when tested with a fork, turning once halfway through grilling and brushing frequently with the reserved marinade for the first 4 minutes of grilling. (For a gas grill, preheat grill. Reduce heat to medium. Place skewers on grill rack over heat. Cover and grill as above.) Discard any remaining brushing marinade. Serve kabobs immediately with reserved marinade for dipping.

*TEST KITCHEN TIP: Because chile peppers contain volatile oils that can burn your skin and eyes, avoid direct contact with them as much as possible. When working with chile peppers, wear plastic or rubber gloves. If your bare hands do touch the peppers, wash your hands and nails well with soap and warm water.

**TEST KITCHEN TIP: If using wooden skewers, soak them in enough water to cover for at least 30 minutes before using.

PER SERVING: 257 cal., 14 g total fat (3 g sat. fat), 32 mg chol., 418 mg sodium, 10 g carb. (1 g fiber, 8 g sugars), 21 g pro. Exchanges: 0.5 vegetable, 0.5 carb., 3 lean meat, 2 fat. Carb choices: 0.5.

Tuna and Noodles

Our taste panel declared this creamy dish is
"even better than regular tuna casserole."

SERVINGS 4 (about 1 cup each)
CARB. PER SERVING 33 g

1 6.5-ounce package light semisoft cheese with cucumber and dill or garlic and herb
4 ounces dried wide rice noodles, broken
1½ cups sliced fresh mushrooms
1 stalk celery, sliced (½ cup)
1 small onion, chopped (⅓ cup)
¼ cup water
⅓ cup fat-free milk
3 4.5-ounce cans very-low-sodium chunk white tuna (water-pack), drained and broken into chunks
½ cup cornflakes or crushed reduced-fat shredded wheat crackers

1. Let cheese stand at room temperature for 30 minutes. Place noodles in a large bowl. Add enough boiling water to cover by several inches. Let stand for 5 minutes, stirring occasionally. Drain and set aside.

2. Meanwhile, in a microwave-safe 2-quart casserole combine mushrooms, celery, onion, and the ¼ cup water. Microwave, covered, on 100 percent power (high) for 3 to 4 minutes or until vegetables are tender, stirring once halfway through cooking.

3. Add cheese and milk to mushroom mixture. Stir until well mixed. Stir in drained noodles and tuna. Microwave, covered, on 100 percent power (high) for 3 to 4 minutes or until heated through, gently stirring once halfway through cooking. Sprinkle with cornflakes.

PER SERVING: 331 cal., 9 g total fat (5 g sat. fat), 73 mg chol., 454 mg sodium, 33 g carb. (1 g fiber, 4 g sugars), 31 g pro. Exchanges: 1 vegetable, 2 starch, 3.5 lean meat. Carb choices: 2.

QUICK TIP

A 4-inch piece of fresh corn makes a diabetes-friendly serving size. Cook as you like—grill, boil, or microwave.

Shrimp Kabobs
with Lemon
Marinade

Shrimp with Curried Lime Carrots

Shrimp Kabobs with Lemon Marinade

The combo of shredded lemon peel, lemon juice, and snipped parsley gives these simple kabobs great fresh flavor.

SERVINGS 4 (2 kabobs and about ¼ cup vegetables each)

CARB. PER SERVING 4 g

1½ pounds fresh or frozen jumbo shrimp in shells
⅓ cup olive oil
2 teaspoons finely shredded lemon peel
¼ cup lemon juice
1 tablespoon snipped fresh parsley
8 cherry tomatoes, quartered
2 green onions, sliced

1. Thaw shrimp, if frozen. Peel and devein shrimp, leaving tails intact if desired. Rinse shrimp; pat dry with paper towels.
2. In a large bowl combine olive oil, lemon peel, lemon juice, and parsley. Set aside half of the oil mixture. Toss shrimp with the remaining oil mixture. Cover and marinate in the refrigerator for 15 minutes (do not marinate any longer or shrimp will start to toughen).
3. Drain shrimp, discarding marinade. Thread shrimp onto eight 8-inch skewers.*
4. For a charcoal grill, place skewers on the grill rack directly over medium coals. Cover and grill for 4 to 6 minutes or until shrimp are opaque, turning once halfway through grilling. (For a gas grill, preheat grill. Reduce heat to medium. Place skewers on grill rack over heat. Grill as above.)
5. Transfer shrimp to a serving dish. Drizzle with the reserved oil mixture. Serve with cherry tomatoes and green onions.
***TEST KITCHEN TIP:** If using wooden skewers, soak them in enough water to cover for at least 30 minutes before using.
PER SERVING: 271 cal., 12 g total fat (2 g sat. fat), 259 mg chol., 255 mg sodium, 4 g carb. (1 g fiber, 1 g sugars), 35 g pro. Exchanges: 5 lean meat, 1 fat. Carb choices: 0.

Shrimp with Curried Lime Carrots

This oh-so-pretty combo makes lean eating incredibly appealing.

SERVINGS 4 (1 cup each)

CARB. PER SERVING 12 g

1 pound fresh or frozen large shrimp in shells
½ teaspoon ground cumin
½ teaspoon ground turmeric
¼ teaspoon salt
⅛ teaspoon ground cardamom
⅛ teaspoon cayenne pepper
4 medium carrots, peeled and thinly bias-sliced
2 tablespoons chopped green onion (1)
½ teaspoon finely shredded lime peel (set aside)
2 tablespoons lime juice
1 tablespoon honey

1. Thaw shrimp, if frozen. Peel and devein shrimp, leaving tails intact if desired. In a medium bowl combine cumin, turmeric, salt, cardamom, and cayenne pepper. Remove ¾ teaspoon of the mixture to another medium bowl. Add shrimp to one bowl and carrots to the second bowl with seasoning. Toss each to coat.
2. Place a steamer basket in a saucepan. Add water to just below the bottom of the basket. Bring water to boiling. Add carrots to steamer basket. Cover and reduce heat. Steam for 3 minutes. Add shrimp. Cover and steam for 3 to 5 minutes more or until shrimp are opaque and carrots are tender.
3. Transfer shrimp and carrots to a bowl. Sprinkle with green onion. Combine lime juice and honey. Drizzle over shrimp and carrots. Sprinkle with lime peel.
PER SERVING: 167 cal., 2 g total fat (0 g sat. fat), 172 mg chol., 357 mg sodium, 12 g carb. (2 g fiber, 7 g sugars), 24 g pro. Exchanges: 1 vegetable, 0.5 carb., 3 lean meat. Carb choices: 1.

Lobster Mac and Cheese Casserole

Look for panko near the coating and crumb mixtures in the supermarket.

SERVINGS 6 (1 cup each)
CARB. PER SERVING 35 g

1½ cups dried whole wheat rigatoni or rotini (6 ounces)
1 large lobster tail (8 to 10 ounces)
2 cups small broccoli florets
Nonstick cooking spray
1 medium red sweet pepper, chopped (¾ cup)
⅓ cup chopped onion
1 6.5-ounce container light semisoft cheese with garlic and herb
2 cups fat-free milk
1 tablespoon flour
1 cup shredded reduced-fat Italian-style cheese blend (4 ounces)
½ teaspoon finely shredded lemon peel
¼ teaspoon black pepper
⅓ cup whole wheat or regular panko (Japanese-style bread crumbs)

1. Preheat oven to 375°F. In a 4-quart Dutch oven cook pasta according to package directions, adding the lobster tail for the last 7 minutes of cooking and adding the broccoli for the last 3 minutes of cooking. Drain and set aside. When lobster tail is cool enough to handle, remove the lobster meat and coarsely chop the meat.
2. Meanwhile, coat a large nonstick skillet with cooking spray; heat skillet over medium heat. Add sweet pepper and onion to skillet. Cook about 5 minutes or until tender, stirring frequently. Remove skillet from heat. Stir in semisoft cheese until melted.
3. In a medium bowl whisk together milk and flour until smooth. Add all at once to sweet pepper mixture. Cook and stir over medium heat until thickened and bubbly. Reduce heat to low. Stir in Italian-blend cheeses until melted. Stir in cooked pasta, broccoli, chopped lobster, lemon peel, and black pepper.
4. Transfer mixture to a 2-quart casserole. Sprinkle with panko. Bake for 15 to 20 minutes or until heated through and top is golden brown.
PER SERVING: 322 cal., 10 g total fat (6 g sat. fat), 68 mg chol., 402 mg sodium, 35 g carb. (4 g fiber, 9 g sugars), 25 g pro. Exchanges: 2 starch, 3 lean meat, 1 fat. Carb choices: 2.

Pan-Seared Scallops with Tomato, Olives, and Fresh Basil

Toss the tomato-wine sauce with hot cooked pasta, top with browned scallops and shredded basil, and voilà—dinner is ready to serve.

SERVINGS 4 (¾ cup pasta, 4 scallops, and about ⅓ cup sauce each)
CARB. PER SERVING 42 g

6 ounces packaged dried whole grain or multigrain fettuccine
1¼ pounds fresh or frozen sea scallops (16 scallops)
¼ teaspoon black pepper
1 14.5-ounce can no-salt-added diced tomatoes, undrained
2 teaspoons olive oil
½ cup dry red wine
2 cloves garlic, minced
½ cup reduced-sodium chicken broth
¼ cup Kalamata olives, pitted and quartered
1 tablespoon thinly sliced fresh basil

1. Cook pasta according to package directions. Meanwhile, thaw scallops, if frozen. Rinse scallops; pat dry with paper towels. Sprinkle scallops with pepper; set aside. Set aside half of the diced tomatoes. In a blender or food processor combine the remaining diced tomatoes and the liquid from the can. Cover and blend or process until smooth; set aside.
2. Preheat a very large skillet over medium-high heat for 2 to 3 minutes. Add oil to hot skillet; swirl to lightly coat skillet. Add scallops to hot skillet; cook about 4 minutes or until golden brown and opaque, turning once. Transfer scallops to a warm platter; cover to keep warm.
3. For sauce, add wine and garlic to skillet, stirring to scrape up any browned bits from bottom of skillet. Cook for 1 to 2 minutes or until wine mixture is reduced by one-third. Add the reserved diced tomatoes, the pureed tomato mixture, and the broth. Bring to boiling; reduce heat. Simmer, uncovered, for 4 to 5 minutes or until sauce begins to thicken slightly.
4. Remove from heat; stir in olives. Divide hot cooked fettuccine among four shallow pasta bowls. Spoon sauce over fettuccine; toss to combine. Arrange scallops on top of fettuccine mixture. Sprinkle with basil. Serve immediately.
PER SERVING: 356 cal., 5 g total fat (1 g sat. fat), 47 mg chol., 439 mg sodium, 42 g carb. (5 g fiber, 5 g sugars), 31 g pro. Exchanges: 1 vegetable, 2.5 starch, 3 lean meat. Carb choices: 3.

Pan-Seared Scallops with Tomato, Olives, and Fresh Basil

Lobster Mac and Cheese

Tex-Mex Bean Tostadas
recipe on page 36

Simple Sides

Some meals need a vegetable side dish to help round them out nutritionally. Try one of these good-for-you ideas.

1. **Stir-fry** zucchini with a little garlic.

2. **Brush** fresh asparagus spears with a little olive oil and grill.

3. **Steam** trimmed fresh green beans and sprinkle with a few toasted sliced almonds.

4. **Blanch** broccoli and/or cauliflower florets.

5. **Drizzle** a little olive oil over halved Brussels sprouts and roast in the oven.

6. **Thread** sweet pepper pieces on a skewer and grill.

7. **Wilt** fresh spinach in a little olive oil.

8. **Bake** a small sweet potato in the oven or microwave.

9. **Cook** julienned carrots and a handful of fresh peas in a little boiling water.

10. **Toss** grape tomatoes in a little olive oil and roast in the oven.

Chile Rellenos

Freshen up the presentation of this puffy egg bake with a few fresh cilantro leaves.

SERVINGS 4 (1 dish each)
CARB. PER SERVING 17 g

- 2 large fresh poblano chile peppers,* Anaheim chile peppers,* or green sweet peppers (8 ounces)
- 1 cup shredded reduced-fat Mexican-style cheese blend (4 ounces)
- 1 to 2 fresh jalapeño chile peppers, seeded and finely chopped*
- 1½ cups refrigerated or frozen egg product, thawed, or 6 eggs, beaten
- ⅓ cup fat-free milk
- ⅓ cup flour
- ½ teaspoon baking powder
- ¼ teaspoon cayenne pepper
  Picante sauce and/or light sour cream (optional)

1. Preheat oven to 450°F. Halve the peppers and remove seeds, stems, and veins. Immerse peppers into boiling water for 3 minutes; drain. Invert peppers on paper towels to drain well. Place one pepper half in each of four greased 12- to 16-ounce au gratin dishes. Top each with cheese and jalapeño pepper.
2. In a medium bowl combine egg and milk. Add flour, baking powder, and cayenne pepper. Beat until smooth. Pour egg mixture evenly over peppers and cheese in dishes.

Chile Rellenos

3. Bake, uncovered, about 15 minutes or until a knife inserted into the egg mixture comes out clean. Let stand about 5 minutes. If desired, serve with picante sauce and/or sour cream.
*TEST KITCHEN TIP: Because chile peppers contain volatile oils that can burn your skin and eyes, avoid direct contact with them as much as possible. When working with chile peppers, wear plastic or rubber gloves. If your bare hands do touch the peppers, wash your hands and nails well with soap and warm water.
PER SERVING: 203 cal., 5 g total fat (4 g sat. fat), 15 mg chol., 470 mg sodium, 17 g carb. (1 g fiber, 2 g sugars), 19 g pro. Exchanges: 0.5 vegetable, 1 starch, 2 lean meat, 0.5 fat. Carb choices: 1.

Tex-Mex Bean Tostadas

Purchase a salsa with 100 mg sodium or less per serving. Pictured on page 35.

SERVINGS 4 (1 tostada each)
CARB. PER SERVING 27 g

- 4 packaged tostada shells
- 1 15-ounce can no-salt-added pinto beans, rinsed and drained
- ½ cup purchased salsa
- ½ teaspoon salt-free Southwest chipotle seasoning blend
- ½ cup shredded reduced-fat cheddar cheese (2 ounces)
- 1½ cups packaged shredded iceberg lettuce
- 1 cup chopped tomato
- ¼ cup shredded reduced-fat cheddar cheese (1 ounce) (optional)
  Lime wedges (optional)

1. Preheat oven to 350°F. Place tostada shells on a baking sheet. Bake for 3 to 5 minutes or until warm.
2. Meanwhile, in a medium bowl combine beans, salsa, and seasoning blend. Using a potato masher or fork, coarsely mash the mixture. Divide bean mixture among tostada shells, spreading evenly. Top with the ½ cup cheese.
3. Bake about 5 minutes or until cheese melts. Top tostadas with lettuce, tomato, and, if desired, the ¼ cup cheese. If desired, serve with lime wedges.
PER SERVING: 211 cal., 7 g total fat (2 g sat. fat), 8 mg chol., 294 mg sodium, 27 g carb. (7 g fiber, 3 g sugars), 10 g pro. Exchanges: 0.5 vegetable, 2 starch, 1 lean meat. Carb choices: 2.

Easy Pasta and
Pepper Primavera

Easy Pasta and Pepper Primavera

Cannellini beans (white kidney beans) provide plenty of protein in this vegetarian main dish. Look for them with the other canned beans at the supermarket.

SERVINGS 4 (1¼ cups each)

CARB. PER SERVING 37 g

- 4 ounces dried multigrain spaghetti
- 2 teaspoons bottled minced garlic or 4 cloves garlic, minced
- 1 tablespoon olive oil or canola oil
- 1 16-ounce package frozen peppers and onions mix or sugar snap stir-fry vegetable mix
- 1 15-ounce can cannellini beans (white kidney beans), rinsed and drained
- ¼ cup dry white wine or reduced-sodium chicken broth
- ½ teaspoon finely shredded lemon peel (set aside)
- 1 tablespoon lemon juice
- ½ teaspoon dried thyme, crushed
- ¼ teaspoon salt
- ¼ teaspoon freshly ground black pepper
- ¼ teaspoon crushed red pepper
- 1 tablespoon butter
- 1 ounce Parmesan cheese, shaved

1. Cook pasta according to package directions.

2. Meanwhile, in a large skillet cook and stir garlic in hot oil over medium heat for 30 seconds. Add frozen vegetables. Cook and stir for 2 minutes. Add beans, wine, lemon juice, thyme, salt, black pepper, and crushed red pepper. Bring to boiling; reduce heat. Cook, uncovered, about 4 minutes or until vegetables are crisp-tender, stirring occasionally. Remove from heat. Stir in butter.

3. Drain pasta. Add pasta to vegetable mixture in skillet. Toss gently to combine.

4. To serve, divide pasta mixture among four shallow bowls. Sprinkle with Parmesan and lemon peel.

PER SERVING: 272 cal., 9 g total fat (3 g sat. fat), 12 mg chol., 410 mg sodium, 37 g carb. (7 g fiber, 5 g sugars), 13 g pro. Exchanges: 1 vegetable, 2 starch, 1 lean meat, 1 fat. Carb choices: 2.5.

Lentil and Veggie
Shepherd's Pie

Lentil and Veggie Shepherd's Pie

*The mashed potato layer is seasoned with garlic,
Parmesan, and basil in this flavorful meatless
version of an all-time favorite.*

SERVINGS 8 (1⅓ cups each)

CARB. PER SERVING 41 g

- 1 14-ounce can vegetable broth or 14.5-ounce can
  reduced-sodium chicken broth
- 1 cup water
- 1 cup dry brown lentils, rinsed and drained
- 3 cloves garlic, minced
- 4 medium carrots, peeled and bias-sliced into ½-inch
  slices (2 cups)
- 3 small parsnips, peeled and bias-sliced into ½-inch
  slices (1½ cups)
- 6 white boiling onions (8 ounces), quartered, or 1 medium
  onion, cut into thin wedges
- 4 cups coarsely shredded trimmed fresh chard or kale
- 1 14.5-ounce can no-salt-added diced tomatoes,
  undrained
- 2 tablespoons no-salt-added tomato paste
- 2 tablespoons snipped fresh basil or 2 teaspoons
  dried basil, crushed
- 4 medium potatoes, peeled and cut up
- 4 cloves garlic, peeled
- 1 tablespoon butter
- 3 to 4 tablespoons fat-free milk
- ½ cup finely shredded Parmesan cheese
- 1 tablespoon snipped fresh basil or ½ teaspoon
  dried basil, crushed

1. In a large saucepan combine broth, the water, lentils,
and minced garlic. Bring to boiling; reduce heat.
Simmer, covered, for 20 minutes. Add carrots, parsnips,
and onions. Return to boiling; reduce heat. Simmer,
covered, for 10 to 15 minutes more or just until
vegetables and lentils are tender. Stir in chard; remove
from heat. Stir in tomatoes, tomato paste, and the
2 tablespoons fresh basil or 2 teaspoons dried basil.

2. Preheat oven to 350°F. Meanwhile, in a covered large
saucepan cook potatoes and whole garlic cloves in
enough boiling lightly salted water to cover for 20 to
25 minutes or until tender; drain. Mash with a potato
masher or beat with an electric mixer on low speed. Add
butter. Gradually beat in enough of the milk to make
potatoes light and fluffy. Fold in cheese and the
1 tablespoon fresh basil or ½ teaspoon dried basil.

3. Spread lentil mixture in a 2- to 2½-quart casserole
or au gratin dish. Spoon potato mixture over lentil
mixture, spreading evenly.

4. Bake, uncovered, about 35 minutes or until heated
through.

MAKE-AHEAD DIRECTIONS: Prepare as directed through Step 3.
Cover baking dish with plastic wrap; store in the
refrigerator for up to 24 hours. To serve, preheat oven to
350°F. Remove plastic wrap. Cover dish with foil. Bake for
50 minutes. Uncover and bake for 10 to 15 minutes more
or until heated through.

PER SERVING: 234 cal., 3 g total fat (2 g sat. fat), 8 mg chol.,
386 mg sodium, 41 g carb. (13 g fiber, 8 g sugars), 12 g pro.
Exchanges: 2 vegetable, 2 starch, 0.5 fat. Carb choices: 3.

◗ QUICK TIP

Rinse and drain the entire can of black beans, then store the remaining beans in an airtight container in the refrigerator for up to 3 days. For another meal, toss them with salad greens, sliced onion, halved grape tomatoes, and shredded reduced-fat cheese for a Mexican-style salad.

Stuffed Zucchini with Black Beans, Corn, and Poblano Pepper

To make cleanup easy, line the baking pan with foil before adding the zucchini.

SERVINGS 2 (2 zucchini halves each)

CARB. PER SERVING 31 g

- 2   medium zucchini (about 8 ounces each)
- 1   fresh poblano chile pepper, seeded and finely chopped*
- ¼   cup finely chopped onion
- 1   teaspoon olive oil
- 2   cloves garlic, minced
- ½   cup fresh or frozen whole kernel corn
- 1   small tomato, chopped (⅓ cup)
- ⅓   cup canned no-salt-added black beans, rinsed and drained
- ½   cup shredded reduced-fat Monterey Jack cheese (2 ounces)
- 2   tablespoons snipped fresh cilantro

1. Preheat oven to 400°F. Trim ends of zucchini; cut each zucchini in half lengthwise. Using a melon baller or a small measuring spoon, scoop out and discard pulp, leaving ¼-inch-thick shells. Place zucchini shells, cut sides up, in a shallow baking pan.

2. In a large nonstick skillet cook chile pepper and onion in hot oil over medium heat about 6 minutes or until tender, stirring occasionally. Add garlic; cook and stir for 1 minute more. Stir in corn, tomato, and black beans. Cook about 2 minutes or until heated through, stirring occasionally. Remove from heat. Stir in ¼ cup of the cheese and the cilantro.

3. Using a small spoon, divide bean mixture evenly among zucchini halves, packing filling lightly and mounding as needed. Sprinkle with the remaining ¼ cup cheese. Bake, uncovered, about 20 minutes or until zucchini is tender.

*TEST KITCHEN TIP: Because chile peppers contain volatile oils that can burn your skin and eyes, avoid direct contact with them as much as possible. When working with chile peppers, wear plastic or rubber gloves. If your bare hands do touch the peppers, wash your hands and nails well with soap and warm water.

PER SERVING: 243 cal., 9 g total fat (4 g sat. fat), 20 mg chol., 274 mg sodium, 31 g carb. (6 g fiber, 6 g sugars), 15 g pro. Exchanges: 2.5 vegetable, 1 starch, 1 medium-fat meat, 0.5 fat. Carb choices: 2.

Stuffed Zucchini with Black Beans, Corn, and Poblano Pepper

Fresh and tasty creations with good-for-you ingredients make main-dish salads perfect to serve for lunch or dinner. Enjoy bite after bite of one of these beauties, lightly dressed and loaded with leafy greens, crunchy veggies, sweet fruits, lean meats, tender pasta, and more.

Turkey and Mango Salad with Chutney Vinaigrette

Pumpkin seeds are rich in protein and essential fatty acids. Roast at 350°F for 10 minutes, stirring once. Sprinkle over salads, stir into cereal, or swirl into yogurt.

SERVINGS 4 (2 cups salad, 2½ ounces turkey, and about 1½ tablespoons vinaigrette each)
CARB. PER SERVING 29 g

- 1 teaspoon ground coriander
- 1 teaspoon ground cumin
- ¼ teaspoon salt
- ¼ teaspoon ground ginger
- ¼ teaspoon black pepper
- ⅛ teaspoon cayenne pepper
- 1 12-ounce turkey breast tenderloin
- 2 teaspoons canola oil
- 6 cups packaged fresh baby spinach
- ¼ of a medium red onion, thinly sliced
- 1 cup fresh snow pea pods, trimmed
- 1 medium mango, seeded, peeled, and cubed
- 1 recipe Chutney Vinaigrette
- 2 tablespoons roasted pumpkin seeds (pepitas)

1. In a small bowl combine coriander, cumin, salt, ginger, black pepper, and cayenne pepper. Cut turkey tenderloin in half horizontally to make two thin steaks. Sprinkle both sides of turkey pieces evenly with coriander mixture; rub in with your fingers.

2. In a large skillet cook turkey tenderloin pieces in oil over medium heat for 6 to 8 minutes or until no longer pink (170°F), turning once halfway through cooking. Transfer turkey to a cutting board and thinly slice.

3. Toss spinach, red onion, pea pods, mango, and Chutney Vinaigrette in a large bowl to coat. To serve, divide salad among four serving plates. Arrange turkey slices on top. Sprinkle with pumpkin seeds.

CHUTNEY VINAIGRETTE: Spoon ¼ cup mango chutney into a small bowl. Use kitchen shears to finely snip any large pieces in the chutney. Stir 1 tablespoon canola oil and 4½ teaspoons rice vinegar into the chutney.

PER SERVING: 308 cal., 9 g total fat (1 g sat. fat), 53 mg chol., 426 mg sodium, 29 g carb. (4 g fiber, 18 g sugars), 26 g pro. Exchanges: 1.5 vegetable, 1.5 starch, 2.5 lean meat, 1 fat. Carb choices: 2.

Turkey Chopped Salad with Orange-Poppy Seed Dressing

While the corn is pan-roasting, give the skillet a few shakes to evenly brown the kernels.

SERVINGS 4 (2 cups salad, 2 tablespoons dressing, and tortilla strips from ½ of a tortilla each)
CARB. PER SERVING 36 g

- 2 6-inch corn tortillas
- 2 cups frozen whole kernel corn
- 1 teaspoon olive oil
- 6 cups chopped romaine lettuce
- 2 cups chopped cooked turkey breast
- 2 medium tomatoes, seeded and chopped (1 cup)
- 1 small orange sweet pepper, chopped (½ cup)
- ⅓ cup red onion slivers
- 2 slices turkey bacon, cooked according to package directions and chopped
- 1 recipe Orange-Poppy Seed Dressing

1. Preheat oven to 350°F. Cut the tortillas into ¼-inch strips. Spread the strips in a single layer on a baking sheet. Bake for 8 to 10 minutes or until crisp. Set aside.
2. In a large skillet cook corn in olive oil over medium heat for 6 to 8 minutes or until light brown. Remove from heat. Set aside.
3. In a large bowl combine romaine, turkey, tomatoes, sweet pepper, onion, turkey bacon, and roasted corn. Add the Orange-Poppy Seed Dressing; toss to combine.

To serve, arrange salad on four serving plates. Top evenly with tortilla strips.

ORANGE-POPPY SEED DRESSING: In a small bowl whisk together ¼ cup orange juice, 1 tablespoon olive oil, 1 tablespoon lime juice, 1 tablespoon honey, and 1 teaspoon poppy seeds.

PER SERVING: 334 cal., 8 g total fat (2 g sat. fat), 76 mg chol., 188 mg sodium, 36 g carb. (5 g fiber, 11 g sugars), 32 g pro. Exchanges: 1.5 vegetable, 1 starch, 1 carb., 3.5 lean meat, 0.5 fat. Carb choices: 2.

Turkey Spinach Salad with Beets

It's hard to beat the good-for-you trio of spinach, beets, and blueberries in this fresh-tasting salad. They provide over 100 percent of the vitamin A and just under 50 percent of the vitamin C you need for the day.

SERVINGS 1 (3¼ cups)
CARB. PER SERVING 23 g

- 2 cups packaged fresh baby spinach
- ½ cup packaged refrigerated cooked whole baby beets or canned small whole beets, cut into thin wedges*
- 1½ ounces lower-sodium sliced smoked turkey breast, cut into strips, or ¼ cup chopped cooked chicken breast
- ¼ cup blueberries
- 2 tablespoons slivered red onion
- 2 tablespoons crumbled semisoft goat cheese (chèvre) (½ ounce)
- 1 tablespoon orange juice
- 1 tablespoon balsamic vinegar
- 1½ teaspoons olive oil

1. Place spinach in a salad bowl or on a plate. Top with beets, turkey, blueberries, red onion, and goat cheese.
2. For dressing, in a small airtight container combine orange juice, vinegar, and oil. Cover and shake well. Drizzle dressing over salad.

*TEST KITCHEN TIP: If you prefer, roast your own beets. Preheat oven to 375°F. Scrub 3 fresh baby beets; trim off stem and root ends. Halve beets and place in a 1-quart casserole. Lightly coat beets with nonstick cooking spray. Roast, covered, for 35 minutes. Roast, uncovered, about 10 minutes more or until beets are tender. Cool to room temperature.

PER SERVING: 242 cal., 11 g total fat (3 g sat. fat), 29 mg chol., 382 mg sodium, 23 g carb. (4 g fiber, 17 g sugars), 15 g pro. Exchanges: 2.5 vegetable, 0.5 fruit, 2 lean meat, 1.5 fat. Carb choices: 1.5.

Turkey Chopped Salad with Orange-Poppy Seed Dressing

Warm Chicken and New Potato Salad

If you don't feel like firing up the grill,
cook the chicken under the broiler.

SERVINGS 4 (about 2 cups each)
CARB. PER SERVING 30 g or 28 g

- 12 ounces skinless, boneless chicken breast halves
- ¼ teaspoon salt
- 1 pound 2-inch round red-skin potatoes, scrubbed and quartered
- 1 pound asparagus, trimmed and cut into 2-inch pieces
- 1 medium onion, chopped (½ cup)
- 1 stalk celery, thinly sliced (½ cup)
- 1 tablespoon light butter
- ⅓ cup water
- ¼ cup white wine vinegar
- 2 tablespoons snipped fresh chives
- 1 tablespoon sugar*
- 1 tablespoon coarse ground mustard
- ¾ teaspoon cornstarch
- 2 cups packaged fresh baby spinach
- 4 slices turkey bacon, cooked according to package directions and chopped

1. Sprinkle chicken with ⅛ teaspoon of the salt. For a charcoal grill, place chicken on the grill rack directly over medium coals. Grill, uncovered, for 12 to 15 minutes or until chicken is no longer pink (170°F), turning once halfway through grilling. (For a gas grill, preheat grill. Reduce heat to medium. Place chicken on grill rack over heat. Cover and grill as above.) Thinly slice chicken.

2. In a large saucepan cook potatoes in enough gently boiling water to cover for 12 to 15 minutes or until tender, adding asparagus pieces for the last 2 minutes of cooking. Drain potatoes and asparagus.

3. Meanwhile, in a large skillet cook onion and celery in hot butter over medium heat for 5 minutes or just until tender, stirring occasionally. In a small bowl combine the water, vinegar, chives, sugar, mustard, cornstarch, and remaining ⅛ teaspoon salt. Stir until cornstarch is dissolved. Add to onion mixture. Cook and stir until thickened and bubbly. Gently stir in the potato mixture and chicken. Cook, stirring gently, for 1 to 2 minutes more or until heated through. Stir in spinach and bacon just before serving.

***SUGAR SUBSTITUTES:** Choose from Splenda Granular or Sweet'N Low bulk or packets. Follow package directions to use product amount equivalent to 1 tablespoon sugar.

▶ QUICK TIP

Mixed baby lettuces make a tasty substitution for the fresh baby spinach.

Warm Chicken and New Potato Salad

PER SERVING: 293 cal., 6 g total fat (2 g sat. fat), 64 mg chol., 608 mg sodium, 30 g carb. (6 g fiber, 8 g sugars), 29 g pro. Exchanges: 1 vegetable, 1.5 starch, 3 lean meat. Carb choices: 2.
PER SERVING WITH SUBSTITUTE: Same as above, except 282 cal., 28 g carb. (5 g sugars).

Orzo Chicken Salad with Avocado-Lime Dressing

Using whole wheat instead of regular orzo pasta helps boost the fiber in this colorful chicken salad. The avocado dressing adds just a hint of Southwestern flavor.

SERVINGS 4 (about 1 cup salad and ¼ cup dressing each)

CARB. PER SERVING 30 g

- ⅔ cup dried whole wheat or regular orzo pasta (3 ounces)
- 1 cup fresh or frozen whole kernel corn
- 2 cups shredded or chopped cooked chicken breast
- 1 cup grape tomatoes, halved
- ¼ cup snipped fresh cilantro
- ½ cup crumbled reduced-fat feta cheese (2 ounces)
- 1 recipe Avocado-Lime Dressing

1. In a medium saucepan cook orzo according to package directions, adding corn during the last 1 minute of cooking; drain. Rinse with cold water to cool quickly; drain well. In a large bowl combine orzo mixture, chicken, tomatoes, and cilantro. Sprinkle with cheese.
2. Cover and chill for 2 to 24 hours. To serve, divide salad among four serving plates or bowls. Drizzle with Avocado-Lime Dressing.

AVOCADO-LIME DRESSING: In a blender or food processor combine 1 small avocado, seeded, peeled, and cut up; ⅓ cup water; ½ teaspoon finely shredded lime peel; ¼ cup lime juice; 4 cloves garlic, minced; ½ teaspoon crushed red pepper; and ¼ teaspoon salt. Cover and blend or process until smooth. Transfer dressing to a small bowl. Cover and chill for 2 to 24 hours.

PER SERVING: 321 cal., 10 g total fat (3 g sat. fat), 65 mg chol., 439 mg sodium, 30 g carb. (7 g fiber, 3 g sugars), 30 g pro. Exchanges: 2 starch, 3.5 lean meat. Carb choices: 2.

Orange and Fennel Chicken Salad

Fennel has a licorcelike flavor. Chop the extra and stir into a veggie soup or even a fresh tomato sauce.

SERVINGS 4 (2 cups salad, 3 tablespoons dressing, and 4 ounces cooked chicken each)

CARB. PER SERVING 12 g

- 1 tablespoon olive oil
- ½ teaspoon dried thyme, crushed
- ¼ teaspoon salt
- ¼ teaspoon black pepper
- 4 skinless, boneless chicken breast halves (1¼ to 1½ pounds total)
- 3 cups torn Bibb or Boston lettuce
- 3 cups torn fresh spinach
- 1 medium orange, peeled and sliced
- ½ fennel bulb, cut into slivers (reserve 2 tablespoons snipped fronds for garnish)
- ⅓ cup bias-sliced green onions
- 1 recipe Orange Dressing
- 2 tablespoons sliced almonds, toasted
  Cracked black pepper (optional)

1. In a small bowl combine olive oil, thyme, salt, and pepper. Brush oil mixture on the chicken.
2. For a charcoal grill, place chicken on the grill rack directly over medium coals. Grill, uncovered, for 12 to 15 minutes or until chicken is tender and no longer pink (170°F), turning once halfway through grilling. (For a gas grill, preheat grill. Reduce heat to medium. Place chicken on grill rack over heat. Cover and grill as above.)
3. Meanwhile, arrange lettuce and spinach on four serving plates. Top evenly with orange slices, fennel, and green onions.
4. Cut chicken into bite-size pieces. Top salads evenly with chicken. Drizzle Orange Dressing evenly over salads and sprinkle with fennel fronds, almonds, and, if desired, cracked black pepper.

ORANGE DRESSING: In a small bowl stir together ½ cup light sour cream, 1 teaspoon finely shredded orange peel, and 3 tablespoons orange juice. If necessary, stir in additional orange juice, 1 teaspoon at a time, to make dressing drizzling consistency.

PER SERVING: 279 cal., 9 g total fat (3 g sat. fat), 91 mg chol., 292 mg sodium, 12 g carb. (3 g fiber, 5 g sugars), 36 g pro. Exchanges: 1 vegetable, 0.5 carb., 4.5 lean meat, 0.5 fat. Carb choices: 1.

Orzo Chicken Salad with
Avocado-Lime Dressing

Chicken Salad with Creamy Tarragon-Shallot Dressing

If you wish, use a paring knife to trim the ends of the green beans.

SERVINGS 4 (about 2 cups salad, 1 chicken thigh, and about 3 tablespoons dressing each)

CARB. PER SERVING 11 g

4 skinless, boneless chicken thighs (about 12 ounces total)
⅛ teaspoon salt
⅛ teaspoon black pepper
8 ounces fresh green beans
  Nonstick cooking spray
1½ cups sliced fresh mushrooms
6 cups torn Bibb lettuce
4 hard-cooked eggs, peeled and thinly sliced
¾ cup grape or cherry tomatoes, halved (optional)
1 recipe Creamy Tarragon-Shallot Dressing

Chicken Salad with Creamy Tarragon-Shallot Dressing

1. Trim fat from chicken. Sprinkle chicken with the salt and pepper. For a charcoal grill, place chicken thighs on the grill rack directly over medium coals. Grill, uncovered, for 12 to 15 minutes or until no longer pink (180°F), turning once halfway through grilling. (For a gas grill, preheat grill. Reduce heat to medium. Place chicken thighs on grill rack over heat. Cover and grill as above.) Slice chicken thighs into strips. Set aside.

2. Meanwhile, in a medium saucepan cook beans, covered, in enough boiling water to cover for 8 to 10 minutes or until tender. Drain and rinse with cold water to cool quickly; drain again and set aside.

3. Coat an unheated large nonstick skillet with cooking spray; heat over medium heat. Cook mushrooms in hot skillet for 5 to 7 minutes or until tender and lightly browned, stirring occasionally. Remove from heat and cool slightly.

4. To serve, divide torn lettuce among four serving bowls. Top with green beans, cooked mushrooms, sliced eggs, and, if desired, tomatoes. Arrange grilled chicken strips on salads. Drizzle with Creamy Tarragon-Shallot Dressing.

CREAMY TARRAGON-SHALLOT DRESSING: In a small bowl whisk together ⅓ cup buttermilk and 2 tablespoons light mayonnaise. Stir in ¼ cup finely chopped shallots, 1 tablespoon snipped fresh tarragon, ⅛ teaspoon salt, and a dash black pepper.

PER SERVING: 259 cal., 12 g total fat (3 g sat. fat), 287 mg chol., 359 mg sodium, 11 g carb. (3 g fiber, 5 g sugars), 27 g pro. Exchanges: 1 vegetable, 0.5 starch, 3.5 lean meat, 1 fat. Carb choices: 1.

Grilled Pork and Peach Salad

Prepare this summery recipe when peaches are at their ripest and juiciest.

SERVINGS 4 (1½ cups lettuce, ¾ cup pork mixture, and 1 tablespoon green onions each)

CARB. PER SERVING 20 g

- 1 1-pound pork tenderloin
- 2 medium peaches or nectarines
- 2 tablespoons honey
- 2 tablespoons orange juice
- 1 tablespoon low-sodium soy sauce
- ½ teaspoon curry powder
- ¼ teaspoon black pepper
- 3 cups torn Bibb lettuce
- 3 cups packaged fresh baby spinach
- 2 green onions, bias sliced (¼ cup)

Grilled Pork and Peach Salad

1. Trim pork and cut into 1-inch cubes. Pit peaches and cut into 1-inch cubes. On four 10-inch skewers* thread pork cubes. On three more 10-inch skewers* thread peach cubes. For a charcoal grill, place skewers on the grill rack directly over medium coals. Grill, uncovered, allowing 10 to 12 minutes for pork or until pork is slightly pink in the center, turning occasionally. For peaches, allow 8 to 10 minutes or until peaches are browned. (For a gas grill, preheat grill. Reduce heat to medium. Place skewers on grill rack over heat. Cover and grill as above.)

2. Meanwhile, in a large bowl stir together honey, orange juice, soy sauce, curry powder, and pepper. When pork skewers are done, remove pork and peaches from skewers and place in honey mixture; toss to coat.

3. To serve, arrange lettuce and spinach on four serving plates. Spoon pork and peaches evenly over greens. Sprinkle with green onions.

***TEST KITCHEN TIP:** If using wooden skewers, soak them in enough water to cover for at least 30 minutes before using.

PER SERVING: 207 cal., 3 g total fat (1 g sat. fat), 54 mg chol., 444 mg sodium, 20 g carb. (3 g fiber, 17 g sugars), 26 g pro. Exchanges: 1 vegetable, 0.5 fruit, 0.5 carb., 3.5 lean meat. Carb choices: 1.

Prosciutto Salad with Blue Cheese

Fresh sliced prosciutto is almost buttery. Be sure to request that a paper be added between each slice. Otherwise, the slices will stick together.

SERVINGS 4 (2 cups salad and 1½ tablespoons dressing each)

CARB. PER SERVING 9 g

- 5 cups watercress, tough stems trimmed, or packaged fresh baby spinach
- 1 small head radicchio, cored and coarsely shredded (about 2 cups)
- 2 medium shallots, thinly sliced
- 1 recipe Lemon Vinaigrette
- 1 ounce thinly sliced prosciutto, cut into thin strips
- ¾ cup coarsely chopped cantaloupe
- 2 tablespoons crumbled blue cheese
- 2 tablespoons shelled pistachio nuts, coarsely chopped

1. In a large bowl combine watercress, radicchio, and shallots. Add half of the Lemon Vinaigrette; toss to coat. Divide salad among four serving plates.

2. Top evenly with prosciutto, cantaloupe, blue cheese, and pistachio nuts. Drizzle with remaining Lemon Vinaigrette.

LEMON VINAIGRETTE: In a screw-top jar combine ½ teaspoon finely shredded lemon peel, 3 tablespoons lemon juice, 2 tablespoons olive oil, 1 teaspoon snipped fresh rosemary or thyme, 1 teaspoon honey, and ⅛ teaspoon salt. Cover and shake well.

PER SERVING: 154 cal., 12 g total fat (2 g sat. fat), 3 mg chol., 286 mg sodium, 9 g carb. (1 g fiber, 5 g sugars), 5 g pro. Exchanges: 1 vegetable, 0.5 medium-fat meat, 2 fat. Carb choices: 0.5.

Pork with Fresh Corn Salad

When corn is at peak-season freshness, the kernels are sweet, milky, and tender—just right to use in a salad.

SERVINGS 4 (4 ounces pork and 1¾ cups corn mixture each)

CARB. PER SERVING 24 g

- 1 teaspoon paprika
- ½ teaspoon garlic powder
- ½ teaspoon ground cumin
- ½ teaspoon black pepper
- ¼ teaspoon salt
- 1 1-pound pork tenderloin
-   Nonstick cooking spray
- 3 ears fresh sweet corn, husks and silks removed
- 2 cups packaged fresh baby spinach
- 1 cup fresh blackberries
- ¼ of a medium jicama, peeled and cut into matchstick-size pieces (½ cup)
- 1 recipe Honey-Rosemary Vinaigrette

1. Preheat oven to 400°F. For rub, in a small bowl combine paprika, garlic powder, cumin, pepper, and salt. Sprinkle rub evenly over all sides of tenderloin; rub in with your fingers.

2. Coat an unheated large nonstick oven-going skillet with cooking spray; heat over medium-high heat. Add tenderloin to the hot skillet; cook, turning occasionally, for 5 to 6 minutes or until well browned on all sides. Place skillet in oven. Roast for 15 to 20 minutes or until an instant-read thermometer inserted into thickest part of the tenderloin registers 145°F.

3. Remove tenderloin from oven. Cover tightly with foil; let stand for 3 minutes. The temperature of the meat after standing should be 150°F. Thinly slice pork crosswise.

4. Meanwhile, cut corn kernels off the cobs. Place corn in a large bowl. Add spinach, blackberries, and jicama. Add Honey-Rosemary Vinaigrette; toss to coat. To serve, divide corn mixture among four serving plates. Top with pork slices.

HONEY-ROSEMARY VINAIGRETTE: In a small screw-top jar combine ¼ cup cider vinegar, 1 tablespoon canola oil, 1 tablespoon honey, 1 teaspoon snipped fresh rosemary, and ⅛ teaspoon salt. Cover and shake well.

PER SERVING: 264 cal., 7 g total fat (1 g sat. fat), 74 mg chol., 313 mg sodium, 24 g carb. (6 g fiber, 8 g sugars), 27 g pro. Exchanges: 0.5 vegetable, 1.5 starch, 3 lean meat. Carb choices: 1.5.

▶ QUICK TIP
Plump blueberries or ruby red raspberries make good replacements for the blackberries.

Pork with Fresh Corn Salad

Pork Barley Salad

You can peel the cuplike leaves from the lettuce head and then use a couple to cradle each serving of barley mixture instead of tearing it into bite-size pieces.

SERVINGS 6 (2 ounces pork, ¾ cup barley mixture, and 1 cup greens each)

CARB. PER SERVING 34 g

- 5 cups water
- 1 cup pearl barley
- 1 cup frozen sweet soybeans (edamame)
- 1 recipe Dijon Vinaigrette
- 1 medium red sweet pepper, chopped (¾ cup)
- ⅓ cup sliced green onions
- ¼ cup chopped cornichons
- ¼ cup snipped fresh parsley
- 1 1-pound pork tenderloin, trimmed
- 6 cups torn Bibb or Boston lettuce

1. In a large saucepan bring the water to boiling over high heat. Stir in barley; reduce heat. Cover and simmer for 45 to 50 minutes or just until barley is tender, adding edamame for the last 10 minutes of cooking; drain. Place barley and edamame in a large bowl. Pour Dijon Vinaigrette over warm barley mixture; toss to coat. Add the sweet pepper, green onions, cornichons, and parsley to barley mixture; mix well. Set aside.

Pork Barley Salad

2. Sprinkle pork tenderloin evenly with ¼ teaspoon black pepper. For a charcoal grill, arrange hot coals around a drip pan. Test for medium-high heat above pan. Place meat on grill rack over pan. Cover; grill for 25 to 30 minutes or until a meat thermometer registers 145°F. (For a gas grill, preheat grill. Reduce heat to medium. Adjust for indirect cooking. Grill as directed.)

3. Transfer pork to a cutting board. Cover tightly with foil; let stand for 3 minutes. Cut into ¼-inch-thick slices; cut slices into strips. Add pork to barley mixture; stir to combine. Arrange lettuce on six serving plates; spoon warm salad over lettuce.

DIJON VINAIGRETTE: In a screw-top jar combine ¼ cup white wine vinegar; 2 tablespoons finely chopped red onion; 2 tablespoons olive oil; 2 teaspoons Dijon mustard; 2 cloves garlic, minced; and ¼ teaspoon black pepper. Cover and shake well.

PER SERVING: 308 cal., 8 g total fat (1 g sat. fat), 49 mg chol., 130 mg sodium, 34 g carb. (8 g fiber, 4 g sugars), 24 g pro. Exchanges: 1 vegetable, 2 starch, 2 lean meat, 0.5 fat. Carb choices: 2.

Grilled Flank Steak Salad

To ensure everything is grilled to perfection, start the steak first. After a few minutes, add the corn and then the sweet peppers. Add the green onions last.

SERVINGS 2 (3 ounces cooked steak, 1 cup greens, ½ cup vegetables, and 1½ tablespoons dressing each)

CARB. PER SERVING 31 g

- 1 recipe Cilantro Dressing
- 8 ounces beef flank steak
- 2 small yellow and/or red sweet peppers, halved
- 1 ear fresh sweet corn, husks and silks removed
- 2 green onions, trimmed
  Nonstick cooking spray
- 2 cups torn romaine lettuce
- 4 cherry tomatoes, halved
- ¼ of a small avocado, peeled and thinly sliced (optional)

1. Prepare Cilantro Dressing; divide it into two portions.

2. Trim fat from steak. Score both sides of steak in a diamond pattern by making shallow diagonal cuts at 1-inch intervals. Place steak in a resealable plastic bag set in a shallow dish. Pour one portion of the Cilantro Dressing over steak; set remaining dressing portion aside. Seal bag; turn to coat steak. Marinate in the refrigerator for 30 minutes.

Grilled Flank Steak Salad

3. Coat sweet peppers, corn, and green onions with cooking spray.

4. For a charcoal grill, place steak and corn on the grill rack directly over medium coals. Grill, uncovered, until steak is desired doneness and corn is tender, turning steak once halfway through grilling and turning corn occasionally. For steak, allow 17 to 21 minutes for medium rare (145°F) to medium (160°F). For corn, allow 15 to 20 minutes. Add sweet pepper halves to the grill for the last 8 minutes of grilling and green onions to the grill for the last 4 minutes of grilling, turning frequently. (For a gas grill, preheat grill. Reduce heat to medium. Place meat and then vegetables on grill rack over heat. Cover and grill as above.)

5. Thinly slice steak against the grain. Coarsely chop sweet peppers and green onions; cut corn from cob, leaving kernels in planks. To serve, divide romaine lettuce between two bowls. Place steak, grilled vegetables, tomatoes, and, if desired, avocado slices over romaine. Drizzle salads with the reserved portion of Cilantro Dressing.

CILANTRO DRESSING: In a blender or small food processor combine 3 tablespoons lime juice; 2 tablespoons chopped shallot; 2 tablespoons snipped fresh cilantro; 1 tablespoon water; 2 teaspoons olive oil; 2 teaspoons honey; 1 large clove garlic, quartered; ½ teaspoon chili powder; ¼ teaspoon salt; and ¼ teaspoon ground cumin. Cover and blend or process until combined.

PER SERVING: 337 cal., 12 g total fat (3 g sat. fat), 47 mg chol., 375 mg sodium, 31 g carb. (5 g fiber, 13 g sugars), 29 g pro. Exchanges: 2 vegetable, 0.5 starch, 1 carb., 3.5 lean meat, 1.5 fat. Carb choices: 2.

Carne Asada Salad

Make It Mine

An ingredient addition here or there will personalize your salad without making a critical change in your meal plan numbers. Try one of these ideas.

1. **Serve** a warm corn tortilla alongside.
2. **Crush** a few baked tortilla chips over the top.
3. **Top** the salad with a spoonful of light sour cream.
4. **Add** a slice or two of fresh avocado just before serving.
5. **Sprinkle** on a handful of fresh corn kernels.
6. **Spoon** about ¼ cup of cooked brown rice over the top.
7. **Squeeze** a lime wedge over the salad.

Chilled Salmon and Tabbouleh
recipe on page 54

Carne Asada Salad

The 10-minute stand time before slicing the meat allows the juices to redistribute, making the meat juicier and tastier.

SERVINGS 6 (1 cup lettuce, ⅔ cup bean mixture, and 2½ ounces cooked beef each)

CARB. PER SERVING 17 g

- 1 1-pound beef flank steak
- 1 teaspoon ground ancho chile pepper
- ½ teaspoon dried oregano, crushed
- ½ teaspoon ground cumin
- ¼ teaspoon salt
  Dash ground cinnamon
- 1 small sweet onion, cut into ¼-inch slices
- 4 medium tomatillos, halved and stems removed
- 1 15-ounce can black beans, rinsed and drained
- 1 medium tomato, seeded and chopped (½ cup)
- 1 small fresh jalapeño chile pepper, seeded and finely chopped*
- ¼ cup snipped fresh cilantro
- ¼ cup lime juice
- ¼ teaspoon ground cumin
- 6 cups coarsely torn romaine lettuce

1. Trim fat from steak. Score both sides of steak in a diamond pattern, making shallow diagonal cuts at 1-inch intervals. In a small bowl stir together the ground chile pepper, oregano, ½ teaspoon cumin, salt, and cinnamon. Sprinkle spice mixture evenly over the steak, rubbing it in with your fingers.

2. For a charcoal grill, place steak, onion slices, and tomatillo halves on the grill rack directly over medium coals. Grill steak, uncovered, for 17 to 21 minutes for medium (160°F), turning once halfway through grilling. Grill onion and tomatillos for 10 to 12 minutes or until tender and browned, turning once halfway through grilling. (For a gas grill, preheat grill. Reduce heat to medium. Place steak and then vegetables on grill rack over heat. Cover and grill as above.)**

3. Transfer steak, onion, and tomatillos to a cutting board. Cover steak with foil; let stand for 10 minutes. Meanwhile, chop the onion slices and tomatillos. In a large bowl combine chopped onion and tomatillos, beans, tomato, jalapeño pepper, and cilantro. Add lime juice and ¼ teaspoon cumin; toss to combine. Thinly slice steak across the grain. To serve, arrange romaine on six serving plates. Top with bean mixture and steak slices.

***TEST KITCHEN TIP:** Because chile peppers contain volatile oils that can burn your skin and eyes, avoid direct contact with them as much as possible. When working with chile peppers, wear plastic or rubber gloves. If your bare hands do touch the peppers, wash your hands and nails well with soap and warm water.

****TEST KITCHEN TIP:** To broil steak, place the steak on the unheated rack of a broiler pan. Broil 3 to 4 inches from the heat for 15 to 18 minutes or until medium (160°F), turning once halfway through broiling and adding tomatoes and onions to broiler pan for the last 10 minutes of cooking, turning them once. Continue as directed.

PER SERVING: 191 cal., 5 g total fat (2 g sat. fat), 31 mg chol., 329 mg sodium, 17 g carb. (6 g fiber, 4 g sugars), 22 g pro. Exchanges: 1 vegetable, 1 starch, 2.5 lean meat. Carb choices: 1.

Easy Taco Salad

With the help of precooked seasoned ground beef, you can make this kid-friendly salad in 15 minutes or less.

SERVINGS 2 (2 cups each)

CARB. PER SERVING 27 g

- 4 ounces refrigerated seasoned ground beef (½ cup)
- 3 cups shredded romaine lettuce
- ¾ cup chopped tomatoes
- ½ cup canned no-salt-added black beans, rinsed and drained
- ¼ cup shredded reduced-fat cheddar cheese (1 ounce)
- 1 0.75-ounce package baked nacho-cheese flavor tortilla chips
- 2 tablespoons light sour cream
- 1 tablespoon bottled salsa

1. Prepare seasoned ground beef according to package directions. Divide romaine lettuce between two serving plates or large salad bowls. Top with heated seasoned beef. Top with tomatoes, beans, cheese, and chips. Serve with sour cream and salsa.

PER SERVING: 235 cal., 8 g total fat (4 g sat. fat), 36 mg chol., 549 mg sodium, 27 g carb. (6 g fiber, 5 g sugars), 17 g pro. Exchanges: 1.5 vegetable, 1.5 starch, 1.5 lean meat, 0.5 fat. Carb choices: 2.

Chilled Salmon and Tabbouleh

A lemony veggie-and-bulgur medley helps boost the fiber in this refreshing garlic-seasoned salmon salad. Pictured on page 52.

SERVINGS 4 (about 1½ cups each)
CARB. PER SERVING 22 g

 1 pound fresh or frozen skinless salmon fillets
 1 cup water
 2 cloves garlic, minced
 1 teaspoon finely shredded lemon peel
 1½ cups water
 ½ cup bulgur
 ⅓ cup lemon juice
 2 tablespoons olive oil
 1 cup grape tomatoes or cherry tomatoes, halved
 1 cup frozen artichoke hearts, thawed, drained, and coarsely chopped
 1 cup chopped, seeded cucumber
 ½ cup snipped fresh Italian (flat-leaf) parsley
 ¼ cup snipped fresh mint
 2 green onions, thinly sliced

1. Thaw fish, if frozen. Rinse fish; pat dry with paper towels. In a large skillet bring the 1 cup water to boiling. Add salmon in a single layer. Simmer, covered, for 8 to 10 minutes or until fish flakes easily when tested with a fork. Using a slotted spatula, carefully transfer fish to a platter. Sprinkle all sides of the fish with ¼ teaspoon *salt* and ⅛ teaspoon *black pepper*. In a small bowl combine garlic and lemon peel; sprinkle evenly over one side of each fish fillet, pressing in with your fingers. Cover and chill salmon.
2. Meanwhile, in a large bowl combine the 1½ cups water and the bulgur. Let stand for 1 hour. Drain bulgur through a fine-mesh sieve, using a large spoon to press out any excess water.
3. In the same large bowl whisk together lemon juice, oil, ¼ teaspoon *salt,* and ⅛ teaspoon *black pepper.* Add drained bulgur, tomatoes, artichoke hearts, cucumber, parsley, mint, and green onions. Toss to combine. Break salmon into large chunks. Gently toss salmon into bulgur mixture. Cover and chill for 2 to 24 hours.
4. To serve, divide salmon-bulgur mixture among four serving plates.

PER SERVING: 393 cal., 22 g total fat (4 g sat. fat), 62 mg chol., 390 mg sodium, 22 g carb. (6 g fiber, 3 g sugars), 27 g pro. Exchanges: 1 vegetable, 1 starch, 3 lean meat, 3 fat. Carb choices: 1.5.

Grilled Shrimp Salad with Creamy Garlic Dressing

When peeling and deveining the shrimp, you can leave the tails intact if you wish.

SERVINGS 4 (1 shrimp skewer and 1½ cups salad each)
CARB. PER SERVING 9 g

 1 pound fresh or frozen large shrimp in shells
 ¼ teaspoon salt
 ⅛ teaspoon black pepper
 6 cups mixed spring salad greens
 1 cup coarsely chopped cucumber
 ½ cup shaved, peeled jicama*
 4 radishes, thinly sliced
 1 recipe Creamy Garlic Dressing
 2 ounces semisoft goat cheese (chèvre), crumbled (optional)

1. Thaw shrimp, if frozen. Peel and devein shrimp. Rinse shrimp; pat dry with paper towels. Thread shrimp onto four 12-inch skewers,** leaving a ¼-inch space between each shrimp. Sprinkle shrimp with salt and pepper.
2. For a charcoal grill, place shrimp skewers on the grill rack directly over medium coals. Grill, uncovered, for 6 to 8 minutes or until shrimp are opaque, turning once halfway through grilling. (For a gas grill, preheat grill. Reduce heat to medium. Place skewers on grill rack over heat. Cover and grill as above.)
3. To serve, divide salad greens among four serving plates. Top with cucumber, jicama, and radishes. Top each salad with a shrimp skewer. Spoon Creamy Garlic Dressing over salads. If desired, sprinkle with goat cheese. Serve immediately.

CREAMY GARLIC DRESSING: In a small bowl combine ½ cup plain fat-free yogurt; 3 tablespoons fat-free milk; 2 tablespoons snipped fresh mint; 2 teaspoons snipped fresh dill; 1 large clove garlic, minced; ⅛ teaspoon salt; and dash black pepper.

***TEST KITCHEN TIP:** Use a vegetable peeler to shave enough wide strips of the peeled jicama to make ½ cup.

****TEST KITCHEN TIP:** If using wooden skewers, soak them in enough water to cover for at least 30 minutes before using.

PER SERVING: 165 cal., 2 g total fat (0 g sat. fat), 173 mg chol., 429 mg sodium, 9 g carb. (2 g fiber, 4 g sugars), 27 g pro. Exchanges: 1.5 vegetable, 3 lean meat. Carb choices: 0.5.

Grilled Shrimp Salad with
Creamy Garlic Dressing

Gazpacho Crab and Pasta Salad

All the summery flavors of cold tomato soup combine in this fresh and flavorful pasta salad.

SERVINGS 4 (1½ cups each)
CARB. PER SERVING 36 g

- 5 ounces dried whole grain medium shell macaroni (about 1½ cups)
- 1 recipe Spicy Tomato Dressing
- 2 medium tomatoes, seeded and chopped (1 cup)
- 1 cup chopped cucumber
- 1 small red sweet pepper, chopped (½ cup)
- 1 small green sweet pepper, chopped (½ cup)
- ⅓ cup slivered red onion
- ¼ cup snipped fresh cilantro
- 6 ounces cooked crabmeat, flaked, or 8 ounces cooked, peeled small shrimp

1. Cook pasta according to package directions; rinse with cold water and drain.

2. In a large bowl combine the pasta, Spicy Tomato Dressing, tomatoes, cucumber, sweet peppers, onion, and cilantro; toss to coat. Gently stir in crabmeat. Chill for 1 hour or until ready to serve.* To serve, divide salad among four serving plates.

SPICY TOMATO DRESSING: In a screw-top jar combine 1 cup low-sodium vegetable juice; 1 tablespoon olive oil; 1 tablespoon red wine vinegar; 1 clove garlic, minced; 1 teaspoon smoked paprika; and ¼ teaspoon cayenne pepper. Cover and shake well until combined.

***TEST KITCHEN TIP:** If pasta absorbs dressing while chilling, add a little low-sodium vegetable juice to moisten it.

PER SERVING: 238 cal., 5 g total fat (1 g sat. fat), 38 mg chol., 282 mg sodium, 36 g carb. (3 g fiber, 6 g sugars), 12 g pro. Exchanges: 1 vegetable, 2 starch, 0.5 lean meat, 0.5 fat. Carb choices: 1.5.

Seared Tuna with Fennel Salad

Reach for a mandoline or a very sharp knife to cut the fennel bulbs into very thin slices.

SERVINGS 4 (1¾ cups salad, 4 ounces tuna, and 2 tablespoons dressing each)
CARB. PER SERVING 10 g

- 1 pound fresh or frozen tuna steaks, cut 1 inch thick
- ¼ teaspoon salt
- ¼ teaspoon freshly ground black pepper
- 3 cups torn fresh curly endive or frisée
- 2 medium fennel bulbs, trimmed, cored, and very thinly sliced (3 cups)
- ¼ of a medium red onion, thinly sliced
- ¼ cup pitted Kalamata olives, halved
- Nonstick cooking spray
- 1 recipe Garlic-Lime Aïoli Dressing

1. Thaw fish, if frozen. Rinse fish and pat dry with paper towels. Sprinkle fish evenly with salt and pepper; set aside. In a large bowl toss together endive, fennel, and red onion; divide mixture among four serving plates. Sprinkle evenly with olives. Set aside.

2. Coat an unheated grill pan with cooking spray; heat pan over medium-high heat. Add tuna steaks to the hot pan. Cook about 6 minutes or until steaks are well browned on the outside, turning once; steaks will be pink in the centers. Transfer steaks to a cutting board. Cut steaks into ¼-inch-thick slices.

3. To serve, arrange tuna slices on salads. Drizzle with Garlic-Lime Aïoli Dressing.

GARLIC-LIME AÏOLI DRESSING: In a small bowl combine ⅓ cup light mayonnaise; 3 tablespoons fat-free milk; ½ teaspoon finely shredded lime peel; 1 tablespoon lime juice; and 2 cloves garlic, minced.

PER SERVING: 234 cal., 9 g total fat (1 g sat. fat), 58 mg chol., 443 mg sodium, 10 g carb. (4 g fiber, 2 g sugars), 29 g pro. Exchanges: 1 vegetable, 4 lean meat, 0.5 fat. Carb choices: 0.5.

Edamame and Cabbage Salad with Peanut Dressing

Soybeans, peanuts, and peanut butter provide all the protein this crunchy, slawlike vegetarian salad needs to be a main dish.

SERVINGS 4 (2 cups each)
CARB. PER SERVING 20 g

- 1½ cups frozen sweet soybeans (edamame), thawed
- 4 cups coarsely shredded napa cabbage
- 1 cup packaged coarsely shredded fresh carrots
- ½ of a small red onion, thinly sliced
- 6 radishes, thinly sliced
- 1 recipe Peanut Dressing
- ¼ cup lightly salted peanuts, coarsely chopped (optional)

1. In a small saucepan cook edamame, covered, in a small amount of boiling water for 5 minutes or until

Roasted Tomato and
Mushroom Pasta Salad

▶ QUICK TIP

Use a vegetable peeler to make shavings from a chunk of Parmesan cheese.

Roasted Tomato and Mushroom Pasta Salad

So the tomato halves stay as plump and juicy as possible, place the cut sides up on the baking pan for roasting.

SERVINGS 6 (1¼ cups each)

CARB. PER SERVING 35 g

8	ounces fresh mushrooms, sliced
8	ounces grape tomatoes or cherry tomatoes, halved
4	cloves garlic, thinly sliced
2	teaspoons dried oregano, crushed
1	tablespoon olive oil
6	ounces dried whole grain penne pasta
2	tablespoons olive oil
2	tablespoons white wine vinegar
½	teaspoon cracked black pepper
1	15-ounce can cannellini beans (white kidney beans), rinsed and drained
½	cup snipped fresh basil
2	ounces Parmesan cheese, shaved

1. Preheat oven to 450°F. Line a 15×10×1-inch baking pan with foil. Arrange mushrooms and tomato halves, cut sides up, in the prepared pan. Sprinkle with garlic and oregano. Drizzle with the 1 tablespoon olive oil. Roast, uncovered, for 20 to 25 minutes or until tomatoes are soft and skins begin to split and mushrooms are light brown.

2. Meanwhile, cook pasta according to package directions, lightly salting the pasta water; drain. In a large bowl whisk together the 2 tablespoons olive oil, the vinegar, and pepper. Add warm pasta to the bowl; toss to coat. Let cool to room temperature, stirring occasionally.

3. To pasta, add mushroom-tomato mixture and any drippings from the pan, beans, basil, and shaved Parmesan. Toss to combine. Serve at room temperature.

PER SERVING: 264 cal., 10 g total fat (3 g sat. fat), 6 mg chol., 271 mg sodium, 35 g carb. (4 g fiber, 2 g sugars), 13 g pro. Exchanges: 1 vegetable, 2 starch, 1 lean meat, 1 fat. Carb choices: 2.

tender, stirring once or twice. Drain; rinse with cold water to cool quickly. Drain again.

2. In a large bowl combine drained edamame, cabbage, carrots, red onion, and radishes.

3. Drizzle Peanut Dressing over salad and toss to coat. To serve, divide salad among four serving plates. If desired, sprinkle with peanuts.

PEANUT DRESSING: In a small saucepan combine 3 tablespoons creamy peanut butter, 2 tablespoons rice vinegar, 2 tablespoons water, 1 tablespoon honey, ½ teaspoon grated fresh ginger, and ⅛ teaspoon crushed red pepper. Heat and whisk over medium-low heat until combined and smooth.

PER SERVING: 209 cal., 10 g total fat (2 g sat. fat), 0 mg chol., 92 mg sodium, 20 g carb. (6 g fiber, 11 g sugars), 12 g pro. Exchanges: 1.5 vegetable, 1 starch, 1 lean meat, 1.5 fat. Carb choices: 1.

comforting
soups and stews

From humble bean chilies and hearty meat stews to brothy noodle soups and creamy vegetable chowders, these one-pot wonders are easy to make and soothing to eat. Loaded with nutrient-rich ingredients, spoonable combos are meals you can feel good about serving and your family will enjoy eating.

Pasta e Fagioli

Any shape of whole grain pasta is good in this soup, so if you have a partial bag or box, add that.

SERVINGS 8 (1 cup each)
CARB. PER SERVING 35 g

1 tablespoon olive oil
2 ounces prosciutto or turkey bacon, chopped
2 large onions, chopped (2 cups)
1 stalk celery, chopped (½ cup)
1 medium carrot, chopped (½ cup)
12 cloves garlic, minced
1 tablespoon dried oregano, crushed
1 teaspoon anchovy paste (optional)
1 teaspoon crushed red pepper
2 14.5-ounce cans reduced-sodium chicken broth
1 28-ounce can no-salt-added diced tomatoes, undrained
1 cup whole grain medium pasta shells
2 15-ounce cans no-salt-added cannellini beans (white kidney beans), rinsed and drained
½ cup snipped fresh parsley
2 tablespoons lemon juice
¼ cup finely shredded Parmesan cheese (1 ounce)

1. In a Dutch oven heat oil over medium-high heat. Add prosciutto; cook for 2 to 3 minutes or until crisp. Using a slotted spoon, transfer prosciutto to paper towels; let drain. Set aside.
2. Add onions, celery, carrot, and garlic to the Dutch oven; cook over medium heat for 3 to 4 minutes or until softened, stirring frequently. Stir in oregano, anchovy paste (if desired), and crushed red pepper. Cook and stir for 1 minute. Add broth, tomatoes, and pasta shells. Bring to boiling; reduce heat. Simmer, uncovered, about 15 minutes or until pasta is tender.
3. Meanwhile, use a fork to mash one can of the beans. Stir the whole and mashed beans into pasta mixture. Simmer about 5 minutes or until heated through.
4. Stir in parsley and lemon juice. To serve, ladle soup into bowls. Sprinkle with Parmesan and the crispy prosciutto.

PER SERVING: 235 cal., 5 g total fat (1 g sat. fat), 2 mg chol., 490 mg sodium, 35 g carb. (9 g fiber, 7 g sugars), 13 g pro. Exchanges: 1 vegetable, 2 starch, 1 lean meat, 0.5 fat. Carb choices: 2.

Vegetable Garden Soup with Turkey

Turkey Meatball Soup

To make equal-size meatballs, use a measuring teaspoon to portion out the turkey mixture and then roll it into balls.

SERVINGS 6 (1⅓ cups each)
CARB. PER SERVING 20 g

Nonstick cooking spray
¾ cup soft whole wheat bread crumbs (1½ slices)
¼ cup bottled light ranch salad dressing
1 egg white, lightly beaten
¼ teaspoon black pepper
1 pound ground turkey breast
2 medium carrots, thinly sliced (1 cup)
1 stalk celery, thinly sliced (½ cup)
1 tablespoon olive oil
3 cups water
1 14.5-ounce can reduced-sodium chicken broth
1 cup multigrain elbow macaroni
1 cup cherry or grape tomatoes, halved
4 cups packaged fresh baby spinach
2 ounces Parmesan cheese, coarsely shredded (optional)

1. Preheat oven to 350°F. Line a 15×10×1-inch baking pan with foil; coat foil with cooking spray. In a large bowl combine bread crumbs, dressing, egg white, and pepper. Add ground turkey; mix well. Shape mixture into ¾-inch meatballs (about 72). Place meatballs in the prepared baking pan. Bake about 10 minutes or until done (165°F). Set aside.

2. In a 4-quart Dutch oven cook carrots and celery in hot oil over medium heat for 5 minutes, stirring occasionally. Add the water and broth; bring to boiling. Add macaroni. Return to boiling; reduce heat. Simmer, covered, for 7 minutes or until macaroni is just tender, stirring occasionally.

3. Add meatballs and tomatoes to soup; heat through. Stir in spinach just before serving. To serve, ladle soup into bowls. If desired, sprinkle with Parmesan cheese.

PER SERVING: 230 cal., 6 g total fat (1 g sat. fat), 39 mg chol., 409 mg sodium, 20 g carb. (3 g fiber, 3 g sugars), 24 g pro. Exchanges: 1 vegetable, 1 starch, 3 lean meat. Carb choices: 1.

Vegetable Garden Soup with Turkey

For a quick substitute, use rotisserie chicken instead of the shredded cooked turkey.

SERVINGS 6 (1½ cups each)
CARB. PER SERVING 14 g

1 medium onion, chopped (½ cup)
1 stalk celery, thinly sliced (½ cup)
1 tablespoon olive oil
3 cloves garlic, minced
2 14.5-ounce cans reduced-sodium chicken broth
1 cup water
8 ounces 2-inch-diameter new potatoes, quartered
6 ounces fresh green beans, trimmed and cut into 1-inch pieces (1½ cups)
9 ounces yellow summer squash, halved lengthwise and cut into thick slices
2 cups coarsely shredded cooked fresh turkey breast
1 large tomato, coarsely chopped
1 tablespoon snipped fresh thyme or lemon thyme
2 teaspoons snipped fresh sage
¼ teaspoon black pepper

1. In a 4-quart Dutch oven cook onion and celery in hot oil over medium heat for 5 minutes, stirring occasionally. Add garlic; cook and stir for 30 seconds. Add broth and the water. Bring to boiling. Add potatoes, beans, and squash. Return to boiling; reduce heat. Simmer, covered, for 10 to 12 minutes or until vegetables are tender.

2. Stir in turkey, tomato, thyme, sage, and pepper. Heat through. To serve, ladle soup into bowls.

PER SERVING: 155 cal., 3 g total fat (1 g sat. fat), 35 mg chol., 368 mg sodium, 14 g carb. (3 g fiber, 4 g sugars), 19 g pro. Exchanges: 1 vegetable, 0.5 starch, 2 lean meat. Carb choices: 1.

BBQ Bean Chili

Turkey Chipotle Chili

Spoon leftover tomato paste into 1-tablespoon portions in ice cube trays and freeze until solid. Pop the tomato paste cubes from the tray and store them in a freezer bag in the freezer.

SERVINGS 6 (1⅔ cups each)

CARB. PER SERVING 34 g

- 2 large onions, chopped (2 cups)
- 1 medium green sweet pepper, chopped (¾ cup)
- ½ cup frozen whole kernel corn
- 12 cloves garlic, minced
- 2 tablespoons olive oil
- 2 tablespoons finely chopped canned chipotle chile peppers in adobo sauce (see tip, page 63)
- 1 tablespoon tomato paste
- 1 tablespoon chili powder
- 1 tablespoon dried oregano, crushed
- 2 teaspoons ground cumin
- 1 teaspoon ground coriander
- 4 cups reduced-sodium chicken broth
- 3 cups chopped or shredded roasted turkey breast
- 1 15-ounce can no-salt-added tomato sauce
- 1 15-ounce can no-salt-added black beans, rinsed and drained
- 1 14.5-ounce can no-salt-added diced tomatoes, undrained
- ¼ cup finely snipped fresh cilantro
- 2 green onions, chopped (¼ cup)
- 2 tablespoons lime juice
- 6 tablespoons plain low-fat Greek yogurt or sour cream
  Snipped fresh cilantro (optional)

1. In a 4-quart Dutch oven cook onions, sweet pepper, corn, and garlic in hot oil about 5 minutes or until vegetables are tender. Stir in chile peppers and tomato paste; cook for 1 minute more.
2. Stir in chili powder, oregano, cumin, and coriander. Stir in broth, turkey, tomato sauce, black beans, and diced tomatoes. Bring to boiling; reduce heat to medium-low. Simmer, covered, for 20 minutes.
3. Stir in the ¼ cup cilantro, the green onions, and lime juice. Simmer, uncovered, for 2 minutes. To serve, ladle chili into bowls. Top each with 1 tablespoon of the yogurt and, if desired, snipped cilantro.
PER SERVING: 338 cal., 6 g total fat (1 g sat. fat), 71 mg chol., 549 mg sodium, 34 g carb. (10 g fiber, 12 g sugars), 37 g pro. Exchanges: 1 vegetable, 2 starch, 4 lean meat. Carb choices: 2.

BBQ Bean Chili

For a spicier chili, add ¼ teaspoon cayenne pepper along with the chili powder.

SERVINGS 6 (1½ cups each)

CARB. PER SERVING 43 g

- Nonstick cooking spray
- 1 medium green sweet pepper, chopped (¾ cup)
- 1 medium onion, cut into thin wedges (½ cup)
- 2 large ripe tomatoes, chopped (2 cups)
- 2 15-ounce cans no-salt-added red kidney beans, rinsed and drained
- 1 15-ounce can no-salt-added navy beans, rinsed and drained
- 1 14.5-ounce can reduced-sodium chicken broth
- 1 8-ounce can no-salt-added tomato sauce
- 8 ounces smoked turkey sausage, chopped
- 1 tablespoon chili powder
- 1 tablespoon molasses or sugar-free or light pancake syrup
- 6 tablespoons plain low-fat Greek yogurt

1. Coat an unheated 4-quart nonstick saucepan or Dutch oven with cooking spray. Heat over medium heat. Add sweet pepper and onion; cook for 5 to 10 minutes or until tender, stirring occasionally.
2. Stir in tomatoes, kidney beans, navy beans, broth, tomato sauce, sausage, chili powder, and molasses. Bring to boiling; reduce heat. Simmer, covered, for 30 minutes, stirring occasionally. To serve, ladle chili into bowls. Top each with 1 tablespoon of the yogurt. If desired, garnish with *fresh cilantro sprigs.*
PER SERVING: 293 cal., 4 g total fat (1 g sat. fat), 26 mg chol., 572 mg sodium, 43 g carb. (19 g fiber, 9 g sugars), 23 g pro. Exchanges: 1 vegetable, 2.5 starch, 2 lean meat. Carb choices: 3.

Spicy Pork Tenderloin Green Chili

Bottled minced garlic is convenient and easy to use, but if you prefer fresh garlic, substitute 18 cloves.

SERVINGS 6 (1½ cups each)
CARB. PER SERVING 26 g

8	ounces fresh Anaheim chile peppers (3 to 4 peppers)
1½	pounds pork tenderloin, trimmed of fat and cut into ¾-inch pieces
2	tablespoons canola oil
3	large onions, chopped (3 cups)
18	cloves garlic, minced
1	pound fresh tomatillos, peeled and diced (about 4 cups)
1	tablespoon ground cumin
2	teaspoons dried oregano, crushed
3	cups reduced-sodium chicken broth
1	cup water
1	15-ounce can no-salt-added navy beans, rinsed and drained
1	tablespoon lime juice
2	tablespoons snipped fresh cilantro

1. Preheat oven to 400°F. Arrange chile peppers on a baking sheet. Roast for 25 to 30 minutes or until skins are dark, turning once halfway through roasting. Place chile peppers in a bowl; cover with plastic wrap and let stand for 10 minutes. Carefully remove skins, stems, and seeds; chop chile peppers.* Set aside.

2. Trim pork. Cut pork into ¾-inch pieces. In a 5- to 6-quart Dutch oven cook pork in hot oil over medium-high heat until browned. Add onions and garlic; cook about 5 minutes more or just until onions are tender, stirring occasionally. Add tomatillos, cumin, and oregano; cook for 3 minutes more, stirring occasionally.

3. Stir in broth and the water. Bring to boiling; reduce heat. Simmer, uncovered, for 15 minutes, stirring occasionally. Stir in beans, lime juice, and chopped chile peppers. Simmer for 5 minutes more. To serve, ladle chili into bowls. Sprinkle with cilantro.

***TEST KITCHEN TIP:** Because chile peppers contain volatile oils that can burn your skin and eyes, avoid direct contact with them as much as possible. When working with chile peppers, wear plastic or rubber gloves. If your bare hands do touch the peppers, wash your hands and nails well with soap and warm water.

PER SERVING: 304 cal., 8 g total fat (1 g sat. fat), 74 mg chol., 364 mg sodium, 26 g carb. (10 g fiber, 8 g sugars), 32 g pro. Exchanges: 1.5 vegetable, 1.5 starch, 3.5 lean meat. Carb choices: 2.

▶ QUICK TIP

Choose tomatillos that are small, firm to the touch, and free of defects, with paper husks that are light brown and look fresh.

Spicy Pork Tenderloin Green Chili

Turkey Chipotle Chili

Miso Soup with
Pork and Edamame

Miso Soup with Pork and Edamame

*Look for red miso paste in the Asian food section
of large supermarkets or in Asian food markets.*

SERVINGS 6 (1¾ cups each)

CARB. PER SERVING 14 g

- 12 ounces boneless pork loin roast
- 4 teaspoons canola oil
- 1 medium red sweet pepper, chopped (¾ cup)
- 1 medium onion, chopped (½ cup)
- 1 tablespoon grated fresh ginger
- 2 cloves garlic, minced
- ¼ teaspoon black pepper
- 8 cups water
- ¼ cup red miso paste
- 1 10- to 12-ounce package frozen shelled sweet
  soybeans (edamame)
- 4 cups thinly sliced savoy cabbage
- 2 or 3 medium radishes, very thinly sliced

1. Trim fat from pork. Cut pork into 1-inch cubes. In a
4-quart nonstick Dutch oven cook pork in 2 teaspoons of
the oil over medium-high heat until browned, stirring

occasionally. Remove pork from pan and set aside. Drain off any fat from the pan.

2. In the same pan cook sweet pepper and onion in the remaining 2 teaspoons oil over medium heat for 5 minutes, stirring occasionally. Add ginger, garlic, and black pepper; cook and stir for 30 seconds more. Add 7 cups of the water. In a small bowl gradually whisk remaining 1 cup water into the miso paste. Add to pan and bring to boiling.

3. Add soybeans and pork to the soup. Return to boiling; reduce heat. Simmer, covered, for 3 minutes. Add cabbage. Cook for 2 minutes more, stirring occasionally. To serve, ladle soup into bowls. Garnish with radish slices.

PER SERVING: 216 cal., 9 g total fat (1 g sat. fat), 39 mg chol., 486 mg sodium, 14 g carb. (5 g fiber, 6 g sugars), 20 g pro. Exchanges: 1 vegetable, 0.5 starch, 2.5 lean meat, 1 fat. Carb choices: 1.

Beer Pork Soup

The flavors of bratwurst—pork, onion, fennel, and sage—take to a bowl. Add a mustard-topped toasted bread plank for that favorite sandwich taste. Pictured on page 67.

SERVINGS 4 (2 cups each)
CARB. PER SERVING 15 g

- 12 ounces lean ground pork
- 1 medium onion, chopped (½ cup)
- 1 teaspoon fennel seeds, crushed
- ½ teaspoon dried sage, crushed
- ¼ teaspoon black pepper
- 2 14.5-ounce cans lower-sodium beef broth
- 1 12-ounce can light beer or nonalcoholic beer
- 2 medium carrots, thinly sliced (1 cup)
- 2 cups shredded green cabbage
- 4 ½-inch-thick slices whole grain baguette-style French bread, toasted
- 1 tablespoon country Dijon-style mustard

1. In a large saucepan cook pork, onion, fennel seeds, sage, and pepper about 10 minutes or until pork is browned and onion is tender, stirring to break up pork as it cooks. Drain off fat if necessary.

2. Add broth, beer, and carrots. Bring to boiling; reduce heat. Simmer, covered, for 5 minutes. Add cabbage. Cook, covered, about 5 minutes more or until carrots and cabbage are tender.

3. To serve, ladle soup into bowls. Spread tops of bread slices with mustard. Float a bread slice on top of each bowl of soup.

PER SERVING: 215 cal., 4 g total fat (1 g sat. fat), 59 mg chol., 579 mg sodium, 15 g carb. (4 g fiber, 4 g sugars), 24 g pro. Exchanges: 1 vegetable, 0.5 starch, 3 lean meat. Carb choices: 1.

Pork Picadillo Soup

Picadillo, a Latin American or Spanish dish, combines ground meat, olives, raisins, and spices. This soup version features lean pork.

SERVINGS 6 (1¼ cups each)
CARB. PER SERVING 22 g

- 12 ounces pork tenderloin or lean beef sirloin
- 1 teaspoon dried oregano, crushed
- ½ teaspoon ground coriander
- ¼ teaspoon ground cinnamon
- ⅛ teaspoon cayenne pepper
- 4 teaspoons olive oil
- 1 medium onion, chopped (½ cup)
- 1 14.5-ounce can reduced-sodium chicken broth
- ½ cup quick-cooking barley
- 1 medium zucchini or yellow summer squash, halved lengthwise and thinly sliced crosswise
- 2 medium tomatoes, chopped
- ¼ cup pitted green olives, chopped
- ¼ cup raisins

1. Cut meat into 1-inch pieces. In a large bowl combine the four spices. Add meat pieces; toss to coat. In a large saucepan cook half the meat in 2 teaspoons of the oil over medium-high heat until browned, stirring occasionally. Remove meat from pan. Add remaining oil to the pan. Add remaining meat and the onion. Cook until meat is browned, stirring occasionally. Drain off any fat. Return all the meat to the pan.

2. Add broth, 1½ cups water, and barley to the pan. Bring to boiling; reduce heat. Simmer, covered, for 10 minutes. Add zucchini. Return to boiling; reduce heat. Simmer, covered, about 5 minutes more or until barley and zucchini are tender.

3. Add tomatoes, olives, and raisins. Cook 1 minute to heat through. To serve, ladle soup into bowls.

PER SERVING: 195 cal., 6 g total fat (1 g sat. fat), 37 mg chol., 297 mg sodium, 22 g carb. (3 g fiber, 6 g sugars), 16 g pro. Exchanges: 1 vegetable, 1 starch, 1.5 lean meat, 0.5 fat. Carb choices: 1.5.

Cheeseburger Soup

Use your fingers to crumble the raw ground beef into pieces as you add it to the Dutch oven.

SERVINGS 6 (1⅓ cups each)
CARB. PER SERVING 23 g

- 1 pound 93% or leaner ground beef
- 2 cups sliced fresh mushrooms
- 1 medium red or green sweet pepper, cut into thin bite-size strips (1 cup)
- 1 medium onion, cut into thin wedges (½ cup)
- 1 cup lower-sodium beef broth
- ¼ cup all-purpose flour
- 3½ cups fat-free milk
- 8 slices reduced-fat American-flavor process cheese product, torn (5 ounces)
- ⅛ teaspoon black pepper
- 3 cups coarsely chopped fresh spinach (about 2½ ounces)
- ½ of a medium cucumber, sliced (optional)
- 1 medium tomato, thinly sliced or chopped
- 1 cup whole grain croutons
- 2 tablespoons snipped fresh chives

1. In a 4-quart Dutch oven cook ground beef, mushrooms, sweet pepper, and onion over medium heat until beef is browned and vegetables are tender, stirring to break up meat as it cooks. Drain off fat.
2. In a small bowl whisk together broth and flour until smooth. Add broth mixture to beef mixture; bring to boiling. Stir in milk. Cook and stir until bubbly; cook and stir for 1 minute more. Reduce heat to low. Add cheese and black pepper. Cook and stir until cheese is melted. Stir in spinach just before serving. To serve, ladle soup into bowls. If desired, top with cucumber. Garnish with tomato, croutons, and chives.
PER SERVING: 313 cal., 12 g total fat (4 g sat. fat), 56 mg chol., 619 mg sodium, 23 g carb. (3 g fiber, 11 g sugars), 29 g pro. Exchanges: 0.5 milk, 1 vegetable, 1 starch, 3 lean meat, 1 fat. Carb choices: 1.5.

Lamb and Chickpea Stew

Dried herbs are usually added to mixtures at the beginning of the cooking time so the flavors have time to release. Fresh herbs should be stirred in during the last few minutes of cooking.

SERVINGS 6 (1½ cups each)
CARB. PER SERVING 24 g

- 1 pound boneless leg of lamb
- 4 teaspoons olive oil
- 1 medium onion, cut into thin wedges (½ cup)
- 2 cups water
- 1 14.5-ounce can reduced-sodium chicken broth
- 1 15-ounce can garbanzo beans (chickpeas), rinsed and drained
- 1 cup fresh green beans, trimmed and cut into 1½-inch pieces
- 1 tablespoon snipped fresh oregano or 1 teaspoon dried oregano, crushed
- 2 teaspoons snipped fresh rosemary or ½ teaspoon dried rosemary, crushed
- ¼ teaspoon black pepper
- 4 cups coarsely chopped fresh spinach
- 2 medium tomatoes, chopped (1 cup)
- ½ of a 6-ounce can (⅓ cup) no-salt-added tomato paste

1. Trim fat from lamb. Cut lamb into 1-inch cubes. In a 4-quart Dutch oven cook half the lamb in 2 teaspoons of the oil over medium-high heat until browned, stirring occasionally. Remove lamb from pan. Add remaining oil to the pan. Add remaining lamb and the onion wedges. Cook until meat is browned, stirring occasionally. Drain off any fat. Return all the lamb to the pan.
2. Add the water and broth. Bring to boiling; reduce heat. Simmer, covered, for 45 minutes to 1 hour. Add garbanzo beans, green beans, dried oregano (if using), dried rosemary (if using), and pepper. Return to boiling; reduce heat. Simmer, covered, for 5 to 10 minutes or until lamb and green beans are tender.
3. Stir in spinach, tomatoes, tomato paste, fresh oregano (if using), and fresh rosemary (if using). Heat through. To serve, ladle stew into bowls.
PER SERVING: 249 cal., 7 g total fat (2 g sat. fat), 47 mg chol., 393 mg sodium, 24 g carb. (6 g fiber, 7 g sugars), 22 g pro. Exchanges: 1 vegetable, 1.5 starch, 2 lean meat, 0.5 fat. Carb choices: 1.5.

Lamb and Chickpea Stew

Beer Pork Soup
recipe on page 65

Cheeseburger Soup

Soup On Call

Soups and stews can often be made in larger batches—simply double a recipe that makes four to six servings and you'll likely have leftovers to freeze for another day. Keep these pointers in mind when planning for soup for the freezer.

1. **Choose** soups that have a broth or tomatoey base.

2. **Avoid** freezing soups that are thickened with cornstarch or flour.

3. **Cool soup** quickly by placing the pot in a sink of ice water, stirring to cool.

4. **Ladle soup** into individual- or family-size freezer containers.

5. **Leave** about a ½-inch headspace between the top of the soup and the rim of the bowl. This will provide room for the food to expand while it freezes.

6. **Freeze soups and stews** for up to 6 months.

7. **Thaw** the soup in the fridge before reheating.

8. **Heat soup** to 160°F to serve.

Cream of Chicken
and Rice Florentine

Cream of Chicken and Rice Florentine

*Speed up the prep time by purchasing sliced
fresh mushrooms and shredded carrot.*

SERVINGS 6 (1⅓ cups each)
CARB. PER SERVING 31 g

- 2 tablespoons olive oil
- 1 pound skinless, boneless chicken breast halves
- 3 medium onions, finely chopped (1½ cups)
- 1 8-ounce package fresh mushrooms, sliced
- 1 medium carrot, shredded (½ cup)
- 6 cloves garlic, minced
- ⅓ cup uncooked long grain rice
- 1 14.5-ounce can reduced-sodium chicken broth
- 1 cup water
- ½ teaspoon black pepper
- ¼ teaspoon ground nutmeg
- 2 12-ounce cans fat-free evaporated milk
- 2 tablespoons flour
- 4 cups packed fresh spinach
- 2 teaspoons finely shredded lemon peel
- 2 tablespoons lemon juice
- Black pepper (optional)

1. In a Dutch oven heat oil over medium-high heat; reduce heat to medium. Add chicken; cook for 12 to 15 minutes or until no longer pink (170°F), turning once halfway through cooking. Transfer chicken to a plate and let cool. When cool enough to handle, use two forks to pull chicken apart into coarse shreds.

2. Meanwhile, add onions, mushrooms, carrot, and garlic to the Dutch oven; cook for 5 minutes, stirring occasionally. Stir in rice; cook for 1 minute more. Add broth, the water, the ½ teaspoon pepper, and the nutmeg. Bring to boiling; reduce heat. Simmer, covered, for 15 minutes.

3. In a small bowl stir together 1 can evaporated milk and flour; stir into mixture in Dutch oven. Stir in remaining can of milk. Cook and stir until bubbly.

4. Stir in spinach and the shredded chicken. Simmer for 5 minutes. Stir in lemon peel and lemon juice. To serve, ladle soup into bowls. If desired, sprinkle with additional pepper.

PER SERVING: 300 cal., 6 g total fat (1 g sat. fat), 48 mg chol., 365 mg sodium, 31 g carb. (2 g fiber, 16 g sugars), 30 g pro. Exchanges: 1 vegetable, 1.5 starch, 3.5 lean meat. Carb choices: 2.

QUICK TIP

If you don't own a ladle, a dry measuring cup with a handle works well for scooping up soups and stews.

Chicken Parmesan Soup

Slightly crush the croutons before sprinkling them on the soup so each spoonful will have some of the crispy topping.

SERVINGS 6 (1⅔ cups each)
CARB. PER SERVING 24 g

- 1 pound skinless, boneless chicken breast halves or turkey breast tenderloin, cut into thin bite-size strips
- 2 teaspoons dried Italian seasoning, crushed
- 1 tablespoon olive oil
- 1 medium yellow sweet pepper, cut into bite-size strips (1 cup)
- 1 medium onion, chopped (½ cup)
- 4 cloves garlic, minced
- 2 14.5-ounce cans reduced-sodium chicken broth
- 2 cups water
- ¼ teaspoon black pepper
- 1 medium zucchini, quartered lengthwise and cut into ½-inch-thick slices
- 1 cup dried multigrain or whole grain penne pasta (about 2⅔ ounces)
- 1 14.5-ounce can no-salt-added diced tomatoes, undrained
- ½ of a 6-ounce can (⅓ cup) no-salt-added tomato paste
- ½ cup whole grain croutons
- ¼ cup finely shredded Parmesan cheese (1 ounce)

1. In a medium bowl toss chicken strips and Italian seasoning to coat. In a 4-quart Dutch oven cook chicken in hot oil over medium-high heat until browned and no longer pink. Remove all chicken from the pan; set aside.
2. Add sweet pepper and onion to the Dutch oven; cook for 5 minutes, stirring occasionally. Stir in garlic. Add broth, the water, and black pepper. Bring to boiling. Add zucchini and pasta. Return to boiling; reduce heat. Simmer, covered, for 10 minutes or until pasta is tender.
3. Stir in diced tomatoes and tomato paste. Add cooked chicken. Cook and stir for 2 to 3 minutes to heat through. To serve, ladle soup into bowls. Sprinkle with croutons and cheese just before serving.

PER SERVING: 245 cal., 6 g total fat (1 g sat. fat), 46 mg chol., 528 mg sodium, 24 g carb. (3 g fiber, 7 g sugars), 25 g pro. Exchanges: 1 vegetable, 1.5 starch, 3 lean meat. Carb choices: 1.5.

Indonesian Chicken and Soba Noodle Soup

For a little crunch, sprinkle each serving with a few chopped unsalted dry-roasted peanuts.

SERVINGS 6 (1 cup soup and ⅔ cup cooked noodles each)
CARB. PER SERVING 35 g

- 1 cup sliced onion
- 2 tablespoons grated fresh ginger
- 1 tablespoon canola oil
- 2 cups shredded green cabbage or napa cabbage
- 1 small sweet potato, peeled and diced (1 cup)
- 1 stalk celery, sliced (½ cup)
- 4 cups reduced-sodium chicken broth
- 1 tablespoon reduced-sodium soy sauce
- ½ teaspoon crushed red pepper
- 8 ounces cooked chicken breast, coarsely chopped
- 1 tablespoon lime juice
- 2 green onions, chopped (¼ cup)
- ¼ cup snipped fresh cilantro
- 8 ounces whole grain soba or udon noodles, cooked according to package directions

1. In a large saucepan cook onion and ginger in hot oil over medium-high heat for 3 minutes, stirring occasionally.
2. Add cabbage, sweet potato, and celery. Cook for 4 minutes more, stirring occasionally. Stir in broth, soy sauce, and crushed red pepper. Bring to boiling; reduce heat. Simmer, covered, about 15 minutes or until vegetables are tender.
3. Stir in chicken and lime juice. Just before serving, stir in green onions and cilantro. To serve, ladle soup and noodles into bowls.

PER SERVING: 266 cal., 5 g total fat (1 g sat. fat), 32 mg chol., 581 mg sodium, 35 g carb. (4 g fiber, 4 g sugars), 20 g pro. Exchanges: 0.5 vegetable, 2 starch, 2 lean meat. Carb choices: 2.

Indonesian Chicken and Soba Noodle Soup

Ratatouille Stew

Ratatouille Stew

Serve this chunky summer vegetable stew alongside a grilled piece of meat such as lean beef sirloin or boneless pork loin.

SERVINGS 4 (1-cup side dish each)
CARB. PER SERVING 13 g

- 1 medium yellow or orange sweet pepper, chopped (¾ cup)
- ½ of a medium sweet onion, chopped
- 2 teaspoons olive oil
- 4 cloves garlic, minced
- 2 cups coarsely chopped unpeeled eggplant
- 1 small zucchini, halved lengthwise and cut into ½-inch-thick slices
- 1 cup lower-sodium vegetable broth
- ⅛ teaspoon black pepper
- 4 medium roma tomatoes, coarsely chopped
- ¼ cup snipped fresh basil
- 3 tablespoons coarsely shredded Parmesan cheese
- 1 tablespoon pine nuts, toasted
- Small fresh basil leaves

1. In a large saucepan cook sweet pepper and onion in hot oil over medium heat for 5 minutes, stirring occasionally. Add garlic; cook and stir for 1 minute. Add eggplant, zucchini, broth, and black pepper. Bring to boiling; reduce heat. Simmer, covered, for 10 to 15 minutes or until vegetables are just tender.
2. Meanwhile, place half of the chopped tomatoes in a blender; cover and blend until smooth. Add blended tomatoes and remaining chopped tomatoes to the eggplant mixture. Cook, covered, for 3 to 4 minutes more or until chopped tomatoes are just softened.
3. Stir in snipped basil just before serving. To serve, ladle stew into shallow bowls. Sprinkle with cheese, pine nuts, and small basil leaves.
PER SERVING: 108 cal., 5 g total fat (1 g sat. fat), 3 mg chol., 205 mg sodium, 13 g carb. (4 g fiber, 6 g sugars), 4 g pro. Exchanges: 2 vegetable, 1 fat. Carb choices: 1.

Strawberry-Lemon Thyme Soup

A swirl of buttermilk and a little fresh thyme dress up this berry-fresh chilled soup.

SERVINGS 4 (¾-cup side dish each)
CARB. PER SERVING 20 g

- 3 cups sliced fresh strawberries
- 1 cup low-fat buttermilk
- 2 teaspoons finely shredded lemon peel
- 1 teaspoon snipped fresh lemon thyme or thyme
- 2 tablespoons honey
- 2 tablespoons low-fat buttermilk (optional)
- Fresh thyme sprigs (optional)

1. In a blender or food processor combine strawberries and the 1 cup buttermilk. Cover and blend or process until very smooth. Transfer to a medium bowl. Stir in lemon peel and the snipped thyme. Cover and chill for 4 to 24 hours to blend flavors.
2. To serve, strain soup, discarding lemon peel and snipped thyme. Stir in honey. Ladle chilled soup into small bowls. If desired, swirl ½ tablespoon buttermilk into each serving and garnish with fresh thyme sprigs.
PER SERVING: 92 cal., 1 g total fat (0 g sat. fat), 2 mg chol., 66 mg sodium, 20 g carb. (2 g fiber, 17 g sugars), 3 g pro. Exchanges: 1 fruit. Carb choices: 1.

Strawberry-Lemon Thyme Soup

Spicy Broccoli
and Bean Soup

to boiling. Add broccoli, carrot, and noodles. Return to boiling; reduce heat. Simmer, uncovered, for 4 minutes.

3. Add tofu and any liquid remaining in the bowl, the sprouts, and the crushed red pepper. Return to boiling; reduce heat. Simmer for 1 to 2 minutes more or until broccoli and noodles are tender and soup is heated through. To serve, ladle soup into bowls. Top with peanuts, green onion tops, and, if desired, basil.

PER SERVING: 265 cal., 11 g total fat (1 g sat. fat), 0 mg chol., 615 mg sodium, 32 g carb. (3 g fiber, 5 g sugars), 11 g pro. Exchanges: 1 vegetable, 2 starch, 0.5 lean meat, 1.5 fat. Carb choices: 2.

Spicy Broccoli and Bean Soup

Shredded napa cabbage makes a simple substitute for the fresh bean sprouts, which can be hard to find.

SERVINGS 4 (2 cups each)
CARB. PER SERVING 32 g

- 2 tablespoons lime juice
- 2 tablespoons reduced-sodium soy sauce
- 8 ounces firm or extra-firm tofu (fresh bean curd), drained and cut into 1-inch cubes
- 4 green onions, thinly sliced
- 3 cloves garlic, minced
- 1 tablespoon canola oil
- 4 cups water
- 2 cups lower-sodium vegetable broth
- 2 cups small fresh broccoli florets
- 1 medium carrot, coarsely shredded (½ cup)
- 3 ounces banh pho (Vietnamese wide rice noodles), broken
- ¾ cup fresh bean sprouts, well rinsed
- ¼ teaspoon crushed red pepper
- ¼ cup chopped unsalted peanuts
- ¼ cup thinly sliced green onion tops
- ¼ cup snipped fresh basil (optional)

1. In a medium bowl combine lime juice and soy sauce. Add tofu; toss gently to coat. Cover and let stand at room temperature for 10 minutes.

2. In a large saucepan cook the 4 green onions and the garlic in hot oil over medium heat for 3 minutes, stirring occasionally. Add the water and vegetable broth. Bring

Wild Mushroom and Leek Soup

The dynamic duo of bacon and tomato makes a terrific topper for this bowl of mushroomy bliss.

SERVINGS 8 (¾-cup side dish each)
CARB. PER SERVING 22 g

- 3 medium leeks, trimmed and thinly sliced (about 1 cup)
- 3 cups sliced fresh wild mushrooms (such as chanterelle, stemmed shiitake, and/or stemmed oyster mushrooms)
- 1 tablespoon olive oil
- 2 cloves garlic, minced
- 1 14.5-ounce can reduced-sodium chicken broth
- 1 cup water
- ⅛ teaspoon black pepper
- 2¾ cups fat-free milk
- ⅓ cup all-purpose flour
- 2 slices turkey bacon, cooked according to package directions and crumbled
- 1 medium tomato, chopped
- 1 tablespoon snipped fresh chives

1. In a large nonstick skillet cook leeks and mushrooms in hot oil over medium heat about 10 minutes or until leeks and mushrooms are tender and lightly browned, stirring occasionally. Add garlic; cook and stir for 30 seconds.

2. Add broth, the water, and pepper to mushroom mixture. In a medium bowl whisk together milk and flour until smooth. Add all at once to the mushroom mixture. Cook and stir over medium heat until thickened and bubbly. Cook and stir for 1 minute more. To serve, ladle soup into shallow bowls. Sprinkle with bacon, chopped tomato, and chives.

PER SERVING: 129 cal., 3 g total fat (1 g sat. fat), 5 mg chol., 213 mg sodium, 22 g carb. (2 g fiber, 6 g sugars), 6 g pro. Exchanges: 1 vegetable, 1 starch, 0.5 fat. Carb choices: 1.5.

Roasted Corn and Poblano Chowder

If fresh sweet corn is out of season, substitute 3 cups frozen whole kernel corn, thawed and patted dry with paper towels.

SERVINGS 6 (1-cup side dish each)
CARB. PER SERVING 25 g

Nonstick cooking spray
- 3 cups fresh corn kernels
- 1 medium red sweet pepper, chopped (¾ cup)
- 1 medium fresh poblano pepper, seeded and chopped*
- 1 medium onion, chopped (½ cup)
- 1 fresh jalapeño pepper, seeded and chopped*
- 2 cloves garlic, minced
- ½ teaspoon ground cumin
- 2 teaspoons canola oil
- 2½ cups lower-sodium vegetable broth
- 2½ cups water
- 2 medium tomatillos, husked and chopped (1 cup)
- ¼ cup snipped fresh cilantro
- ⅓ cup light sour cream
- Fresh cilantro sprigs (optional)

1. Preheat oven to 450°F. Coat two 15×10×1-inch baking pans with cooking spray. Add corn, sweet pepper, poblano pepper, onion, and jalapeño in even layers in the pans. Roast, uncovered, about 35 minutes or until vegetables are lightly charred, stirring once.

2. Meanwhile, in a large saucepan cook and stir garlic and cumin in hot oil over medium-low heat for 30 to 60 seconds or until fragrant. Add broth and the water. Bring to boiling. Add roasted corn mixture and the tomatillos. Return to boiling; reduce heat. Simmer, covered, for 5 minutes.

3. Cool slightly. Ladle half of the soup into a blender. Cover and blend until smooth. Return blended portion to the saucepan with the remaining soup. Stir in snipped cilantro. To serve, ladle soup into bowls. Top each serving with a spoonful of sour cream and, if desired, a sprig of fresh cilantro.

*TEST KITCHEN TIP: Because hot chile peppers contain volatile oils that can burn your skin and eyes, avoid direct contact with them as much as possible. When working with chile peppers, wear plastic or rubber gloves. If your bare hands do touch the peppers, wash your hands and nails well with soap and warm water.

PER SERVING: 135 cal., 4 g total fat (1 g sat. fat), 4 mg chol., 247 mg sodium, 25 g carb. (3 g fiber, 5 g sugars), 4 g pro. Exchanges: 0.5 vegetable, 1.5 starch, 0.5 fat. Carb choices: 1.5.

Roasted Corn and Poblano Chowder

Seafood Stew with Toasted Baguette Slices

The baguette slices should be crispy like croutons, so cut them about ½ inch thick and then toast.

SERVINGS 4 (2 cups stew and 2 baguette slices each)
CARB. PER SERVING 29 g

8   ounces fresh or frozen large shrimp in shells
8   ounces fresh or frozen skinless halibut, cut 1 inch thick
4   medium fresh or frozen sea scallops
2   tablespoons canola oil
    Nonstick cooking spray
1   medium green sweet pepper, chopped (¾ cup)
1   medium onion, chopped (½ cup)
1   medium jalapeño pepper, seeded and finely chopped*
3   cloves garlic, minced
2   cups water
1   14.5-ounce can no-salt-added stewed tomatoes, undrained
1   14.5-ounce can reduced-sodium chicken broth
½   cup snipped fresh cilantro
8   small baguette slices, toasted

1. Thaw shrimp, halibut, and scallops, if frozen. Peel and devein shrimp. Rinse shrimp, halibut, and scallops and pat dry with paper towels. In a large nonstick skillet heat 1 tablespoon of the oil over medium heat. Add shrimp, halibut, and scallops to separate spots in the hot skillet. Cook shrimp and scallops for 2 to 4 minutes or until opaque, turning once halfway through cooking and transferring them to a plate when they are finished cooking. Cook halibut for 8 to 12 minutes or until fish

flakes when tested with a fork. Transfer halibut to a cutting board; cut into 1-inch pieces. Cut scallops in half. Set seafood aside.

2. Meanwhile, coat an unheated nonstick 4-quart Dutch oven with cooking spray; heat over medium heat. Add sweet pepper and onion. Cook for 8 minutes or until vegetables are tender, stirring occasionally. Add jalapeño pepper and garlic; cook and stir for 2 minutes more. Add the water, tomatoes, and broth. Bring to boiling; reduce heat. Simmer, covered, for 10 minutes.

3. Add shrimp, scallops, and halibut pieces to the hot stew. Cook for 1 to 2 minutes or until heated through. Stir in cilantro just before serving. To serve, ladle stew into bowls. Top with toasted baguette slices.

*****TEST KITCHEN TIP:** Because hot chile peppers contain volatile oils that can burn your skin and eyes, avoid direct contact with them as much as possible. When working with chile peppers, wear plastic or rubber gloves. If your bare hands do touch the peppers, wash your hands and nails well with soap and warm water.

PER SERVING: 368 cal., 11 g total fat (1 g sat. fat), 123 mg chol., 666 mg sodium, 29 g carb. (4 g fiber, 8 g sugars), 38 g pro. Exchanges: 1 vegetable, 1.5 starch, 4.5 lean meat, 0.5 fat. Carb choices: 2.

Dilled Salmon and Asparagus Soup

If the salmon you purchase has its skin, use a long, thin-blade knife to cut the skin from the meat.

SERVINGS 5 (about 1½ cups each)
CARB. PER SERVING 25 g

12   ounces fresh or frozen skinless salmon fillet
     Nonstick cooking spray
1   pound fresh asparagus, trimmed and cut into 1-inch pieces
1   medium onion, chopped (½ cup)
1   tablespoon canola oil
2   14.5-ounce cans reduced-sodium chicken broth
2½   cups fat-free milk
½   cup flour
⅛   teaspoon salt
1   tablespoon snipped fresh dill weed or 1 teaspoon dried dill weed
2   cups coarsely chopped fresh spinach
5   tablespoons light sour cream
1   slice rye bread, toasted and cut into ½-inch cubes
⅓   cup chopped cucumber

Seafood Stew with
Toasted Baguette Slices

Dilled Salmon and Asparagus Soup

4. To serve, ladle soup into shallow bowls. Top each serving with a spoonful of sour cream and sprinkle with rye bread cubes and chopped cucumber.

PER SERVING: 318 cal., 14 g total fat (3 g sat. fat), 44 mg chol., 603 mg sodium, 25 g carb. (2 g fiber, 9 g sugars), 24 g pro. Exchanges: 1 vegetable, 1 starch, 2.5 medium-fat meat. Carb choices: 1.5.

Ginger-Sesame Scallop Soup

Place any leftover unpeeled ginger in a freezer bag and store in the freezer. It will keep indefinitely.

SERVINGS 4 (1½ cups each)
CARB. PER SERVING 20 g

- 12 small fresh or frozen sea scallops, cut into quarters (about 1¼ pounds)
- 1 medium onion, chopped (½ cup)
- 1 tablespoon toasted sesame oil
- 1 tablespoon grated fresh ginger
- 2 cloves garlic, minced
- 3 cups unsalted vegetable stock
- 2 cups seafood stock
- ¼ teaspoon black pepper or crushed red pepper
- 2 cups fresh sugar snap pea pods, trimmed and halved crosswise (8 ounces)
- 2 medium carrots, cut into matchstick-size pieces (1 cup)
- 2 cups coarsely chopped fresh spinach (2 ounces)
- 1 tablespoon sesame seeds, toasted

1. Thaw salmon, if frozen. Rinse salmon and pat dry with paper towels. Preheat oven to 450°F. Line a 15×10×1-inch baking pan with foil. Coat foil with cooking spray. Place salmon on one side of the pan. Measure thickness of fish. Add asparagus to the other side of the pan, spreading in an even layer. Lightly coat asparagus with cooking spray. Roast asparagus and salmon, uncovered, for 4 to 6 minutes per ½-inch thickness of salmon or until salmon flakes easily when tested with a fork and asparagus is just tender. Using two forks, flake salmon, removing and discarding any bones.

2. In a 4-quart Dutch oven cook onion in hot oil over medium heat about 5 minutes or until tender but not browned, stirring occasionally. Add broth. In a medium bowl whisk together milk, flour, and salt until smooth. Add all at once to broth mixture. Cook and stir over medium heat until thickened and bubbly. Cook and stir for 1 minute more.

3. Add flaked salmon, asparagus pieces, and dill to the soup. Cook for 1 to 2 minutes or until heated through. Stir in spinach just before serving.

1. Thaw scallops, if frozen. Rinse with cold water and pat dry with paper towels. Set aside.

2. In a large saucepan cook onion in hot sesame oil over medium heat for 5 minutes, stirring occasionally. Add ginger and garlic; cook and stir for 30 seconds more. Add vegetable stock, seafood stock, and pepper; bring to boiling. Add pea pods and carrots. Return to boiling; reduce heat. Simmer, covered, for 2 to 3 minutes or until pea pods are crisp-tender.

3. Add scallops. Cook about 1 minute more or until scallops are opaque. Stir in spinach. Cook for 1 minute more. To serve, ladle soup into shallow bowls. Garnish with toasted sesame seeds.

PER SERVING: 243 cal., 6 g total fat (1 g sat. fat), 47 mg chol., 678 mg sodium, 20 g carb. (3 g fiber, 7 g sugars), 28 g pro. Exchanges: 1.5 vegetable, 0.5 starch, 3.5 lean meat. Carb choices: 1.

sensational sandwiches

When you're craving a sit-back-and-chill kind of meal, turn to these stacked, stuffed, and rolled favorites, all loaded with healthful ingredients. Your family will love every bite of them.

Peppered Pork Burgers

Serve this juicy grilled burger with the cool and crunchy Jicama Radish Slaw on page 103.

SERVINGS 4 (1 burger and bun each)
CARB. PER SERVING 26 g

- 1 recipe Honey-Mustard Spread
- 12 ounces lean ground pork*
- ½ teaspoon black pepper
- ½ teaspoon paprika
- ¼ teaspoon garlic powder
- ¼ teaspoon ground cumin
- ⅛ teaspoon salt
- 4 whole wheat hamburger buns, split and toasted
- 2 romaine lettuce leaves, halved
- ¾ cup bottled roasted red sweet peppers, drained and cut into large pieces

1. Prepare Honey-Mustard Spread; cover and chill. In a medium bowl combine pork, black pepper, paprika, garlic powder, cumin, and salt. Shape into four ½-inch-thick patties.

2. For a charcoal grill, place patties on the grill rack directly over medium coals. Grill, uncovered, for 10 to 12 minutes or until an instant-read thermometer inserted into side of each patty registers 160°F, turning patties once halfway through grilling. (For a gas grill, preheat grill. Reduce heat to medium. Place patties on the grill rack over heat. Cover and grill as above.)

3. To assemble, spread Honey-Mustard Spread on cut sides of bun tops. Place lettuce leaves, grilled burgers, and roasted red peppers on bun bottoms. Add bun tops, spread sides down.

HONEY-MUSTARD SPREAD: In a small bowl combine 3 tablespoons light mayonnaise, 1 tablespoon Dijon-style mustard, and 1 teaspoon honey.

*TEST KITCHEN TIP: Instead of purchasing preground pork, which can be high in fat, buy a whole piece of lean pork loin and grind it in a food processor.

PER SERVING: 272 cal., 8 g total fat (2 g sat. fat), 63 mg chol., 510 mg sodium, 26 g carb. (3 g fiber, 6 g sugars), 23 g pro. Exchanges: 2 starch, 2.5 lean meat, 0.5 fat. Carb choices: 2.

Asian Pork Quesadillas

Here's fusion cooking at its best. Asian-style Peanut Sauce hooks up with Mexican-style whole grain tortillas stuffed with ginger-seasoned pork loin and napa cabbage. It's a perfect marriage.

SERVINGS 4 (1 quesadilla each)
CARB. PER SERVING 19 g

- 8 ounces pork tenderloin, cut into thin bite-size strips
- ½ teaspoon ground ginger
- ½ teaspoon black pepper
- 2 to 3 teaspoons olive oil or canola oil
- ½ of a medium red onion, cut into thin wedges
- 3 cups shredded napa cabbage
- 4 7- to 8-inch whole wheat, low-carb tortillas
- Nonstick cooking spray
- 1 recipe Peanut Sauce

Asian Pork Quesadillas

1. In a medium bowl toss pork with ginger and pepper to coat. In a large nonstick skillet heat 2 teaspoons of the oil over medium-high heat. Add pork; stir-fry about 3 minutes or until pork is cooked through. Remove pork from skillet; cover to keep warm.
2. Add onion to skillet, adding the remaining 1 teaspoon oil if needed. Stir-fry for 2 minutes. Add the 3 cups cabbage; stir-fry about 2 minutes more or just until onion is tender and cabbage starts to wilt. Stir pork into cabbage mixture in skillet.
3. To assemble, coat one side of each tortilla lightly with cooking spray. Place tortillas, coated sides down, on a work surface. Using a slotted spoon, spoon pork mixture on top side of each tortilla. Drizzle with Peanut Sauce. Fold each over filling.
4. Preheat a large skillet over medium heat for 1 minute. Place two of the quesadillas in the hot skillet; cook for 4 to 6 minutes or until browned, turning once. Remove quesadillas from skillet; place on a baking sheet. Keep warm in a 300°F oven. Repeat to cook the remaining quesadillas. If desired, serve with *lime wedges*.
PEANUT SAUCE: In a small saucepan stir together 3 tablespoons creamy peanut butter; 2 tablespoons water; 1 tablespoon reduced-sodium soy sauce; ½ teaspoon bottled minced garlic or 1 clove garlic, minced; and ¼ teaspoon ground ginger. Heat over very low heat until melted and smooth, whisking constantly.
PER SERVING: 253 cal., 12 g total fat (2 g sat. fat), 37 mg chol., 463 mg sodium, 19 g carb. (10 g fiber, 3 g sugars), 19 g pro. Exchanges: 1 vegetable, 1 starch, 2 lean meat, 1.5 fat. Carb choices: 1.

Avocado BLT Sandwiches

To choose an avocado that is just right for slicing and for mashing into a creamy spread, squeeze it gently in your hand. If it yields to the pressure, it is ripe and ready to use.

SERVINGS 4 (1 sandwich each)
CARB. PER SERVING 28 g

- 1 large ripe avocado
- 2 tablespoons fat-free mayonnaise or salad dressing
- 1 teaspoon lemon juice
- 1 clove garlic, minced
- 4 slices bacon, crisp-cooked, drained, and halved crosswise
- 4 leaves romaine lettuce
- 1 large tomato, thinly sliced
- 8 slices whole wheat bread, toasted

1. Halve, seed, and peel avocado. Transfer one of the avocado halves to a small bowl; mash with a potato masher or the back of a wooden spoon. Stir in mayonnaise, lemon juice, and garlic; set aside. Thinly slice the remaining avocado half.
2. Arrange avocado slices, bacon, lettuce, and tomato on four of the toast slices. Spread the mashed avocado mixture over the remaining four toast slices; place on top of the filled slices, spread sides down. To serve, cut sandwiches in half.
PER SERVING: 238 cal., 12 g total fat (2 g sat. fat), 8 mg chol., 433 mg sodium, 28 g carb. (7 g fiber, 5 g sugars), 9 g pro. Exchanges: 2 starch, 2 fat. Carb choices: 2.

Hot Ham and Pear Melts

Whole grain French bread, low-sugar apricot preserves, lower-sodium ham, fresh pear, arugula, and goat cheese add up to one scrumptious sandwich. It's a cut above any melt you've ever had!

SERVINGS 4 (¼ baguette, 1½ ounces ham, and ¼ cup pear slices each)

CARB. PER SERVING 36 g

1   10- to 12-ounce whole grain baguette
2   tablespoons lower-sugar apricot preserves
2   cups arugula or fresh spinach
1   medium pear, quartered, cored, and thinly sliced
6   ounces thinly sliced lower-sodium cooked ham
1   4-ounce package goat cheese (chèvre), softened
1   teaspoon snipped fresh chives
    Nonstick cooking spray

1. Preheat oven to 350°F. Cut baguette crosswise into four portions. Split each portion in half horizontally. Scoop out the soft centers of tops and bottoms of baguette portions, leaving about a ½-inch shell. (Save soft bread centers for another use.)

2. Spread preserves on cut sides of bottom halves of baguette portions. Top with half of the arugula, the pear slices, ham, and the remaining arugula. In a small bowl stir together goat cheese and chives; spread on cut sides of the top halves of the baguette portions. Place over arugula, cheese sides down. Lightly coat tops and bottoms of sandwiches with cooking spray.

3. Place sandwiches in a shallow baking pan. Cover with foil. Bake for 10 to 15 minutes or until heated through. Serve warm.

PER SERVING: 300 cal., 10 g total fat (5 g sat. fat), 32 mg chol., 647 mg sodium, 36 g carb. (3 g fiber, 10 g sugars), 16 g pro. Exchanges: 0.5 vegetable, 0.5 fruit, 1.5 starch, 2 medium-fat meat. Carb choices: 2.5.

¼ teaspoon black pepper, and, if desired, several dashes bottled hot pepper sauce. Cover and shake well. In a medium bowl combine 2 cups packaged shredded broccoli (broccoli slaw mix), 2 tablespoons thinly sliced green onion, and 1 tablespoon snipped fresh parsley. Pour vinegar mixture over vegetable mixture, tossing to coat. Cover and chill for 2 to 24 hours before serving.

PER SERVING: 310 cal., 10 g total fat (1 g sat. fat), 55 mg chol., 560 mg sodium, 31 g carb. (3 g fiber, 10 g sugars), 23 g pro. Exchanges: 0.5 vegetable, 2 starch, 2.5 lean meat, 1 fat. Carb choices: 2.

Pork Tenderloin Sandwiches

Serve the crunchy slaw on top of the meat for a meal in a bun, or serve it alongside for a salad and sandwich lunch.

SERVINGS 4 (about 3 ounces pork, 1 bun, and ½ cup broccoli slaw each)

CARB. PER SERVING 31 g

12 ounces pork tenderloin
2 tablespoons flour
¼ teaspoon salt
¼ teaspoon onion powder or garlic powder
¼ teaspoon cayenne pepper
¼ teaspoon black pepper
2 tablespoons vegetable oil
4 whole wheat hamburger buns, split and toasted
   Ketchup, yellow mustard, and/or pickles (optional)
1 recipe Broccoli Slaw

1. Cut pork crosswise into four pieces. Place one pork piece between two pieces of clear plastic wrap. Pound lightly with the flat side of a meat mallet, working from center to edges until ¼ inch thick. Remove plastic wrap. Repeat with remaining pork pieces.
2. In a shallow dish combine flour, salt, onion powder, cayenne pepper, and black pepper. Dip meat into the flour mixture, turning to coat. In a very large skillet heat oil over medium heat. Add pork; cook for 8 to 10 minutes or until no pink remains and juices run clear, turning once. (If all the pork slices won't fit in the skillet, cook in two batches, adding additional oil if necessary.)
3. Place pork on buns. If desired, top with ketchup, mustard, and/or pickles. Serve with Broccoli Slaw.
BROCCOLI SLAW: In a screw-top jar combine 2 tablespoons vinegar, 1 tablespoon honey, ¼ teaspoon salt, ⅛ to

Greek Feta Burgers

Forget the mustard, pickles, and ketchup—these lean, cheese-studded burgers taste fantastic topped with a slice of fresh tomato and a spoonful of Cucumber Sauce.

SERVINGS 2 (1 burger and ½ bun each)

CARB. PER SERVING 14 g

1 recipe Cucumber Sauce
8 ounces 93% or leaner ground beef
1 tablespoon crumbled reduced-fat feta cheese
1½ teaspoons snipped fresh Italian (flat-leaf) parsley
1 clove garlic, minced
⅛ teaspoon black pepper
1 whole wheat hamburger bun, split and toasted
½ cup fresh spinach leaves
2 tomato slices

1. Prepare Cucumber Sauce; set aside. In a medium bowl combine ground beef, cheese, parsley, garlic, and pepper. Shape mixture into two ½-inch-thick patties.
2. In a large nonstick skillet cook patties over medium-high heat for 8 to 10 minutes or until an instant-read thermometer inserted into side of each patty registers 160°F, turning once halfway through cooking.
3. Top each bun half with spinach. Top each with a burger, tomato slice, and half of the sauce.
CUCUMBER SAUCE: In a small bowl combine 3 tablespoons chopped, seeded cucumber; 2 tablespoons light sour cream; 1 clove garlic, minced; ½ teaspoon snipped fresh Italian (flat-leaf) parsley; ¼ teaspoon snipped fresh mint; and ⅛ teaspoon sea salt.

PER SERVING: 262 cal., 10 g total fat (4 g sat. fat), 66 mg chol., 361 mg sodium, 14 g carb. (2 g fiber, 3 g sugars), 27 g pro. Exchanges: 0.5 vegetable, 1 starch, 3 lean meat, 1 fat. Carb choices: 1.

Pepper-Stuffed Burgers

Biting into these mesquite-seasoned burgers is a delight. Inside you'll find roasted miniature sweet peppers oozing with pepper cheese.

SERVINGS 4 (1 burger and roll each)
CARB. PER SERVING 30 g

- 4 miniature red sweet peppers (about ½ ounce each)
- 1 ounce Monterey Jack cheese with jalapeño peppers or reduced-fat Monterey Jack cheese, cut into 4 small cubes
- 1 pound 93% or leaner ground beef
- ½ teaspoon mesquite seasoning
- 4 whole grain or multigrain ciabatta rolls or whole wheat hamburger buns, split and toasted

1. Cut the tops off the sweet peppers. Remove any ribs and seeds. For a charcoal grill, grill peppers on the rack of an uncovered grill directly over medium coals for 5 to 7 minutes or until pepper skins are lightly blistered and peppers are just tender, turning occasionally. (For a gas grill, preheat grill. Reduce heat to medium. Place peppers on grill rack over heat. Cover and grill as directed.) Remove peppers from the grill; cool slightly. Stuff peppers with the cheese cubes.

2. In a medium bowl combine ground beef and mesquite seasoning. Divide mixture into four portions. Shape each portion of the beef mixture around one of the stuffed peppers to completely enclose the pepper. Flatten slightly to form ¾-inch-thick patties.

3. For a charcoal grill, place patties on the grill rack directly over medium coals. Grill, uncovered, for 14 to 18 minutes or until an instant-read thermometer inserted into side of each patty registers 160°F (insert the thermometer into the meat to the side of the pepper). (For a gas grill, place patties on grill rack over heat. Cover and grill as above.)

4. Place burgers on rolls.

PER SERVING: 344 cal., 11 g total fat (4 g sat. fat), 66 mg chol., 551 mg sodium, 30 g carb. (2 g fiber, 1 g sugars), 29 g pro. Exchanges: 2 starch, 3.5 lean meat, 0.5 fat. Carb choices: 2.

▶ QUICK TIP
If you wish, add fresh spinach leaves and thin red onion slices when serving these oozy-good burgers.

Pepper-Stuffed Burgers

Cheesesteaks with Sweet Peppers and Mushrooms

For easy slicing, freeze the steak for 30 minutes and then cut with a sharp knife.

SERVINGS 6 (⅙ loaf, 2½ ounces beef, and ¼ cup vegetables each)
CARB. PER SERVING 34 g

- 4 teaspoons canola oil
- 1 pound boneless beef sirloin steak, trimmed and cut into thin strips
- ¼ teaspoon black pepper
- ⅛ teaspoon salt
- 1 large portobello mushroom, stems and gills removed, cut into thin strips
- 1 large yellow sweet pepper, cut into thin strips
- 1 medium fresh poblano chile pepper, seeded and cut into thin strips*
- 1 medium onion, halved and thinly sliced
- 2 cloves garlic, minced
- 1 14- to 16-ounce loaf French bread
- 1 cup shredded reduced-fat Monterey Jack cheese (4 ounces)

1. In a very large nonstick skillet heat 2 teaspoons of the oil over medium-high heat. Add beef strips; sprinkle with black pepper and salt. Cook for 4 to 6 minutes or just until beef is slightly pink in the center, stirring frequently. Remove beef from skillet; cover and set aside.
2. In the same skillet combine the remaining 2 teaspoons oil, the mushroom strips, sweet pepper, chile pepper, onion, and garlic. Cook for 8 to 10 minutes or until vegetables are tender, stirring occasionally.

3. Meanwhile, preheat broiler. Split bread loaf in half horizontally. Scoop out the soft centers of the top and bottom of the loaf, leaving about a ½-inch shell. (Save soft bread centers for another use.) Place bread halves, cut sides up, on a large baking sheet.
4. Broil bread 5 to 6 inches from the heat for 1 to 2 minutes or until toasted. Spoon vegetable mixture into bottom half of the loaf. Top with steak strips and cheese. Remove loaf top from the baking sheet. Broil filled bottom half of loaf for 1 to 2 minutes or until cheese is melted. Place loaf top over filling. To serve, cut crosswise into six portions.

*****TEST KITCHEN TIP:** Because chile peppers contain volatile oils that can burn your skin and eyes, avoid direct contact with them as much as possible. When working with chile peppers, wear plastic or rubber gloves. If your bare hands do touch the peppers, wash your hands and nails well with soap and warm water.

PER SERVING: 348 cal., 11 g total fat (4 g sat. fat), 45 mg chol., 562 mg sodium, 34 g carb. (2 g fiber, 3 g sugars), 28 g pro. Exchanges: 1 vegetable, 2 starch, 3 lean meat, 0.5 fat. Carb choices: 2.

Cheesesteaks with Sweet Peppers and Mushrooms

Grilled Turkey Gyros

Pita bread and a drizzle of cucumber-yogurt sauce add loads of traditional flavor to this grilled turkey version of gyros.

SERVINGS 4 (1 pita round, 3 turkey patties, ½ cup vegetables, and about 3 tablespoons sauce each)
CARB. PER SERVING 37 g

- 12 ounces uncooked ground turkey breast
- ¼ cup finely chopped onion
- 1 egg, lightly beaten
- 1 tablespoon fine dry bread crumbs
- 2 cloves garlic, minced
- 1 teaspoon ground coriander
- ½ teaspoon ground cumin
- ⅛ teaspoon salt
- ⅛ teaspoon black pepper
- 1 tablespoon olive oil
- 4 whole wheat pita bread rounds
- 1 cup thinly sliced cucumber
- 1 cup diced tomato
- 2 tablespoons snipped fresh Italian (flat-leaf) parsley
- 1 recipe Cucumber-Yogurt Sauce

Grilled
Turkey Gyros

1. For patties, in a large bowl combine turkey breast, onion, egg, bread crumbs, garlic, coriander, cumin, salt, and pepper. Shape mixture into 12 patties, flattening each to about ½-inch thickness. Brush all sides of the patties with olive oil. Wrap pita bread rounds in foil.

2. For a charcoal grill, place patties and foil-wrapped pita bread on the greased grill rack directly over medium coals. Grill, uncovered, about 6 minutes or until an instant-read thermometer inserted into each patty registers 165°F* and pitas are heated through, turning once halfway through grilling. (For a gas grill, preheat grill; reduce heat to medium. Place patties and foil-wrapped pita bread on grill rack directly over heat. Cover and grill as above.)

3. Divide cucumber slices among grilled pita bread rounds. Top each with three patties, ¼ tomato, and parsley. Drizzle with Cucumber-Yogurt Sauce. Fold pitas around fillings; secure with toothpicks.

CUCUMBER-YOGURT SAUCE: In a small bowl combine ⅓ cup plain fat-free yogurt; ¼ cup shredded, seeded cucumber; 1 tablespoon tahini (sesame seed paste); 2 cloves garlic, minced; and ⅛ teaspoon salt. Cover and chill for at least 20 minutes.

*TEST KITCHEN TIP: The internal color of a burger is not a reliable doneness indicator. A chicken or turkey patty cooked to 165°F is safe, regardless of color. To measure the doneness of a patty, insert an instant-read thermometer through the side to the center of the patty.

PER SERVING: 332 cal., 9 g total fat (1 g sat. fat), 95 mg chol., 560 mg sodium, 37 g carb. (6 g fiber, 6 g sugars), 31 g pro. Exchanges: 0.5 vegetable, 2.5 starch, 3 lean meat, 0.5 fat. Carb choices: 2.5.

Italian Meatball Rolls

Refrigerated Italian-style turkey meatballs take the work out of this favorite—and help lower the calories and fat, too.

SERVINGS 4 (2 meatballs and 1 bun each)
CARB. PER SERVING 36 g

Nonstick cooking spray
2½ cups thinly sliced cremini mushrooms
1 medium onion, chopped (½ cup)
2 cloves garlic, minced
1 8-ounce can no-salt-added tomato sauce
2 tablespoons balsamic vinegar
½ teaspoon dried rosemary, crushed
½ teaspoon dried oregano, crushed
8 ounces refrigerated Italian-style cooked turkey meatballs (8 meatballs), halved
4 whole wheat hot dog buns
½ cup shredded part-skim mozzarella cheese (2 ounces)
Snipped fresh oregano (optional)

1. Preheat broiler. Coat an unheated large nonstick skillet with cooking spray; preheat over medium heat. Add mushrooms, onion, and garlic to hot skillet; cook for 5 to 10 minutes or until tender, stirring occasionally. Add tomato sauce, balsamic vinegar, rosemary, and the dried oregano. Bring to boiling; reduce heat. Simmer, covered, for 2 minutes. Stir in meatballs. Cook about 5 minutes more or until meatballs are heated through.
2. Meanwhile, open buns so they lie flat and place on a baking sheet, cut sides up. Broil 4 to 5 inches from the heat about 1 minute or until lightly toasted. Divide meatball mixture among buns. Sprinkle with cheese. Broil for 1 to 2 minutes more or until cheese melts. If desired, sprinkle with fresh oregano.

PER SERVING: 344 cal., 12 g total fat (4 g sat. fat), 70 mg chol., 644 mg sodium, 36 g carb. (4 g fiber, 10 g sugars), 21 g pro. Exchanges: 1 vegetable, 2 starch, 2 medium-fat meat. Carb choices: 2.5.

Turkey Mango Sandwiches

If fresh mangoes are out of season, substitute jarred mango slices found in the produce section of the supermarket.

SERVINGS 4 (1 open-face sandwich each)
CARB. PER SERVING 25 g

¼ cup light mayonnaise or salad dressing
1 green onion, thinly sliced
1 tablespoon snipped fresh cilantro
½ teaspoon finely shredded lime peel
4 1-ounce slices whole grain bakery bread
1 cup fresh spinach leaves
6 ounces packaged lower-sodium sliced cooked turkey breast
1 medium mango, seeded, peeled, and thinly sliced
1 small fresh poblano chile pepper, stemmed, seeded, and thinly sliced into rings*

1. In a small bowl stir together mayonnaise, green onion, cilantro, and lime peel. Spread on one side of each of the bread slices.

2. To assemble, on the spread-topped side of each slice layer spinach, turkey, mango slices, and pepper rings.

***TEST KITCHEN TIP:** Because chile peppers contain volatile oils that can burn your skin and eyes, avoid direct contact with them as much as possible. When working with chile peppers, wear plastic or rubber gloves. If your bare hands do touch the peppers, wash your hands and nails well with soap and warm water.

PER SERVING: 211 cal., 7 g total fat (1 g sat. fat), 28 mg chol., 470 mg sodium, 25 g carb. (4 g fiber, 9 g sugars), 14 g pro. Exchanges: 1 starch, 0.5 carb., 1.5 lean meat, 1 fat. Carb choices: 1.5.

Curried Chicken Sandwiches

The longer the red onion is left to pickle, the lighter the color will be.

SERVINGS 6 (1 sandwich each)
CARB. PER SERVING 39 g

1 pound skinless, boneless chicken breast halves, cut into 1-inch pieces
1 tablespoon olive oil
1 tablespoon lemon juice
1 teaspoon ground coriander
½ teaspoon ground cumin
¼ teaspoon garam masala
¼ teaspoon salt
⅛ teaspoon cayenne pepper
⅛ teaspoon ground turmeric
¼ cup chopped fresh cilantro
6 whole-wheat pita bread rounds or whole-wheat naan loaves
1 cup shredded lettuce
½ cup chopped, seeded tomato
1 recipe Pickled Red Onion and Cucumber

1. Place chicken in a medium bowl. Add oil, lemon juice, coriander, cumin, garam masala, salt, cayenne pepper, and turmeric; toss to coat.

2. In a large nonstick skillet cook and stir chicken over medium-high heat for 6 to 8 minutes or until no longer pink. Remove from heat; stir in cilantro.

3. To serve, top each pita bread with lettuce, chicken, tomato, and Pickled Red Onion and Cucumber.

PICKLED RED ONION AND CUCUMBER: In a small saucepan cook ½ cup thinly sliced red onion and ½ cup thinly sliced, peeled cucumber in lightly salted boiling water for 45 seconds; drain. In a medium bowl combine the red onion and cucumber; ½ cup cold water; ½ cup rice vinegar; 1 clove garlic, halved; and ½ teaspoon cumin seeds. Cover and chill for 3 to 24 hours. Drain before using.

PER SERVING: 286 cal., 5 g total fat (1 g sat. fat), 44 mg chol., 627 mg sodium, 39 g carb. (5 g fiber, 2 g sugars), 24 g pro. Exchanges: 0.5 vegetable, 2.5 starch, 2 lean meat. Carb choices: 2.5.

Turkey Mango Sandwiches

Grilled Chicken
and Peach Wraps

Shrimp Po'Boys

Crunchy Egg
Salad Sandwiches
recipe on page 89

Egg-citing Sandwich

The simplicity of egg salad sandwiches offers versatility. For something different, start with the recipe on page 89 and try one of these simple swaps.

1. **Use finely chopped** zucchini or yellow summer squash in place of the cucumber.

2. **Try toasted** sliced almonds instead of the walnuts.

3. **Trade yellow, orange, or green** sweet pepper for the red sweet pepper.

4. **Change out the chives** with sliced green onion.

5. **Switch the herb** from dill weed to thyme.

6. **Omit** the Dijon-style mustard.

8. **Spoon the salad** on whole wheat bagel thins or whole wheat buns in place of the sandwich thins.

9. **Try leaf lettuce or arugula** for the spinach.

10. **Add a slice** of fresh tomato.

Grilled Chicken and Peach Wraps

You can use smooth-skin nectarines instead of the fuzzy-skin peaches.

SERVINGS 4 (1 wrap each)
CARB. PER SERVING 36 g

- 4 small skinless, boneless chicken breast halves (1 pound total)
- 2 medium fresh peaches, halved and pitted
- ¼ cup peach preserves (snip any large pieces)
- 1 tablespoon white wine vinegar
- 1 teaspoon grated fresh ginger
- ¼ teaspoon salt
- ¼ teaspoon crushed red pepper
- ½ cup plain fat-free Greek yogurt
- ¼ cup reduced-fat crumbled blue cheese
- 4 8-inch whole wheat low-carb flour tortillas
- 4 lettuce leaves
- 4 thin slices red or sweet onion, separated into rings

1. Place each chicken breast half between two pieces of plastic wrap. Using the flat side of a meat mallet, pound the chicken lightly to about ¼-inch thickness. Remove plastic wrap. Set aside.

2. For a charcoal grill, place chicken and peach halves on the greased grill rack directly over medium-hot coals. Grill, uncovered, for 6 to 8 minutes or until chicken is no longer pink and peaches are lightly browned, turning once halfway through grilling. Remove chicken and peaches from grill; set aside and cover to keep warm. (For a gas grill, preheat grill. Reduce heat to medium-high. Place chicken and peach halves on grill rack over heat. Cover and grill as above.)

3. For peach sauce, in a medium bowl stir together the peach preserves, vinegar, ginger, salt, and crushed red pepper. Slice chicken breasts and peaches; add to peach sauce mixture and toss to coat. In another small bowl stir together the yogurt and blue cheese.

4. Spread blue cheese mixture evenly on wraps. Divide lettuce and onion slices among wraps. Place peach and chicken mixture evenly in wraps. Tightly roll up wraps and secure with toothpicks. Serve immediately.

PER SERVING: 343 cal., 6 g total fat (2 g sat. fat), 72 mg chol., 595 mg sodium, 36 g carb. (10 g fiber, 18 g sugars), 34 g pro. Exchanges: 0.5 vegetable, 0.5 fruit, 1.5 starch, 3.5 lean meat. Carb choices: 2.5.

Shrimp Po'Boys

Take a bite of this sandwich and you'll discover sassy Cajun-spiced shrimp enhanced by a cool and creamy veggie spread. Not only that, the combo boasts 73 percent of the Daily Value for vitamin A and 105 percent for vitamin C.

SERVINGS 4 (1 sandwich each)
CARB. PER SERVING 22 g

- 1¼ pounds fresh or frozen large shrimp in shells
- ⅓ cup tub-style light cream cheese, softened
- 1 tablespoon fat-free milk
- 1 stalk celery, finely chopped (½ cup)
- ½ cup jarred roasted red sweet peppers, drained and chopped
- 2 green onions, thinly sliced
- 1 teaspoon Cajun seasoning
- 2 teaspoons canola oil
- 4 ½-inch slices French bread, toasted
- 3 cups torn or shredded romaine lettuce
- Snipped fresh parsley (optional)

1. Thaw shrimp, if frozen. Peel and devein shrimp. Rinse shrimp; pat dry with paper towels. Set aside. In a small bowl combine cream cheese and milk, stirring until smooth. Stir in celery, roasted red peppers, and green onions; set aside.

2. In a medium bowl toss shrimp with Cajun seasoning to coat. In a large nonstick skillet heat oil over medium-high heat. Add shrimp; cook and stir for 3 to 4 minutes or until opaque. Remove from heat.

3. Divide bread slices among four serving plates. Top with cream cheese mixture, lettuce, and shrimp. If desired, sprinkle with snipped parsley.

PER SERVING: 280 cal., 8 g total fat (3 g sat. fat), 182 mg chol., 486 mg sodium, 22 g carb. (2 g fiber, 3 g sugars), 29 g pro. Exchanges: 1 vegetable, 1 starch, 3.5 lean meat, 0.5 fat. Carb choices: 1.5.

▶ QUICK TIP
Give the veggies
stacked on the bagels
a sprinkle of freshly
ground black pepper.

Vegetable Sandwiches
with Feta-Yogurt Spread

Salmon Melts

Fixing salmon for dinner one night? Cook extra to use for these easy open-face sandwiches the next.

SERVINGS 4 (1 topped muffin half each)
CARB. PER SERVING 17 g

- 8 ounces cooked salmon, flaked
- ¼ cup finely chopped green onions (2)
- ¼ cup finely chopped red sweet pepper
- 2 tablespoons fat-free mayonnaise dressing
- 2 tablespoons light sour cream
- 2 teaspoons lemon juice
- ¼ teaspoon bottled hot pepper sauce
- 2 whole-wheat English muffins, split and toasted
- 4 slices tomato
- 1 cup arugula or watercress
- ½ cup shredded part-skim mozzarella cheese (2 ounces)

1. Preheat broiler. In a medium bowl stir together salmon, onions, sweet pepper, mayonnaise, sour cream, lemon juice, and hot pepper sauce. Arrange English muffin halves on a baking sheet. Top evenly with tomato slices, arugula, salmon mixture, and cheese. Broil 4 to 5 inches from the heat for 3 to 4 minutes or until cheese melts and bubbles.
PER SERVING: 244 cal., 11 g total fat (3 g sat. fat), 48 mg chol., 348 mg sodium, 17 g carb. (3 g fiber, 5 g sugars), 20 g pro. Exchanges: 0.5 vegetable, 1 starch, 2 medium-fat meat. Carb choices: 1.

Vegetable Sandwiches with Feta-Yogurt Spread

Use up leafy salad greens—they make a good substitute for the baby spinach.

SERVINGS 4 (1 sandwich each)
CARB. PER SERVING 29 g

- 1 recipe Feta-Yogurt Spread
- 4 whole wheat bagel thins or multigrain sandwich rounds, split
- 1 cup lightly packed packaged fresh baby spinach
- 1 cup thinly sliced English cucumber
- ½ cup halved and thinly sliced red onion
- ½ cup thinly sliced radishes
- 1 roma tomato, thinly sliced

1. Prepare Feta-Yogurt Spread. To assemble, spread cut sides of bagel halves evenly with yogurt mixture. On half of the bagel halves layer spinach, cucumber, red onion, radishes, and tomato on top of yogurt mixture.

Top with remaining bagel halves, spread sides down.
FETA-YOGURT SPREAD: In a small bowl stir together ½ cup plain fat-free Greek yogurt, ½ cup crumbled fat-free or reduced-fat feta cheese, 1 teaspoon snipped fresh mint, 1 teaspoon snipped fresh oregano, and ⅛ teaspoon black pepper.
PER SERVING: 157 cal., 1 g total fat (0 g sat. fat), 1 mg chol., 397 mg sodium, 29 g carb. (6 g fiber, 6 g sugars), 10 g pro. Exchanges: 0.5 milk, 1 vegetable, 1 starch. Carb choices: 2.

Crunchy Egg Salad Sandwiches

The tasty egg salad also makes a summery stuffing for hollowed-out garden-fresh tomato halves.
Pictured on page 87.

SERVINGS 4 (1 sandwich each)
CARB. PER SERVING 26 g

- 4 hard-cooked eggs,* finely chopped
- ½ cup seeded and finely chopped, peeled cucumber
- ¼ cup coarsely chopped walnuts, toasted
- ¼ cup finely chopped red sweet pepper
- 2 tablespoons snipped fresh chives
- 2 tablespoons fat-free mayonnaise
- 2 tablespoons light sour cream
- 1½ teaspoons snipped fresh dill weed or ¼ teaspoon dried dill weed
- 1 teaspoon Dijon-style mustard
- ¼ teaspoon salt
- ¼ teaspoon black pepper
- 4 round whole grain sandwich thins
- 1 cup fresh spinach leaves

1. In a medium bowl combine eggs, cucumber, walnuts, sweet pepper, chives, mayonnaise, sour cream, dill weed, mustard, salt, and black pepper. Line bottoms of sandwich thins with spinach leaves. Divide egg salad evenly over spinach. Top with sandwich thin tops.
*TEST KITCHEN TIP: To hard-cook eggs, place eggs in a single layer in a medium saucepan. Add enough cold water to cover the eggs by 1 inch. Bring to a rapid boil over high heat. Remove from heat, cover, and let stand for 15 minutes; drain. Run cold water over the eggs until cool enough to handle. To peel eggs, gently tap each egg on the countertop. Roll the egg between the palms of your hands. Peel off eggshell, starting at the large end.
PER SERVING: 246 cal., 12 g total fat (3 g sat. fat), 215 mg chol., 537 mg sodium, 26 g carb. (6 g fiber, 4 g sugars), 12 g pro. Exchanges: 0.5 vegetable, 1.5 starch, 1 medium-fat meat, 1 fat. Carb choices: 2.

simple sides
and salads

A well-rounded meal consists of lean meat, poultry, fish, or other protein coupled with an assortment of nutrient-rich vegetables, fruits, and grains. Take your pick from this collection of healthful side dishes to bring the vibrant hues and tastes of freshness to your plate.

Cinnamon-Almond Topped Carrots

If you can't find baby carrots with tops, substitute packaged peeled fresh baby carrots.

SERVINGS 4 (½ cup carrots and 1 tablespoon almonds each)
CARB. PER SERVING 8 g

- 12 ounces baby carrots with tops
- ¼ cup slivered almonds
  Butter-flavor nonstick cooking spray
- ⅛ teaspoon ground cinnamon
- 1 tablespoon light butter, melted
  Fresh marjoram sprigs (optional)

1. Trim green tops of carrots to 1 inch. Scrub carrots. Halve any thick carrots lengthwise. Place a steamer insert in a large skillet or 4-quart Dutch oven with a tight-fitting lid. Add water to the skillet to just below the steamer insert. Bring water to boiling. Place carrots in the steamer insert. Cover and steam over medium heat for 8 to 10 minutes or until carrots are tender, adding more water as needed to maintain steam.

2. Place almonds in a small bowl. Lightly coat with cooking spray and sprinkle with cinnamon; toss gently to coat. In a medium nonstick skillet cook spiced almonds over medium heat for 3 to 5 minutes or until toasted, stirring occasionally. Remove from heat.

3. Transfer carrots to a serving platter; drizzle with melted butter. Toss to coat. Sprinkle with spiced almonds. If desired, garnish with marjoram.

PER SERVING: 76 cal., 4 g total fat (1 g sat. fat), 4 mg chol., 91 mg sodium, 8 g carb. (3 g fiber, 4 g sugars), 2 g pro. Exchanges: 1 vegetable, 1 fat. Carb choices: 0.5.

Broccolini with
Bacon and Feta

Broccolini with Bacon and Feta

*Preserve the bright green color of Broccolini by serving it
with lemon wedges instead of squeezing the juice over all.*

SERVINGS 6 (2 to 3 spears each)
CARB. PER SERVING 4 g

- 1   pound Broccolini*
- ¼   cup dry white wine or reduced-sodium chicken broth
- ⅛   teaspoon black pepper
- ⅓   cup crumbled reduced-fat feta cheese
- 2   slices turkey bacon, cooked according to package
     directions and crumbled
     Lemon wedges

1. In a large skillet cook Broccolini, covered, in a small
amount of boiling water for 6 to 8 minutes or until just
tender. Drain off water. Add wine or broth and pepper. If
using wine, add ⅛ teaspoon *salt*. Cook, uncovered, over
medium heat for 2 to 3 minutes or until liquid is
evaporated, stirring frequently to coat Broccolini evenly
in the liquid.

2. Transfer Broccolini to a serving platter. Sprinkle with
cheese and bacon. Serve with lemon wedges.

*TEST KITCHEN TIP: If desired, substitute 1¼ pounds broccoli
for the Broccolini. Trim off stems and discard; cut
broccoli into florets. Cook as directed above.

PER SERVING: 64 cal., 2 g total fat (1 g sat. fat), 7 mg chol.,
205 mg sodium, 4 g carb. (2 g fiber, 1 g sugars), 5 g pro.
Exchanges: 1 vegetable, 0.5 lean meat. Carb choices: 0.

Roasted Cauliflower Salad

*A large head (about 20 ounces) of cauliflower equals
about 6 cups of florets.*

SERVINGS 6 (¾ cup each)
CARB. PER SERVING 7 g

- 6   cups bite-size fresh cauliflower florets
- 2   tablespoons canola oil
- ¼   teaspoon salt
- ⅛   teaspoon freshly ground black pepper
- 2   tablespoons cider vinegar
- ½   teaspoon stone-ground mustard
- ½   teaspoon caraway seeds, crushed
- ¾   cup packaged coarsely shredded fresh carrots
- 2   green onions, thinly sliced

1. Preheat oven to 425°F. In a 15×10×1-inch baking pan
arrange cauliflower in a single layer. Drizzle with
1 tablespoon of the oil and sprinkle with ⅛ teaspoon of
the salt and the pepper. Toss to coat. Roast, uncovered,
for 25 minutes or until cauliflower is lightly browned
and just tender, stirring twice. Cool slightly.

2. For dressing, in a small screw-top jar combine
remaining 1 tablespoon oil, remaining ⅛ teaspoon salt,
the vinegar, mustard, and caraway seeds.

3. Transfer cauliflower to a large bowl. Stir in carrots
and green onions. Add dressing and toss to coat.

PER SERVING: 74 cal., 5 g total fat (0 g sat. fat), 0 mg chol.,
147 mg sodium, 7 g carb. (3 g fiber, 3 g sugars), 2 g pro.
Exchanges: 1 vegetable, 1 fat. Carb choices: 0.5.

Green Beans with Caramelized Mushrooms

Keep the mushrooms spread in a single layer as they cook—this will help each turn caramelly brown.

SERVINGS 6 (½ cup each)
CARB. PER SERVING 5 g

- 8 ounces fresh green beans, trimmed
- 1 8-ounce package sliced fresh mushrooms
- 2 teaspoons olive oil
- ¼ teaspoon salt
- ⅛ teaspoon black pepper
- ¼ cup chopped walnuts, toasted
- ¼ cup snipped fresh basil

1. In a large skillet cook beans, covered, in a small amount of boiling water for 6 to 8 minutes or until crisp-tender. Drain and rinse beans under cold water to stop cooking; drain again. Pat dry with paper towels.
2. Carefully wipe the skillet dry. In the same skillet cook mushrooms in hot oil over medium heat for 5 to 10 minutes or until tender and lightly browned, stirring occasionally. Add beans and sprinkle with the salt and pepper. Cook for 2 to 3 minutes or until beans are heated through, tossing frequently. Transfer bean mixture to a serving platter. To serve, sprinkle with walnuts and basil.
PER SERVING: 66 cal., 5 g total fat (1 g sat. fat), 0 mg chol., 101 mg sodium, 5 g carb. (2 g fiber, 1 g sugars), 3 g pro. Exchanges: 1 vegetable, 1 fat. Carb choices: 0.

Corn on the Cob with Cilantro-Lime Butter

The creamy butter boasts big flavor, so it doesn't take much to spread over the corn.

SERVINGS 8 (1 piece corn and about 1 teaspoon butter each)
CARB. PER SERVING 9 g

- 4 ears of fresh sweet corn, husked and scrubbed
- 3 tablespoons light butter, softened
- 1 tablespoon snipped fresh cilantro
- ¼ teaspoon salt
- ¼ teaspoon finely shredded lime peel
- ⅛ to ¼ teaspoon crushed red pepper

1. Carefully cut each ear of corn crosswise in half. In a Dutch oven cook corn, covered, in enough boiling water to cover for 5 to 7 minutes or until kernels are tender. Remove from water.

2. Meanwhile, in a small bowl combine butter, cilantro, salt, lime peel, and crushed red pepper. Serve with warm corn.
PER SERVING: 58 cal., 3 g total fat (1 g sat. fat), 6 mg chol., 117 mg sodium, 9 g carb. (1 g fiber, 1 g sugars), 1 g pro. Exchanges: 0.5 starch, 0.5 fat. Carb choices: 0.5.

▶ QUICK TIP

If you're lucky enough to have some of this zippy butter left over, drizzle it over cooked green beans, broccoli, or carrots at another meal.

Corn on the Cob with Cilantro-Lime Butter

Moroccan-Style
Simmered Beans

Quick Sautéed Vegetables

This colorful and flavorful combo certainly qualifies as vitamin-packed; each serving provides 34 percent of your vitamin A and 287 percent of your vitamin C daily values.

SERVINGS 4 (¾ cup each)
CARB. PER SERVING 9 g

- 1 red sweet pepper, thinly sliced
- 1 yellow sweet pepper, thinly sliced
- 2 teaspoons olive oil
- 1 small zucchini, thinly sliced
- 4 ounces fresh asparagus spears, trimmed and cut into 2-inch pieces
- 2 cloves garlic, minced
- ⅛ teaspoon salt
- ⅛ teaspoon black pepper
- 1½ teaspoons butter
- ½ teaspoon finely snipped fresh thyme

1. In a large skillet cook sweet peppers in hot oil over medium-high heat for 2 minutes. Stir in zucchini and asparagus. Cook and stir for 6 to 7 minutes or just until asparagus is tender.

2. Stir in garlic, salt, and black pepper; cook and stir for 1 minute. Add butter and thyme, stirring just until combined. Serve immediately.

PER SERVING: 75 cal., 4 g total fat (1 g sat. fat), 4 mg chol., 90 mg sodium, 9 g carb. (2 g fiber, 4 g sugars), 2 g pro. Exchanges: 1.5 vegetable, 1 fat. Carb choices: 0.5.

Moroccan-Style Simmered Beans

Put the extra lima beans to good use—stir them into a pot of baked beans or use them to make hummus.

SERVINGS 8 (½ cup each)
CARB. PER SERVING 24 g

- ½ cup chopped sweet onion
- 1 medium carrot, chopped (½ cup)
- 2 teaspoons canola oil
- 1 clove garlic, minced
- ¼ teaspoon ground cumin
- ¼ teaspoon ground coriander
- ⅛ teaspoon crushed red pepper
- ⅛ teaspoon ground cinnamon
- 1 15-ounce can garbanzo beans (chickpeas), rinsed and drained
- 1 15-ounce can Great Northern beans, rinsed and drained
- ½ cup frozen baby lima beans
- ½ cup chopped tomatoes
- ⅓ cup water
- 1 tablespoon lemon juice
- Ground cumin and/or crushed red pepper (optional)

1. In a large saucepan cook onion and carrot in hot oil over medium heat for 8 to 10 minutes or until very tender, stirring occasionally. Stir in garlic, the ¼ teaspoon cumin, the coriander, the ⅛ teaspoon crushed red pepper, and the cinnamon. Cook and stir for 1 minute.

2. Add garbanzo beans, Great Northern beans, lima beans, tomatoes, and the water. Bring to boiling; reduce heat. Cook, covered, for 20 minutes to blend flavors, stirring occasionally. Stir in lemon juice just before serving. If desired, sprinkle with additional cumin and/or crushed red pepper.

PER SERVING: 127 cal., 2 g total fat (0 g sat. fat), 0 mg chol., 202 mg sodium, 24 g carb. (6 g fiber, 2 g sugars), 8 g pro. Exchanges: 1.5 starch, 0.5 lean meat. Carb choices: 1.5.

Herbed Potatoes and Peas

Stir the potatoes and peas gently to keep the potato slices from breaking up.

SERVINGS 4 (¾ cup each)
CARB. PER SERVING 21 g

12 ounces 2- to 3-inch-diameter new potatoes, scrubbed and thinly sliced
1 tablespoon light butter
2 teaspoons olive oil
2 cups fresh pea pods, trimmed
¼ teaspoon salt
⅛ teaspoon black pepper
2 tablespoons snipped fresh chives
2 tablespoons snipped fresh mint

1. In a large skillet cook potatoes, covered, in a small amount of boiling water for 10 to 12 minutes or until potatoes are just tender. Drain off water.
2. Add butter and oil to the skillet. Add pea pods and sprinkle with salt and pepper. Cook, uncovered, over medium-high heat for 3 to 5 minutes or until potatoes are lightly browned and pea pods are crisp-tender, stirring occasionally. Sprinkle with chives and mint; toss to coat. Serve immediately.
PER SERVING: 126 cal., 4 g total fat (1 g sat. fat), 4 mg chol., 176 mg sodium, 21 g carb. (3 g fiber, 3 g sugars), 3 g pro. Exchanges: 0.5 vegetable, 1 starch, 0.5 fat. Carb choices: 1.5.

Barley-Vegetable Pilaf

Barley is done when it is slightly chewy. The veggies should be crisp-tender, so be careful not to overcook.

SERVINGS 4 (⅔ cup each)
CARB. PER SERVING 29 g

1¾ cups lower-sodium vegetable broth
¾ cup quick-cooking barley
½ cup small fresh broccoli florets
½ cup ½-inch pieces zucchini
½ cup chopped red sweet pepper
2 tablespoons snipped fresh chives
1 teaspoon finely shredded lemon peel
2 tablespoons finely shredded Parmesan cheese (optional)

1. In a medium saucepan heat broth to boiling. Stir in barley. Return to boiling; reduce heat. Simmer, covered, for 8 minutes. Add broccoli, zucchini, and sweet pepper. Return to boiling. Cook, covered, about 3 minutes more or until barley and vegetables are tender. Remove from heat and stir in chives and lemon peel. If desired, sprinkle with cheese.
PER SERVING: 141 cal., 1 g total fat (0 g sat. fat), 0 mg chol., 251 mg sodium, 29 g carb. (7 g fiber, 2 g sugars), 5 g pro. Exchanges: 0.5 vegetable, 1.5 starch. Carb choices: 2.

Chipotle Quinoa with Beans

A little chipotle pepper adds a lot of heat and smoky flavor. Stir a small amount of the extra into a pot of chili.

SERVINGS 6 (⅔ cup each)
CARB. PER SERVING 23 g

1 medium onion, chopped (½ cup)
1 tablespoon canola oil
2 cloves garlic, minced
1 14.5-ounce can reduced-sodium chicken broth
¾ cup quinoa,* rinsed and drained
1 small green sweet pepper, chopped (½ cup)
½ of a 15-ounce can no-salt-added black beans (¾ cup), rinsed and drained
1 teaspoon finely chopped canned chipotle pepper in adobo sauce**
1 medium tomato, seeded and chopped (⅔ cup)
¼ cup snipped fresh cilantro

1. In a large saucepan cook onion in hot oil over medium heat for 5 minutes, stirring occasionally. Add garlic; cook and stir for 30 seconds more. Add broth and quinoa. Bring to boiling; reduce heat. Simmer, covered, for 15 minutes.
2. Stir in sweet pepper, black beans, and chipotle pepper. Cook, covered, for 1 minute. Remove from heat. Let stand, covered, for 10 minutes. Stir in tomato and cilantro.
***TEST KITCHEN TIP:** Look for quinoa at health food stores or in the grains section of large supermarkets.
****TEST KITCHEN TIP:** Because chile peppers contain volatile oils that can burn your skin and eyes, avoid direct contact with them as much as possible. When working with chile peppers, wear plastic or rubber gloves. If your bare hands do touch the peppers, wash your hands and nails well with soap and warm water.
PER SERVING: 146 cal., 4 g total fat (0 g sat. fat), 0 mg chol., 175 mg sodium, 23 g carb. (4 g fiber, 2 g sugars), 6 g pro. Exchanges: 2 vegetable, 1 starch, 0.5 fat. Carb choices: 1.5.

▶ QUICK TIP

This flavorful dish starts with a pouch of cooked rice. To keep it from drying out, simply cook the rice mixture just until heated through.

Spanish-Style Rice

Spanish-Style Rice

Serve this pilaf-style rice dish alongside grilled fish, pork, or poultry.

SERVINGS 5 (½ cup each)

CARB. PER SERVING 17 g

½ cup chopped green sweet pepper
¼ cup chopped onion
½ to 1 whole medium fresh serrano chile pepper, chopped (optional) (see tip, page 95)
2 teaspoons olive oil
2 cloves garlic, minced
1 8.8-ounce pouch cooked brown rice or 2 cups cooked brown rice
½ cup chopped tomato
¼ cup chopped pitted green olives
¼ teaspoon salt
2 tablespoons snipped fresh cilantro

1. In a large skillet cook sweet pepper, onion, and, if desired, serrano pepper in hot oil over medium heat for 3 to 5 minutes or until vegetables are crisp-tender, stirring occasionally. Add garlic and cook for 1 minute more.

2. Stir in cooked rice, tomato, green olives, and salt. Cook and stir for 2 minutes or until heated through. Stir in cilantro and serve immediately.

PER SERVING: 106 cal., 3 g total fat (0 g sat. fat), 0 mg chol., 122 mg sodium, 17 g carb. (1 g fiber, 1 g sugars), 2 g pro. Exchanges: 1 starch, 0.5 fat. Carb choices: 1.

Lemon Couscous with Asparagus

Chèvre can be somewhat creamy, so it may seem a bit sticky when crumbling.

SERVINGS 6 (½ cup each)

CARB. PER SERVING 23 g

12 ounces thin fresh asparagus spears, trimmed and cut into 1½- to 2-inch pieces
2 teaspoons cooking oil
1 cup reduced-sodium chicken broth
¼ teaspoon black pepper
⅔ cup whole wheat couscous
2 teaspoons finely shredded lemon peel
2 ounces semisoft goat cheese (chèvre), crumbled
2 tablespoons chopped fresh chives or thinly sliced green onion tops

1. In a large skillet cook asparagus in hot oil for 3 to 5 minutes or until lightly browned and crisp-tender.

2. Meanwhile, in a medium saucepan bring broth and pepper just to boiling; stir in couscous. Cover and remove from heat. Let stand for 5 minutes.

3. Fluff couscous mixture with a fork. Stir in lemon peel and asparagus. Transfer couscous mixture to a serving dish. Sprinkle with goat cheese and chives.

PER SERVING: 156 cal., 5 g total fat (2 g sat. fat), 7 mg chol., 145 mg sodium, 23 g carb. (4 g fiber, 2 g sugars), 7 g pro. Exchanges: 0.5 vegetable, 1.5 starch, 0.5 fat. Carb choices: 1.5.

Herbed Pasta with Pine Nuts

Pine nuts are high in fat and will turn rancid quicker than other nuts. For longer storage, keep them in the freezer.

SERVINGS 6 (½ cup each)

CARB. PER SERVING 13 g

½ of a medium sweet onion, cut into thin wedges
1 tablespoon olive oil
1 medium red sweet pepper, cut into thin bite-size strips (1 cup)
3 cloves garlic, minced
3 ounces dried multigrain penne pasta (1 cup)
¼ teaspoon salt
⅛ teaspoon black pepper
2 tablespoons snipped fresh oregano
1 teaspoon snipped fresh rosemary or thyme
2 tablespoons pine nuts, toasted

1. In a large nonstick skillet cook onion wedges, covered, in hot oil over medium heat for 8 minutes, stirring occasionally. Uncover and add sweet pepper strips. Cook, uncovered, for 5 to 8 minutes more or until onion wedges are lightly browned and pepper strips are tender, stirring occasionally. Add garlic; cook and stir for 30 seconds more.

2. Meanwhile, cook pasta according to package directions. Drain pasta, reserving ¼ cup of the cooking liquid. Add pasta, reserved ¼ cup cooking liquid, the salt, and black pepper to vegetables in skillet. Cook and stir for 1 to 2 minutes or until well combined. Add oregano and rosemary; toss to coat. Divide pasta among six serving plates. Sprinkle with pine nuts.

PER SERVING: 103 cal., 5 g total fat (0 g sat. fat), 0 mg chol., 105 mg sodium, 13 g carb. (2 g fiber, 2 g sugars), 3 g pro. Exchanges: 1 starch, 1 fat. Carb choices: 1.

Fresh Macaroni Salad

1. In a medium saucepan cook macaroni according to package directions, adding broccoli and pea pods for the last 3 minutes of cooking. Drain pasta mixture. Rinse with cold water; drain again. In a large bowl combine pasta mixture, roasted peppers, and green onions.
2. For dressing, in a small bowl whisk together yogurt, mayonnaise, basil, the 2 tablespoons milk, the garlic, lemon peel, salt, and black pepper.
3. Pour dressing over pasta mixture. If desired, add chopped eggs. Toss lightly to coat. Cover and chill for 4 to 24 hours. Before serving, if necessary to moisten, stir in additional milk, 1 tablespoon at a time.
PER SERVING: 114 cal., 4 g total fat (1 g sat. fat), 4 mg chol., 160 mg sodium, 16 g carb. (2 g fiber, 3 g sugars), 5 g pro. Exchanges: 1 vegetable, 1 starch, 0.5 fat. Carb choices: 1.

Two-Tone Potato Salad
Yukon gold potatoes share the spotlight with sweet potatoes in this version of one of America's favorite potluck salads.
SERVINGS 6 (½ cup each)
CARB. PER SERVING 13 g

- 6 ounces small (about 2-inch) Yukon gold potatoes, cut into ½-inch-thick wedges
- 1 6-ounce sweet potato, peeled and cut into 1-inch cubes
- ⅓ cup light mayonnaise
- 1 tablespoon Dijon-style mustard
- 1 tablespoon fat-free milk
- 2 teaspoons snipped fresh thyme or ½ teaspoon dried thyme, crushed
- ¼ teaspoon black pepper
- 1 stalk celery, thinly sliced
- 2 green onions, thinly sliced
- 2 slices turkey bacon, cooked according to package directions and chopped

1. In a large saucepan cook potatoes, covered, in enough boiling water to cover for 10 to 12 minutes or until just tender. Drain well; cool to room temperature.
2. Meanwhile, for dressing, in a large bowl combine mayonnaise, mustard, milk, thyme, and pepper. Add potatoes, celery, and green onions. Toss to coat. Cover and chill at least 4 hours or up to 24 hours. Gently stir in bacon just before serving.
PER SERVING: 106 cal., 5 g total fat (1 g sat. fat), 10 mg chol., 248 mg sodium, 13 g carb. (2 g fiber, 2 g sugars), 2 g pro. Exchanges: 1 starch, 1 fat. Carb choices: 1.

Fresh Macaroni Salad
Besides all of the vegetables, basil and lemon give this creamy pasta salad a burst of freshness.
SERVINGS 6 (¾ cup each)
CARB. PER SERVING 16 g

- 1 cup dried multigrain elbow macaroni (3 ounces)
- 1 cup small fresh broccoli florets
- ½ cup sugar snap pea pods, trimmed and halved crosswise
- ½ cup chopped, drained roasted red sweet peppers
- 2 green onions, thinly sliced (¼ cup)
- ½ cup plain fat-free yogurt
- ¼ cup light mayonnaise
- 2 tablespoons snipped fresh basil
- 2 tablespoons fat-free milk
- 2 cloves garlic, minced
- 1 teaspoon finely shredded lemon peel
- ⅛ teaspoon salt
  Dash black pepper
- 2 hard-cooked eggs, peeled and coarsely chopped (optional)
  Fat-free milk

Two-Tone Potato Salad

A serving spoon and fork or set of tongs work perfectly for picking up salad ingredients and gently giving them a toss. With a few quick tosses, the leafy greens will be evenly coated with the dressing.

Panzanella Salad with a Twist

The rustic Italian salad known as panzanella is usually loaded with day-old-bread cubes, tomatoes, and fresh mozzarella. The twist in this version is whole grain bread cubes, red grapes, and red onion.

SERVINGS 6 (2 cups each)
CARB. PER SERVING 17 g

- 4 ounces whole grain baguette-style French bread, cut into ½-inch slices
- 1 clove garlic, halved
- 6 cups packaged fresh baby spinach or torn romaine lettuce
- ⅓ cup torn fresh basil
- ½ of a small red onion, cut into thin wedges
- 1½ cups halved seedless red grapes
- ¼ cup bottled reduced-calorie balsamic vinaigrette salad dressing

1. Preheat broiler. Place bread slices on a baking sheet. Broil 2 to 3 inches from the heat about 3 minutes or until lightly toasted, turning once to toast both sides. Cool on a wire rack. Lightly rub bread slices with cut sides of garlic clove. Cut bread into cubes.
2. In a large glass salad bowl combine spinach and basil. Top with red onion, the bread cubes, and grapes. Drizzle with salad dressing and toss to coat. Serve immediately.
MAKE-AHEAD DIRECTIONS: Prepare bread cubes; store in an airtight container. In the salad bowl layer spinach, red onion, and grapes. Cover and chill salad for up to 4 hours. Top with basil and bread cubes and drizzle with salad dressing; toss to coat. Serve immediately.
PER SERVING: 99 cal., 2 g total fat (0 g sat. fat), 0 mg chol., 237 mg sodium, 17 g carb. (3 g fiber, 7 g sugars), 4 g pro. Exchanges: 1 starch, 0.5 fat. Carb choices: 1.

Layered Salad with Spicy Buttermilk Dressing

This go-to potluck salad gets an update with the addition of a fresh chile and a little lemon peel and ground cumin.

SERVINGS 6 (about 1¾ cups salad and 2 tablespoons dressing each)
CARB. PER SERVING 12 g

- 6 cups coarsely chopped romaine lettuce
- 1 cup cherry tomatoes, quartered
- 1 medium yellow sweet pepper, cut into thin bite-size strips (1 cup)
- 1 cup thinly sliced and halved English cucumber or zucchini
- ½ of a small red onion, thinly sliced
- 1 recipe Spicy Buttermilk Dressing
- ¾ cup seasoned whole grain croutons

1. Place romaine in the bottom of a 3-quart clear salad bowl. Top with tomatoes, sweet pepper, cucumber, and red onion. If desired, cover and chill for up to 8 hours.
2. To serve, drizzle Spicy Buttermilk Dressing over the salad; toss to coat. Divide among six salad plates and top with croutons.
SPICY BUTTERMILK DRESSING: In a small bowl whisk together ½ cup buttermilk; ¼ cup light mayonnaise; 1 medium fresh serrano chile pepper, seeded and finely chopped;* 1 teaspoon finely shredded lemon peel; ¼ teaspoon ground cumin; ⅛ teaspoon salt; and ⅛ teaspoon black pepper.
*TEST KITCHEN TIP: Because chile peppers contain volatile oils that can burn your skin and eyes, avoid direct contact with them as much as possible. When working with chile peppers, wear plastic or rubber gloves. If your bare hands do touch the peppers, wash your hands and nails well with soap and warm water.
PER SERVING: 105 cal., 5 g total fat (1 g sat. fat), 4 mg chol., 226 mg sodium, 12 g carb. (3 g fiber, 4 g sugars), 3 g pro. Exchanges: 1.5 vegetable, 0.5 starch, 1 fat. Carb choices: 1.

Panzanella Salad
with a Twist

Jicama Radish Slaw

Fruit Salad with a Crunch

Peach and Spinach
Salad with Feta

Tasty Toppers

A sprinkling of an ingredient or two can turn a simple bowl of salad greens or steamed vegetables into an extra-tasty side dish. Try one of these flavor boosters.

1. **Top with a little** snipped fresh herb, such as basil, oregano, parsley, or thyme.

2. **Sprinkle on** a tablespoon or two of chopped toasted almonds, walnuts, or pecans.

3. **Crumble on** a little reduced-fat feta cheese.

4. **Try a sprinkling** of chopped fresh parsley, garlic, and lemon peel.

5. **Add a bit** of sliced green onion or finely chopped shallot.

6. **Grate on some** fresh Parmesan or Romano cheese.

7. **Shred on** a couple radishes.

8. **Chop a** roma tomato and sprinkle on with a little snipped fresh basil.

9. **Spring for** a bit of crumbled cooked turkey bacon.

Jicama Radish Slaw

SERVINGS 8 (½ cup each)
CARB. PER SERVING 5 g

- ¼ cup snipped fresh cilantro
- 2 tablespoons rice vinegar
- 2 tablespoons toasted sesame oil
- ¼ teaspoon salt
- ⅛ to ¼ teaspoon crushed red pepper
- ½ of a medium jicama, peeled and cut into thin matchstick-size pieces (about 3 cups)
- ¾ cup radishes, trimmed and thinly sliced
- ½ cup julienne or packaged coarsely shredded fresh carrot
- 2 green onions, cut into 2-inch pieces and thinly sliced lengthwise
  Lime wedges (optional)

1. In a large bowl whisk together cilantro, vinegar, oil, salt, and crushed red pepper. Add jicama, radishes, carrot, and green onions. Toss to coat. Serve immediately or cover and chill for up to 2 hours. If desired, garnish with lime wedges.
PER SERVING: 54 cal., 3 g total fat (1 g sat. fat), 0 mg chol., 86 mg sodium, 5 g carb. (3 g fiber, 2 g sugars), 1 g pro. Exchanges: 0.5 vegetable, 0.5 fat. Carb choices: 0.

Peach and Spinach Salad with Feta

SERVINGS 4 (about 1¼ cups each)
CARB. PER SERVING 8 g

- 6 cups packaged fresh baby spinach
- 1 recipe Honey-Mustard Vinaigrette
- 1 medium peach, pitted, or 1 apple, cored and thinly sliced
- 3 tablespoons crumbled reduced-fat feta cheese
- 1 tablespoon pine nuts, toasted

1. In a large bowl toss spinach with Honey-Mustard Vinaigrette. Divide spinach among four salad plates. Top with peach or apple slices, feta cheese, and pine nuts.
HONEY-MUSTARD VINAIGRETTE: In a screw-top jar combine 2 tablespoons white wine vinegar, 1 tablespoon olive oil, 1 tablespoon finely chopped shallot, 2 teaspoons water, 1 teaspoon honey mustard, and ⅛ teaspoon salt. Cover and shake well.
PER SERVING: 99 cal., 6 g total fat (1 g sat. fat), 2 mg chol., 234 mg sodium, 8 g carb. (3 g fiber, 3 g sugars), 4 g pro. Exchanges: 1 vegetable, 1 fat. Carb choices: 0.5.

Fruit Salad with a Crunch

SERVINGS 4 (1 cup each)
CARB. PER SERVING 29 g

- 1 recipe Lime-Honey Dressing
- 2 cups cubed fresh pineapple
- 1 medium red pear, cored, quartered, and thinly sliced
- 2 kiwifruits, peeled, halved, and thinly sliced
- ¼ cup chopped, peeled jicama
- 1 tablespoon shredded coconut, toasted

1. Prepare Lime-Honey Dressing. Pour dressing into a bowl and add pineapple, pear, kiwifruits, and jicama. Toss to coat. Serve immediately or cover and chill for up to 1 hour to blend flavors. Sprinkle with coconut just before serving.
LIME-HONEY DRESSING: In a medium bowl whisk together 2 tablespoons lime juice, 1 tablespoon honey, ½ teaspoon grated fresh ginger, and, if desired, ⅛ teaspoon ground cardamom.
PER SERVING: 116 cal., 1 g total fat (1 g sat. fat), 0 mg chol., 8 mg sodium, 29 g carb. (4 g fiber, 20 g sugars), 1 g pro. Exchanges: 1 fruit, 1 carb. Carb choices: 2.

Fruit Skewers with Goat Cheese Dip

SERVINGS 4 (2 skewers and 2 tablespoons dip each)
CARB. PER SERVING 19 g

- 2 ounces semisoft goat cheese (chèvre), softened
- 2 tablespoons tub-style light cream cheese, softened
- 1 teaspoon honey
- 2 tablespoons fat-free milk
- 1½ cups halved fresh strawberries
- 1 cup 1- to 1½-inch chunks fresh pineapple
- 1 cup large seedless red grapes

1. For dip, in a small bowl stir together goat cheese, cream cheese, and honey until well combined. Gradually stir in milk until smooth. Set aside.
2. For the skewers, alternately thread strawberry halves, pineapple chunks, and grapes on eight 8-inch-long skewers. Serve fruit skewers with dip.
PER SERVING: 124 cal., 4 g total fat (3 g sat. fat), 10 mg chol., 95 mg sodium, 19 g carb. (2 g fiber, 15 g sugars), 4 g pro. Exchanges: 1 fruit, 0.5 medium-fat meat, 0.5 fat. Carb choices: 1.

eye-opening breakfasts

Begin each day with a healthful breakfast. Whether it's pancakes hot off the griddle, coffeecake fresh from the oven, or eggs scrambled in the pan, something fresh, flavorful, and nutritiously balanced will get your eyes open, your taste buds tingling, and your day off to a stellar start.

Oatmeal Pancakes with Maple Fruit

Bananas and blueberries combine with maple syrup for a yummy topping.

SERVINGS 8 (2 pancakes and ⅓ cup maple fruit each)
CARB. PER SERVING 31 g

- 3 medium bananas, peeled and sliced
- ½ cup fresh blueberries
- ¼ cup sugar-free maple-flavor syrup
- 2 teaspoons lemon juice
- ¼ teaspoon ground cinnamon
- 1 cup flour
- ½ cup quick-cooking rolled oats
- 1½ teaspoons baking powder
- ½ teaspoon baking soda
- ⅛ teaspoon salt
- 1 cup low-fat buttermilk or sour milk*
- ¼ cup refrigerated or frozen egg product, thawed, or 1 egg, lightly beaten
- 1 tablespoon canola oil
- 1 tablespoon sugar-free maple-flavor syrup
- 1 teaspoon vanilla

1. For maple fruit, in a medium bowl stir together bananas, blueberries, the ¼ cup syrup, the lemon juice, and cinnamon. Set aside.

2. In a large bowl stir together flour, oats, baking powder, baking soda, and salt. In a medium bowl use a fork to combine buttermilk, egg, oil, the 1 tablespoon syrup, and the vanilla. Add buttermilk mixture all at once to flour mixture. Stir just until moistened. Let stand for 10 minutes to soften oats.

3. For each pancake, spoon 2 slightly rounded tablespoons batter onto a hot, lightly greased griddle or heavy skillet; spread to a 3- to 4-inch circle. Cook over medium heat for 1 to 2 minutes on each side or until pancakes are golden brown. Turn over when edges are slightly dry and bottoms are browned. Serve warm topped with maple fruit.

*TEST KITCHEN TIP: To make 1 cup sour milk, place 1 tablespoon lemon juice or vinegar in a glass measuring cup. Add enough fat-free milk to make 1 cup total liquid; stir. Let the mixture stand for 5 minutes before using.

PER SERVING: 159 cal., 3 g total fat (0 g sat. fat), 1 mg chol., 246 mg sodium, 31 g carb. (2 g fiber, 8 g sugars), 5 g pro. Exchanges: 0.5 fruit, 1 starch, 0.5 carb., 0.5 fat. Carb choices: 2.

Fruit and Nut Quinoa

Citrus Salad with Avocado

Wake your taste buds with this fresh fruit salad for breakfast. Or add some shrimp for a lunchtime treat.
SERVINGS 4 (¾ cup each)
CARB. PER SERVING 27 g

- 2 medium grapefruit
- 3 medium oranges
- 1 tablespoon honey
- 1 tablespoon raspberry vinegar or cider vinegar
- 1 tablespoon snipped fresh mint
- 1 medium avocado, peeled, seeded, and coarsely chopped

1. Peel and section the grapefruit and oranges, reserving juices in a bowl.* Place the grapefruit and orange sections in a medium bowl. In the bowl with the reserved juices, whisk the honey and vinegar with the juices to combine. Pour over the grapefruit and orange sections. Add mint; toss to combine. Add avocado; stir gently to combine. To serve, spoon into four serving bowls.

***TEST KITCHEN TIP:** To section grapefruit and oranges, using a serrated knife, remove the peel. Holding the fruit over a bowl to catch the juices, cut between one section and the membrane, slicing to the fruit's center. Turn the knife and slide it up the other side of the section alongside the membrane. Place the section in a second bowl. Repeat with the remaining sections.

PER SERVING: 154 cal., 5 g total fat (1 g sat. fat), 0 mg chol., 4 mg sodium, 27 g carb. (4 g fiber, 18 g sugars), 2 g pro. Exchanges: 2 fruit, 1 fat. Carb choices: 2.

CITRUS SALAD WITH SHRIMP: Prepare salad as directed. Stir in 8 ounces fresh or frozen cooked shrimp, thawed if frozen.

PER SERVING: 210 cal., 6 g total fat (1 g sat. fat), 111 mg chol., 131 mg sodium, 27 g carb. (4 g fiber, 18 g sugars), 14 g pro. Exchanges: 2 fruit, 2 lean meat, 1 fat. Carb choices: 2.

Fruit and Nut Quinoa

Quinoa, a protein-rich grain commonly used in pilafs, salads, and soups, makes a tasty breakfast cereal when spiced with cinnamon and drizzled with honey.
SERVINGS 4 (¾ cup quinoa mixture, ½ cup berries, and 1 teaspoon honey each)
CARB. PER SERVING 45 g

- 1 cup quinoa, rinsed and well drained
- 1 cup fat-free milk
- 1 cup water
- ½ teaspoon ground cinnamon
- Dash salt
- ½ cup chopped pecans, toasted
- 1 cup fresh blackberries
- 1 cup fresh raspberries
- 4 teaspoons honey

1. In a medium saucepan stir together quinoa, milk, the water, cinnamon, and salt. Bring to boiling over medium-high heat; reduce heat. Simmer, covered, about 15 minutes or until most of the liquid is absorbed. Remove from heat; let stand, covered, for 5 minutes.
2. Stir in pecans. Top each serving evenly with fresh berries. Drizzle each serving with 1 teaspoon honey.
PER SERVING: 325 cal., 13 g total fat (1 g sat. fat), 1 mg chol., 67 mg sodium, 45 g carb. (8 g fiber, 13 g sugars), 10 g pro. Exchanges: 0.5 fruit, 2.5 starch, 2 fat. Carb choices: 3.

Peach-Blueberry Parfaits

Try sliced fresh strawberries or raspberries when peaches are out of season.

SERVINGS 2 (1¼ cups each)
CARB. PER SERVING 34 g

- 1 6-ounce carton vanilla, peach, or blueberry fat-free yogurt
- 1 cup lightly sweetened multigrain clusters cereal or low-fat granola cereal
- 1 ripe peach, pitted and cut up
- ½ cup fresh blueberries
- ¼ teaspoon ground cinnamon

1. Divide half of the yogurt between two dessert glasses or bowls; top with half of the cereal. Top with half of the peach, half of the blueberries, and the cinnamon. Repeat layers with the remaining yogurt, cereal, peaches, and blueberries.

PER SERVING: 166 cal., 1 g total fat (0 g sat. fat), 2 mg chol., 95 mg sodium, 34 g carb. (7 g fiber, 19 g sugars), 11 g pro. Exchanges: 0.5 milk, 0.5 fruit, 1 starch. Carb choices: 2.

Use a pastry brush or a piece of waxed paper to apply shortening inside each muffin cup if you don't have paper bake cups on hand.

Peachy Granola Muffins

Peachy Granola Muffins

For a fruit swap, try a nectarine, pear, or blueberries instead of the peach.

SERVINGS 12 (1 muffin each)
CARB. PER SERVING 25 g or 24 g

Nonstick cooking spray
1   cup all-purpose flour
1   cup whole wheat flour
⅓   cup packed brown sugar*
2   teaspoons baking powder
1   teaspoon ground cinnamon
¼   teaspoon salt
⅛   teaspoon ground nutmeg
1   cup buttermilk
2   eggs, lightly beaten, or ½ cup refrigerated or frozen egg product, thawed
2   tablespoons canola oil
1   medium peach, peeled and chopped (¾ cup)
½   cup low-fat granola
    Powdered sugar (optional)

1. Preheat oven to 375°F. Line twelve 2½-inch muffin cups with paper bake cups or lightly coat with cooking spray. Lightly coat the paper bake cups with cooking spray; set cups aside. In a large bowl stir together all-purpose flour, whole wheat flour, brown sugar, baking powder, cinnamon, salt, and nutmeg. Make a well in the center of the flour mixture; set aside.
2. In a medium bowl combine buttermilk, eggs, and canola oil. Add buttermilk mixture all at once to flour mixture; stir just until moistened (batter should be lumpy). Fold in peach and granola. Spoon batter into the prepared muffin cups, filling each nearly full.
3. Bake for 18 to 20 minutes or until a toothpick inserted in the centers comes out clean. Cool in muffin cups on a wire rack for 5 minutes. Remove muffins from muffin cups. If desired, dust muffins with powdered sugar. Serve warm.
*SUGAR SUBSTITUTE: Choose Splenda Brown Sugar Blend. Follow package directions to use product amount equivalent to ⅓ cup brown sugar.
PER SERVING: 150 cal., 4 g total fat (1 g sat. fat), 36 mg chol., 154 mg sodium, 25 g carb. (2 g fiber, 7 g sugars), 5 g pro. Exchanges: 1.5 starch, 0.5 fat. Carb choices: 1.5.
PER SERVING WITH SUBSTITUTE: Same as above, except 149 cal., 153 mg sodium, 24 g carb. (6 g sugars).

Snickerdoodle Crescent Rolls

heat and stir milk, brown sugar, the 2 tablespoons butter, and the salt just until warm (120°F to 130°F); add to flour mixture along with egg. Beat with an electric mixer on low speed for 30 seconds, scraping sides of bowl constantly. Beat on high speed for 3 minutes. Using a wooden spoon, stir in whole wheat flour and as much of the remaining all-purpose flour as you can.

2. Turn dough out onto a lightly floured surface. Knead in enough of the remaining all-purpose flour to make a slightly soft dough that is smooth and elastic (3 to 5 minutes total). Shape dough into a ball. Place in a lightly greased bowl, turning once to grease surface. Cover and let rise in a warm place until double in size (about 1 hour).

3. Punch dough down. Divide dough in half. Cover and let rest for 10 minutes. Line a large baking sheet with parchment paper or lightly coat with nonstick cooking spray; set aside. Preheat oven to 350°F.

4. On a lightly floured surface roll each dough half into a 12-inch circle. Spread the 1 tablespoon butter evenly over both circles. In a small bowl stir together granulated sugar and cinnamon; sprinkle 1 tablespoon of the mixture evenly over each circle. Cut each circle into six wedges.

5. To shape rolls, begin at wide end of each wedge and loosely roll toward the point. Place, point sides down, 2 to 3 inches apart on prepared baking sheet and curve ends of each to make a crescent shape. Cover; let rise in a warm place until nearly double in size (about 30 minutes). In a small bowl beat together the egg white and the water. Brush evenly over the rolls and sprinkle with remaining cinnamon-sugar mixture.**

6. Bake about 15 minutes or until golden. Transfer rolls to a wire rack and let cool slightly; serve warm.

***SUGAR SUBSTITUTES:** Choose from Sweet'N Low Brown or Sugar Twin Granulated Brown to substitute for the brown sugar. Choose Splenda Granular to substitute for the granulated sugar. Follow package directions to use product amounts equivalent to 2 tablespoons brown sugar and 3 tablespoons granulated sugar.

****TEST KITCHEN TIP:** If using granulated sugar substitute, do not use all of the remaining cinnamon-sugar mixture. Just a light dusting will be fine; otherwise, the tops of the rolls will look dry and powdery. Also, rolls will not brown as darkly when using sugar substitute.

PER SERVING: 130 cal., 3 g total fat (2 g sat. fat), 8 mg chol., 91 mg sodium, 22 g carb. (2 g fiber, 6 g sugars), 4 g pro. Exchanges: 1 starch, 0.5 carb., 0.5 fat. Carb choices: 1.5.
PER SERVING WITH SUBSTITUTES: Same as above, except 110 cal., 17 g carb. (1 g sugars). Exchanges: 0 carb. Carb choices: 1.

Snickerdoodle Crescent Rolls

Reminiscent of the famous cookies, these tender breakfast rolls get a sprinkling of cinnamon-sugar.

SERVINGS 12 (1 roll each)
CARB. PER SERVING 22 g or 17 g

- 1 to 1½ cups all-purpose flour
- 1 package active dry yeast
- ¾ cup fat-free milk
- 2 tablespoons packed brown sugar*
- 2 tablespoons butter
- ¼ teaspoon salt
- ¼ cup refrigerated or frozen egg product, thawed, or 1 egg, lightly beaten
- 1 cup whole wheat flour
- 1 tablespoon butter, softened
- 3 tablespoons granulated sugar*
- 2 teaspoons ground cinnamon
- 1 egg white
- 1 tablespoon water

1. In a large mixing bowl stir together 1 cup of the all-purpose flour and the yeast. In a small saucepan

Mocha Coffeecake

Mocha Coffeecake

Deliciously chocolaty, this morning-style cake pairs perfectly with a cup of coffee anytime.

SERVINGS 12 (1 piece each)
CARB. PER SERVING 24 g or 22 g

- 3   tablespoons packed brown sugar*
- 2   tablespoons flour
- 1   tablespoon unsweetened cocoa powder
- ½   teaspoon ground cinnamon
- 2   tablespoons cold butter
- 1½ cups flour
- ½   cup packed brown sugar**
- 2   tablespoons unsweetened cocoa powder
- 1   tablespoon instant espresso coffee powder
- 1   teaspoon baking powder
- ¼   teaspoon baking soda
- ¼   teaspoon salt
- 2   eggs, lightly beaten, or ½ cup refrigerated or frozen egg product, thawed
- ½   cup fat-free sour cream or plain low-fat yogurt
- ¼   cup water
- 3   tablespoons canola oil
- 1   teaspoon vanilla

1. Preheat oven to 350°F. Lightly coat an 8×8×2-inch or 9×9×2-inch baking pan with *nonstick cooking spray*; set aside. For topping, in a bowl combine the 3 tablespoons brown sugar, 2 tablespoons flour, 1 tablespoon cocoa powder, and the cinnamon. Cut in butter until mixture resembles coarse crumbs. Set aside.
2. In a large bowl stir together the 1½ cups flour, ½ cup brown sugar, 2 tablespoons cocoa powder, the espresso powder, baking powder, baking soda, and salt. Make a well in the center of the flour mixture; set aside.
3. In a medium bowl combine eggs, sour cream, the water, canola oil, and vanilla. Add to flour mixture; stir just until combined. Spread batter evenly in prepared pan. Sprinkle evenly with topping.
4. Bake for 25 to 30 minutes or until a wooden toothpick inserted in the center comes out clean. Cool in pan on a wire rack for 15 minutes. Cut into 12 pieces; serve warm.
***NOTE:** We do not recommend using sugar sustitute for the 3 tablespoons brown sugar in the topping.
****SUGAR SUBSTITUTE:** Choose Splenda Brown Sugar Blend. Follow package directions to use product amount equivalent to ½ cup brown sugar.

PER SERVING: 165 cal., 6 g total fat (2 g sat. fat), 41 mg chol., 148 mg sodium, 24 g carb. (1 g fiber, 8 g sugars), 3 g pro. Exchanges: 1 starch, 0.5 carb., 1 medium-fat meat, 0.5 fat. Carb choices: 1.5.
PER SERVING WITH SUBSTITUTE: Same as original, except 162 cal., 147 mg sodium, 22 g carb. (6 g sugars). Exchanges: 0.5 medium-fat meat.

Breakfast Bars to Go

Here's a great make-ahead breakfast. The kids can serve themselves, and you can grab a wrapped bar to eat on the way to work.

SERVINGS 24 (1 bar each)
CARB. PER SERVING 30 g or 28 g

- 2   cups crisp rice cereal
- 2   cups quick-cooking rolled oats
- ½   cup dry-roasted peanuts
- ½   cup sunflower kernels
- 2   cups chopped dried fruit, such as raisins, apricots, cherries, blueberries, and/or cranberries
- ¾   cup honey
- ¾   cup creamy natural peanut butter
- ¼   cup packed brown sugar*
- 1   teaspoon vanilla

1. Line a 13×9×2-inch baking pan with foil; set aside. In a large bowl combine cereal, oats, peanuts, sunflower kernels, and chopped fruit. Set aside.
2. In a medium microwave-safe bowl combine honey, peanut butter, and brown sugar. Microwave, uncovered, on 100 percent power (high) for 1½ to 2½ minutes or until mixture is bubbly, stirring once. Stir in vanilla. Pour mixture over cereal mixture. Stir until just combined. Press into the prepared pan to form an even layer.
3. Cover and chill for 2 to 24 hours. Cut into 24 bars. If desired, wrap individual bars in plastic wrap and chill for up to 1 week.
***SUGAR SUBSTITUTE:** Choose Splenda Brown Sugar Blend. Follow package directions to use product amount equivalent to ¼ cup brown sugar.

PER SERVING: 196 cal., 8 g total fat (1 g sat. fat), 0 mg chol., 53 mg sodium, 30 g carb. (2 g fiber, 19 g sugars), 5 g pro. Exchanges: 1 starch, 1 carb., 1.5 fat. Carb choices: 2.
PER SERVING WITH SUBSTITUTE: Same as above, except 193 cal., 52 mg sodium, 28 g carb. (18 g sugars).

Baked Eggs
with Tomato
Topper

*TEST KITCHEN TIP: Because chile peppers contain volatile oils that can burn your skin and eyes, avoid direct contact with them as much as possible. When working with chile peppers, wear plastic or rubber gloves. If your bare hands do touch the peppers, wash your hands and nails well with soap and warm water.

PER SERVING: 107 cal., 6 g total fat (2 g sat. fat), 214 mg chol., 231 mg sodium, 2 g carb. (0 g fiber, 2 g sugars), 12 g pro. Exchanges: 2 lean meat, 0.5 fat. Carb choices: 0.

Eggs Benedict with Avocado Cream

If you have an egg-poaching pan or silicon poaching cups, use them for cooking the eggs.

SERVINGS 4 (1 egg, 2 tablespoons Avocado Cream, 1 muffin half, 1 tomato slice, and ½ slice bacon each)

CARB. PER SERVING 18 g

- 4 eggs
- 1 recipe Avocado Cream
- 2 whole wheat English muffins, split and toasted
- 4 slices tomato
- 2 slices bacon, halved, crisp-cooked, and drained

1. Half-fill a nonstick skillet with water. Bring water to boiling; reduce heat to simmering (bubbles should begin to break the surface of the water). Break one of the eggs into a measuring cup. Holding the lip of the cup as close to the water as possible, carefully slide the egg into the simmering water. Repeat with remaining eggs, allowing each egg an equal amount of space.

2. Simmer eggs, uncovered, for 3 to 5 minutes or until the whites are completely set and yolks begin to thicken but are not hard. Remove eggs with a slotted spoon and place them in a large pan of warm water to keep them warm. Prepare Avocado Cream.

3. Place a freshly toasted muffin half on each of four serving plates. Top each with Avocado Cream, a tomato slice, an egg, and a bacon piece.

AVOCADO CREAM: In a blender or food processor combine 1 small ripe avocado, halved, seeded, and peeled; ¼ cup fat-free plain Greek yogurt; 2 tablespoons snipped fresh cilantro; 1 tablespoon lime juice; ¼ teaspoon bottled hot pepper sauce (optional); and ⅛ teaspoon salt.

PER SERVING: 210 cal., 11 g total fat (3 g sat. fat), 216 mg chol., 400 mg sodium, 18 g carb. (4 g fiber, 4 g sugars), 13 g pro. Exchanges: 1 starch, 1.5 medium-fat meat, 0.5 fat. Carb choices: 1.

Baked Eggs with Tomato Topper

It's easy to move the ramekins to and from the oven when they are placed on a baking sheet.

SERVINGS 4 (1 egg dish and 2 tablespoons tomato topper each)

CARB. PER SERVING 2 g

- 1 medium roma tomato, finely chopped (⅓ cup)
- 1 tablespoon finely chopped green onion
- 1 tablespoon snipped fresh cilantro
- 1 teaspoon finely chopped jalapeño pepper*
- 1 teaspoon lime juice
- ⅛ teaspoon salt
-    Nonstick cooking spray
- 4 egg whites
- 4 eggs
- 4 tablespoons fat-free milk
- ¼ teaspoon black pepper
- 2 tablespoons finely shredded reduced-fat cheddar cheese

1. For tomato topper, in a small bowl combine tomato, green onion, cilantro, jalapeño pepper, lime juice, and salt; set aside.

2. Preheat oven to 350°F. Coat four 8-ounce ramekins with cooking spray. Place an egg white in each dish. Top each with a whole egg, positioning the yolk in the center of the ramekin. Add 1 tablespoon milk to each ramekin. Top evenly with black pepper, then cheese. Place ramekins on a baking sheet.

3. Bake, uncovered, for 16 to 18 minutes or until eggs are set around edges but still a little jiggly in the center. Top each serving evenly with the tomato topper.

Eggs Benedict with
Avocado Cream

Roasted Tomato and
Asparagus Crustless Quiche

Breakfast Lasagna Rolls

*For a dash of extra color, sprinkle paprika over
the top of each pasta roll just before serving.*

SERVINGS 8 (1 roll each)

CARB. PER SERVING 26 g

- 8   dried whole grain lasagna noodles
-     Nonstick cooking spray
- 8   eggs or 2 cups refrigerated or frozen egg product, thawed
- 2   teaspoons snipped fresh dill weed or ½ teaspoon dried dill weed
- 2   teaspoons olive oil
- 4   cups fresh spinach
- 4   ounces thinly sliced reduced-sodium cooked ham
- ½   cup bottled roasted red sweet peppers, drained and cut into strips
- 1½ cups sliced fresh mushrooms
- 4   green onions, thinly sliced (½ cup)
- 1   12-ounce can evaporated fat-free milk
- 2   tablespoons flour
- 1   tablespoon Dijon-style mustard
- ¼   teaspoon black pepper
- 1   cup shredded reduced-fat cheddar cheese (4 ounces)

1. Preheat oven to 350°F. Cook lasagna noodles according to package directions. Drain; rinse with cold water. Drain again. Place noodles in a single layer on a sheet of foil; set aside. Lightly coat a 2-quart rectangular baking dish with cooking spray; set aside.

2. Using a whisk, in a bowl beat together eggs, dill weed, and a dash *salt*. In a large nonstick skillet heat 1 teaspoon of the oil over medium heat; pour in egg mixture. Cook over medium heat, without stirring, until eggs begin to set on the bottom and around edges. With a spatula, lift and fold the partially cooked eggs so the uncooked portions flows underneath. Continue cooking over medium heat for 2 to 3 minutes or until eggs are cooked through but still glossy and moist. Remove from heat; set aside. Gently stir spinach into mixture in skillet. Cover and let stand about 3 minutes or until spinach is wilted.

3. Top each lasagna noodle with ham, cutting slices to fit noodles. Divide the egg mixture evenly over ham. Top with sweet pepper strips. Starting from a short end, roll up each noodle. Place the lasagna rolls, seam sides down, in the prepared baking dish; set aside.

4. For sauce, in a large skillet heat the remaining 1 teaspoon oil over medium-high heat. Add mushrooms and green onions; cook and stir about 3 minutes or until tender. In a medium bowl stir together ¼ cup of the evaporated milk and the flour until smooth; stir in the remaining evaporated milk, the mustard, and black pepper. Stir the milk mixture into the mushroom mixture in skillet. Cook and stir until slightly thickened and bubbly. Remove from heat. Stir in the cheese until melted. Pour sauce over the lasagna rolls.

5. Cover and bake about 35 minutes or until heated through. To serve, sprinkle with *paprika* if desired.

PER SERVING: 287 cal., 11 g total fat (4 g sat. fat), 229 mg chol., 437 mg sodium, 26 g carb. (4 g fiber, 6 g sugars), 22 g pro. Exchanges: 1 vegetable, 1.5 starch, 2 medium-fat meat. Carb choices: 2.

Roasted Tomato and Asparagus Crustless Quiche

Wow! Each serving is one-fourth of a standard pie plate.

SERVINGS 4 (¼ quiche each)

CARB. PER SERVING 11 g

- 8   ounces fresh asparagus, cut into 1-inch pieces
- 4   ounces cherry tomatoes or grape tomatoes, halved
-     Nonstick cooking spray
- 2   cups refrigerated or frozen egg product, thawed, or 8 eggs, lightly beaten
- 1   cup fat-free cottage cheese
- ¼   cup finely chopped red onion
- 2   tablespoons flour
- 2   teaspoons snipped fresh rosemary
- ¼   teaspoon black pepper
- ¼   cup finely shredded Asiago cheese (1 ounce)

1. Preheat oven to 400°F. Arrange asparagus and tomatoes, cut sides up, in a single layer in a 15×10×1-inch baking pan. Coat vegetables with cooking spray. Roast, uncovered, for 10 to 12 minutes or until browned and tomatoes are soft. Set aside and let cool.

2. Reduce oven temperature to 375°F. In a large mixing bowl combine egg, cottage cheese, onion, flour, rosemary, and pepper. Stir in the asparagus and tomatoes.

3. Coat a 9-inch deep-dish pie plate with cooking spray. Pour egg mixture into the prepared pie plate. Bake, uncovered, about 40 minutes or until a knife inserted near the center comes out clean. Sprinkle with cheese. Serve immediately.

PER SERVING: 157 cal., 2 g total fat (2 g sat. fat), 10 mg chol., 537 mg sodium, 11 g carb. (1 g fiber, 3 g sugars), 21 g pro. Exchanges: 1 vegetable, 0.5 starch, 2.5 lean meat. Carb choices: 1.

Bacon and Egg Breakfast Wraps

Grab whatever color sweet pepper you have in the fridge—red, yellow, or orange have the same flavor as green.

SERVINGS 4 (1 wrap each)

CARB. PER SERVING 18 g

- 4 slices bacon, chopped
- 1 cup chopped fresh mushrooms
- 1 small green sweet pepper, chopped (½ cup)
- ¼ teaspoon chili powder
- ¼ teaspoon black pepper
- ⅛ teaspoon salt
- 1 cup refrigerated or frozen egg product, thawed
- ¼ cup chopped, seeded tomato
  Bottled hot pepper sauce
- 4 8-inch flour tortillas, warmed*

1. In a large nonstick skillet cook bacon over medium heat until crisp. Using a slotted spoon, remove bacon from skillet, reserving 1 tablespoon of the drippings in the skillet (discard the remaining drippings). Drain bacon on paper towels.

2. Add mushrooms, sweet pepper, chili powder, black pepper, and salt to the reserved drippings in skillet; cook and stir about 3 minutes or until vegetables are tender.

3. Pour egg over vegetable mixture in skillet. Cook over medium heat. As mixture sets, run a spatula around edge of skillet, lifting and folding egg mixture so the uncooked portion flows underneath. Continue cooking over medium heat about 2 minutes or until egg is cooked through but still glossy and moist. Stir in cooked bacon, tomato, and hot pepper sauce to your liking. Divide egg mixture among tortillas; roll up tortillas. To serve, cut wraps in half.

*TEST KITCHEN TIP: To warm tortillas, preheat oven to 350°F. Wrap tortillas tightly in foil. Bake about 10 minutes or until heated through.

PER SERVING: 195 cal., 9 g total fat (3 g sat. fat), 11 mg chol., 462 mg sodium, 18 g carb. (1 g fiber, 2 g sugars), 11 g pro. Exchanges: 0.5 vegetable, 1 starch, 1 lean meat, 1.5 fat. Carb choices: 1.

Huevos Rancheros Breakfast Nachos

Nachos in the morning may sound a bit odd, but these will delight everyone at your breakfast table.

SERVINGS 4 (about 11 chips, 3 tablespoons salsa mixture, and ¼ cup egg each)

CARB. PER SERVING 26 g

- 3 ounces baked tortilla chips
- ¼ teaspoon cumin seeds
- ½ cup canned black beans, rinsed and drained
- ½ cup bottled salsa
- 2 eggs
- 3 egg whites
- 3 tablespoons fat-free milk
- ⅛ teaspoon black pepper
  Nonstick cooking spray
- ½ cup shredded reduced-fat Mexican-style cheese blend (2 ounces)

1. Divide chips among four serving plates, spreading into single layers; set aside. In a dry small saucepan heat cumin seeds over medium heat about 1 minute or until aromatic, stirring frequently. Stir in black beans and salsa. Cook for 1 to 2 minutes or until heated through, stirring occasionally. Remove from heat; cover and keep warm.

2. In a medium bowl whisk together eggs, egg whites, milk, and pepper. Coat an unheated medium nonstick skillet with cooking spray; heat skillet over medium heat. Pour in egg mixture. Cook over medium heat, without stirring, until mixture starts to set on the bottom and around edges. Using a spatula or a large spoon, lift and fold the partially cooked egg mixture so the uncooked portion flows underneath. Continue cooking for 2 to 3 minutes or until egg mixture is cooked through but still glossy and moist. Remove from heat immediately.

3. Break up cooked eggs and spoon over tortilla chips. Top with salsa mixture and cheese. Serve immediately.

PER SERVING: 207 cal., 6 g total fat (3 g sat. fat), 113 mg chol., 503 mg sodium, 26 g carb. (4 g fiber, 2 g sugars), 14 g pro. Exchanges: 1.5 starch, 1.5 medium-fat meat. Carb choices: 2.

Bacon and Egg
Breakfast Wraps

Breakfast Pita Pizza
recipe on page 119

Huevos Rancheros
Breakfast Nachos

Scramble 'Em Up

A batch of scrambled eggs can go from basic to beyond with an additional ingredient or two. Use the ideas below and simply fold in the ingredients or sprinkle them on top.

1. **Try** some sautéed sliced fresh mushrooms and a little chopped shallot.

2. **Opt** for a handful of chopped fresh spinach and a sprinkling of reduced-fat feta cheese.

3. **Add** a few halved grape tomatoes and a bit of snipped fresh basil.

4. **Go for** a little chopped avocado and finely chopped jalapeño pepper.

5. **Freshen up** with some snipped fresh herb, such as parley, basil, or dill weed.

6. **Swirl in** a spoonful of fresh salsa.

7. **Toss in** a little chopped zucchini and a smidge of snipped fresh thyme.

8. **Go green** with a few sautéed tiny broccoli florets or fresh asparagus pieces.

Sausage Skillet

Hearty yet healthful describes this easy-to-fix dish that's reminiscent of restaurant breakfast specialties.

SERVINGS 2 (1 cup each)
CARB. PER SERVING 28 g

- 1 **teaspoon canola oil**
- 2 **ounces smoked turkey sausage, cut diagonally into ½-inch slices**
- 1 **cup frozen diced hash brown potatoes**
- ½ **of a small zucchini, halved lengthwise and cut into ½-inch pieces**
- ½ **of a medium red sweet pepper, coarsely chopped**
- ⅓ **cup thinly sliced red onion**
- 1 **clove garlic, minced**
- ¼ **teaspoon chili powder**
- ⅛ **teaspoon black pepper**
- ¼ **cup bottled salsa**

1. In a large nonstick skillet heat oil over medium heat. Add sausage, potatoes, zucchini, sweet pepper, red onion, garlic, chili powder, and black pepper to skillet.
2. Cook for 4 to 5 minutes or until sausage is lightly browned and vegetables are tender, stirring occasionally. Spoon salsa over sausage mixture.

PER SERVING: 187 cal., 6 g total fat (1 g sat. fat), 19 mg chol., 475 mg sodium, 28 g carb. (4 g fiber, 4 g sugars), 8 g pro. Exchanges: 1 vegetable, 1.5 starch, 1 lean meat. Carb choices: 2.

Mushroom-
Olive Frittata

Mushroom-Olive Frittata

Serve this vegetable-packed frittata with fresh berries (or another fruit) and you'll have a great start on your five-a-day fruit and vegetable goal.

SERVINGS 4 (1 wedge each)
CARB. PER SERVING 4 g

1 cup sliced fresh cremini mushrooms
1 tablespoon olive oil
2 cups coarsely shredded fresh Swiss chard or spinach
1 large shallot, thinly sliced
4 eggs*
2 egg whites*
2 teaspoons snipped fresh rosemary or ½ teaspoon dried rosemary, crushed
¼ teaspoon black pepper
⅛ teaspoon salt
¼ cup thinly sliced, pitted Kalamata olives
⅓ cup shredded Parmesan cheese

1. Preheat broiler. In a broilerproof medium nonstick skillet cook mushrooms in hot oil over medium heat for 3 minutes, stirring occasionally. Add Swiss chard and shallot. Cook about 5 minutes or until mushrooms and chard are tender, stirring occasionally.
2. Meanwhile, in a medium bowl whisk together eggs, egg whites, rosemary, pepper, and salt. Pour egg mixture over vegetables in skillet. Cook over medium heat. As mixture sets, run a spatula around edge of skillet, lifting egg mixture so the uncooked portion flows underneath. Continue cooking and lifting edge until egg mixture is almost set and surface is just slightly moist.
3. Sprinkle with olives; top with cheese. Broil about 4 inches from the heat about 2 minutes or until top is lightly browned and center is set. Let stand for 5 minutes before serving.
*TEST KITCHEN TIP: If desired, substitute 1¼ cups refrigerated or frozen egg product, thawed, for the 4 eggs and 2 egg whites.
PER SERVING: 165 cal., 11 g total fat (3 g sat. fat), 216 mg chol., 416 mg sodium, 4 g carb. (1 g fiber, 1 g sugars), 12 g pro. Exchanges: 1 vegetable, 1.5 medium-fat meat, 0.5 fat. Carb choices: 0.

Breakfast Pita Pizza

Lots of vegetables, protein-packed tofu, and reduced-fat cheddar top a crispy pita crust for a super-duper pizza.

SERVINGS 2 (1 pizza each)
CARB. PER SERVING 24 g

½ cup sliced fresh mushrooms
1 small red or green sweet pepper, chopped (½ cup)
1 teaspoon olive oil
3 ounces firm tub-style tofu (fresh bean curd), drained and crumbled (about ½ cup)
1 green onion, thinly sliced
1 clove garlic, minced
⅛ teaspoon black pepper
1 whole wheat pita bread round, split horizontally
½ cup shredded reduced-fat cheddar cheese (2 ounces)

1. Preheat oven to 375°F. In a medium skillet cook mushrooms and sweet pepper in hot oil over medium heat for 5 to 8 minutes or until tender, stirring occasionally. Stir in tofu, green onion, garlic, and black pepper.
2. Place pita halves, cut sides down, on a baking sheet. Sprinkle pita halves with ¼ cup of the cheese. Top with mushroom mixture. Sprinkle the remaining ¼ cup cheese over mushroom mixture on pita halves. Bake for 8 to 10 minutes or until heated through and cheese melts.
PER SERVING: 256 cal., 11 g total fat (5 g sat. fat), 20 mg chol., 417 mg sodium, 24 g carb. (4 g fiber, 2 g sugars), 15 g pro. Exchanges: 0.5 vegetable, 1.5 starch, 1.5 medium-fat meat. Carb choices: 1.5.

good-for-you
snacks

From veggie-topped flatbread and chicken-filled mini peppers to caramelly fruit dip and crunchy snack mix, these healthful treats make great go-tos for between-meal munching. Each is nutritionally balanced to help keep your blood glucose levels in line.

Veggie-Topped Rye Crisps

Turn snack time into veggie time with these incredible stacks that feature dill-flavor cream cheese slathered on a crispy cracker and topped with cucumber, carrot, and radish.

SERVINGS 4 (2 topped crackers each)
CARB. PER SERVING 21 g

- ½ cup light cream cheese spread, softened
- ½ teaspoon finely shredded lemon peel
- ½ teaspoon snipped fresh dill weed or ¼ teaspoon dried dill weed
- 1 small clove garlic, minced
- 8 3½×1½-inch crisp rye crackers
- ½ cup thin bite-size English cucumber strips
- ½ cup coarsely shredded carrot
- ¼ cup thin bite-size radish strips

1. In a small bowl stir together cream cheese, lemon peel, dill, and garlic. Spread evenly on crackers. Top with cucumber, carrot, and radishes.

MAKE-AHEAD DIRECTIONS: Prepare cream cheese mixture as directed. Transfer to an airtight container; cover. Store in the refrigerator for up to 2 days. Within 4 hours of assembling the crisps, cut up the vegetables and store, covered, in the refrigerator.

PER SERVING: 144 cal., 5 g total fat (3 g sat. fat), 15 mg chol., 217 mg sodium, 21 g carb. (4 g fiber, 3 g sugars), 5 g pro. Exchanges: 1.5 starch, 0.5 fat. Carb choices: 1.5.

BLT Cups

These light and refreshing salad snacks make a great side dish, too.

SERVINGS 4 (about 1 cup each)
CARB. PER SERVING 5 g

- 3 tablespoons light mayonnaise
- 1 tablespoon fat-free milk
- ½ teaspoon finely shredded lemon peel
- 1 clove garlic, minced
- ⅛ teaspoon black pepper
- 3 cups chopped romaine lettuce
- 1 cup cherry tomatoes or grape tomatoes, halved
- 2 slices turkey bacon, cooked according to package directions and chopped
- 4 whole wheat croutons, coarsely crushed

1. In a small bowl stir together mayonnaise, milk, lemon peel, garlic, and pepper. Set aside.

2. In four wide 8-ounce glasses or serving dishes, layer half the lettuce, half the tomatoes, and half the bacon. Top with half the mayonnaise mixture. Repeat layers once. Sprinkle with crushed croutons.

PER SERVING: 83 cal., 6 g total fat (1 g sat. fat), 9 mg chol., 226 mg sodium, 5 g carb. (2 g fiber, 2 g sugars), 3 g pro. Exchanges: 1 vegetable, 1 fat. Carb choices: 0.

Bruschetta Planks

Spoon the warm, chunky veggie topper on the crunchy cracker just before serving to keep it from getting soggy.

SERVINGS 4 (1 cracker and ¼ cup topping each)
CARB. PER SERVING 10 g

- ½ cup chopped red or yellow sweet pepper
- ½ cup chopped fresh button mushrooms or cremini mushrooms
- ¼ cup chopped onion
- 2 teaspoons olive oil
- 1 medium tomato, seeded and chopped (½ cup)
- 1 clove garlic, minced
- 2 tablespoons snipped fresh basil
- 4 thin whole grain flatbread crackers
- 1 ounce Parmesan cheese, thinly shaved

1. In a medium nonstick skillet cook sweet pepper, mushrooms, and onion in hot oil over medium heat for 5 to 7 minutes or until tender, stirring occasionally. Add tomato and garlic. Cook and stir for 1 minute more. Remove from heat. Stir in basil.

2. Spoon tomato mixture evenly on crackers. Top with shaved Parmesan cheese. Serve immediately.

PER SERVING: 107 cal., 6 g total fat (2 g sat. fat), 5 mg chol., 157 mg sodium, 10 g carb. (2 g fiber, 3 g sugars), 4 g pro. Exchanges: 1 vegetable, 0.5 starch, 1 fat. Carb choices: 0.5.

Bruschetta Planks

Spicy Tomato Salsa

To toast the cumin seeds, toss them in a dry small skillet and heat over medium heat about 1 minute or until fragrant.

SERVINGS 6 (⅓ cup salsa and 4 pita wedges each)
CARB. PER SERVING 20 g

- 1 medium tomato, seeded and chopped (½ cup)
- ½ cup finely chopped zucchini
- 2 green onions, thinly sliced (¼ cup)
- 2 tablespoons snipped fresh cilantro
- 1 tablespoon lemon juice
- ½ to 1 small fresh Thai red chile pepper, seeded and finely chopped*
- 1 large clove garlic, minced
- ¼ teaspoon cumin seeds, toasted and crushed
- ⅛ teaspoon ground coriander
- 3 whole wheat pita bread rounds or 6-inch naan rounds, each cut into 8 wedges and toasted

1. In a medium bowl combine tomato, zucchini, green onions, cilantro, lemon juice, Thai pepper, garlic, cumin, and coriander. Cover and chill for 2 to 24 hours. Serve with pita or naan wedges.

*TEST KITCHEN TIP: Because chile peppers contain volatile oils that can burn your skin and eyes, avoid direct contact with them as much as possible. When working with chile peppers, wear plastic or rubber gloves. If your bare hands do touch the peppers, wash your hands and nails well with soap and warm water.

PER SERVING: 96 cal., 1 g total fat (0 g sat. fat), 0 mg chol., 174 mg sodium, 20 g carb. (3 g fiber, 1 g sugars), 4 g pro. Exchanges: 1 vegetable, 1 starch. Carb choices: 1.

For an impressive presentation, arrange four pepper halves on each of four plates and sprinkle with a little snipped fresh cilantro.

Pizza Lettuce Cups

1. In a medium bowl combine tomatoes, cheese, pepperoni, basil, and oregano. Divide tomato mixture among lettuce leaves. Roll up.

PER SERVING: 68 cal., 4 g total fat (2 g sat. fat), 20 mg chol., 257 mg sodium, 2 g carb. (0 g fiber, 0 g sugars), 6 g pro. Exchanges: 0.5 vegetable, 0.5 lean meat, 0.5 fat. Carb choices: 0.

BBQ Chicken Bites

No mini peppers? You can substitute wedges of sweet pepper, but don't bake them quite as long.

SERVINGS 4 (4 stuffed pepper halves each)
CARB. PER SERVING 10 g

Nonstick cooking spray
8   miniature red, yellow, and/or green sweet peppers or large fresh jalapeño chile peppers
½   cup shredded cooked chicken breast
¼   cup shredded reduced-fat cheddar cheese (1 ounce)
2   green onions, thinly sliced (¼ cup)
2   tablespoons snipped fresh cilantro (optional)
⅓   cup low-sodium barbecue sauce

1. Preheat oven to 350°F. Line a baking sheet with foil; coat foil with cooking spray. Set aside. Cut each pepper in half lengthwise (do not remove stem); remove seeds and membranes.* Place pepper halves, cut sides up, on prepared baking sheet. Set aside.

2. For filling, in a small bowl combine chicken, cheese, green onions, and, if desired, cilantro. Add barbecue sauce; stir until combined. Spoon chicken mixture evenly into pepper halves.

3. Bake for 15 to 20 minutes or until heated through and peppers are just tender.

*TEST KITCHEN TIP: If using jalapeño peppers, because chile peppers contain volatile oils that can burn your skin and eyes, avoid direct contact with them as much as possible. When working with jalapeño peppers, wear plastic or rubber gloves. If your bare hands do touch the peppers, wash your hands and nails well with soap and warm water.

PER SERVING: 90 cal., 2 g total fat (1 g sat. fat), 20 mg chol., 87 mg sodium, 10 g carb. (1 g fiber, 7 g sugars), 8 g pro. Exchanges: 0.5 vegetable, 0.5 carb., 1 lean meat, 0.5 fat. Carb choices: 0.5.

Pizza Lettuce Cups

If you love pizza but can't afford the carbohydrate that comes with the crust, try this healthful version.

SERVINGS 4 (2 wraps each)
CARB. PER SERVING 2 g

1¼   cups cherry tomatoes or grape tomatoes, quartered
¾   cup shredded reduced-fat mozzarella cheese (3 ounces)
1   ounce thinly sliced cooked turkey pepperoni, chopped (¼ cup)
¼   cup snipped fresh basil
1   tablespoon snipped fresh oregano
8   large Bibb lettuce leaves

BBQ Chicken Bites

Mediterranean Salmon Spread

Start off your next party with these healthful, yummy veggie pickups. Slices of zucchini and Belgian endive leaves are loaded with a creamy salmon and red pepper spread. Each serving has only 78 calories, 3 grams of fat, and—best of all—0 carb choices.

SERVINGS 4 (¼ cup spread, 4 zucchini slices, and 2 endive leaves each)
CARB. PER SERVING 5 g

 3 tablespoons light sour cream
 2 teaspoons snipped fresh mint
 ⅛ teaspoon garlic powder
 1 6-ounce pouch skinless, boneless pink salmon
 ⅓ cup bottled roasted red sweet pepper, drained and chopped
 16 1-inch diagonal slices zucchini, with centers hollowed out slightly
 8 Belgian endive leaves
    Snipped fresh mint (optional)

1. In a small bowl combine sour cream, the 2 teaspoons mint, and the garlic powder. Stir in salmon and roasted sweet pepper. Cover and chill for 2 to 24 hours.
2. Stir spread. Spoon evenly onto zucchini slices and endive leaves. If desired, garnish with additional snipped mint.

PER SERVING: 78 cal., 3 g total fat (1 g sat. fat), 18 mg chol., 227 mg sodium, 5 g carb. (1 g fiber, 2 g sugars), 9 g pro. Exchanges: 1 vegetable, 1 lean meat. Carb choices: 0.

Mediterranean Salmon Spread

Tangy Tomato and Goat Cheese Dip

You can store this creamy bean dip in the refrigerator for up to three days. Stir it before serving.

SERVINGS 8 (¼ cup dip and 1 cup vegetable dippers each)
CARB. PER SERVING 13 g

 ⅓ cup dried tomatoes
 1 15-ounce can no-salt-added cannellini beans (white kidney beans), rinsed and drained
 4 ounces semisoft goat cheese (chèvre)
 1 teaspoon finely shredded lemon peel (set aside)
 2 tablespoons lemon juice
 2 tablespoons water
 2 cloves garlic, thinly sliced
 ¼ teaspoon salt
 8 cups zucchini slices, red sweet pepper strips, carrot sticks, and/or broccoli florets

1. Place dried tomatoes in a small bowl. Add enough boiling water to cover; let stand for 5 minutes. Drain tomatoes well and finely chop.
2. Meanwhile, in a food processor combine beans, goat cheese, lemon juice, the water, garlic, and salt. Cover and process until smooth. Transfer to a medium bowl. Stir in chopped tomatoes and lemon peel. Serve with vegetable dippers.

PER SERVING: 119 cal., 5 g total fat (3 g sat. fat), 11 mg chol., 221 mg sodium, 13 g carb. (4 g fiber, 3 g sugars), 7 g pro. Exchanges: 1 vegetable, 0.5 starch, 1 fat. Carb choices: 1.

Granola-Topped
Caramel Fruit Dip

Mini Grilled Tomato Sandwiches

*Use a serrated knife to gently cut each toasty sandwich
into four triangles or squares.*

SERVINGS 4 (2 sandwich quarters each)

CARB. PER SERVING 11 g

- 4 very thin slices whole wheat bread
- 2 tablespoons purchased reduced-fat basil pesto
- 1 ounce Parmesan cheese, thinly shaved
- 2 roma tomatoes, trimmed and each cut into 4 slices
- ½ of a small avocado, seeded, peeled, and thinly sliced
  Butter-flavor nonstick cooking spray

1. Spread one side of each bread piece with a thin layer of pesto. Top half the bread pieces evenly with the shaved cheese, tomato slices, and avocado slices. Top with remaining bread pieces, spread sides down. Lightly coat both sides of sandwiches with cooking spray.

2. Preheat a grill pan or large nonstick skillet over medium-high heat. Reduce heat to medium. Place sandwiches on grill pan or in skillet. Weight sandwiches down by placing a skillet on top of the sandwiches. Cook for 2 minutes. Turn sandwiches over, weight down, and cook about 2 minutes more or until golden brown. Cut each sandwich into quarters. Serve warm.

PER SERVING: 125 cal., 7 g total fat (2 g sat. fat), 7 mg chol., 268 mg sodium, 11 g carb. (3 g fiber, 3 g sugars), 6 g pro. Exchanges: 0.5 vegetable, 0.5 starch, 0.5 lean meat, 1 fat. Carb choices: 1.

Thin and Crispy Fruit Pizza

*Watch carefully—the bagel thin halves will toast
quickly in a toaster or under a broiler.*

SERVINGS 4 (1 bagel half each)

CARB. PER SERVING 25 g

- ¼ of an 8-ounce package reduced-fat cream cheese (Neufchâtel), softened
- ¼ cup plain fat-free yogurt
- 2 tablespoons sugar-free caramel-flavor ice cream topping
- 2 whole wheat bagel thins, split and toasted
- 1 cup assorted fresh fruit, such as blueberries, raspberries, chopped strawberries, and/or chopped mango

1. In a small bowl beat cream cheese with an electric mixer on medium speed until smooth. Beat in yogurt and caramel topping.

2. Spread cream cheese mixture evenly on cut sides of bagel thins. Top evenly with fruit. Serve immediately.

PER SERVING: 143 cal., 4 g total fat (2 g sat. fat), 11 mg chol., 169 mg sodium, 25 g carb. (3 g fiber, 7 g sugars), 5 g pro. Exchanges: 1 starch, 0.5 carb., 0.5 fat. Carb choices: 1.5.

Granola-Topped Caramel Fruit Dip

*When you're in the mood for dessert but want to stick
with your diabetes meal plan, try this easy-fix treat.
The combination of fresh fruit, caramel-kissed yogurt,
and a nutty topper is a true delight.*

SERVINGS 4 (about ⅓ cup dip and ¾ cup fruit each)

CARB. PER SERVING 27 g

- 2 tablespoons regular rolled oats
- 1 tablespoon sunflower kernels
- 1 tablespoon sliced almonds
  Butter-flavor nonstick cooking spray
- ⅛ teaspoon ground cinnamon
- 2 6- to 7-ounce cartons plain low-fat Greek yogurt
- 3 tablespoons sugar-free caramel-flavor ice cream topping
- 3 cups sliced apples, sliced kiwifruits, cut-up cantaloupe, and/or whole strawberries

1. In a small bowl combine oats, sunflower kernels, and almonds. Lightly coat with cooking spray and sprinkle with cinnamon; toss gently to coat. In a medium skillet cook oat mixture over medium heat for 3 to 5 minutes or until toasted, stirring occasionally. Remove from heat and cool completely.

2. In a small bowl stir together yogurt and caramel topping until smooth. Transfer to a serving bowl. Sprinkle with oat mixture. Serve with fresh fruit for dipping.

PER SERVING: 168 cal., 4 g total fat (2 g sat. fat), 4 mg chol., 65 mg sodium, 27 g carb. (3 g fiber, 12 g sugars), 9 g pro. Exchanges: 1 milk, 1 fruit, 0.5 fat. Carb choices: 2.

Thai Fruit Skewers

For a quick fix, skip the skewers. Instead divide the fruit mixture among four bowls.

SERVINGS 4 (2 skewers each)
CARB. PER SERVING 21 g

- ½ cup reduced-fat or light unsweetened coconut milk
- 1 tablespoon finely shredded lime peel
- ⅛ teaspoon cayenne pepper
- 2 kiwifruits, peeled and quartered
- 4 to 6 1½-inch fresh peeled pineapple pieces
- 4 to 6 1½-inch fresh peeled papaya pieces
- 4 to 6 1½-inch fresh peeled mango pieces
- ¼ cup snipped fresh mint
- ¼ cup shredded coconut, toasted

1. In a medium bowl combine coconut milk, lime peel, and cayenne pepper. Add kiwifruits, pineapple, papaya, and mango pieces. Toss to coat. Cover and chill for 1 to 4 hours, stirring occasionally.
2. Drain fruit, discarding coconut milk mixture. Thread fruit pieces alternately on eight 6-inch skewers. Sprinkle fruit with mint and coconut.

PER SERVING: 112 cal., 4 g total fat (3 g sat. fat), 0 mg chol., 13 mg sodium, 21 g carb. (4 g fiber, 14 g sugars), 1 g pro. Exchanges: 1 fruit, 0.5 carb., 0.5 fat. Carb choices: 1.5.

Fruit Triangles

Remove four sheets of phyllo and then rewrap and store the remaining for another use.

SERVINGS 4 (3 triangles and 1½ tablespoons sauce each)
CARB. PER SERVING 21 g

- 1 small ripe plum, pitted and chopped (½ cup)
- 2 tablespoons snipped dried apricots
- ¼ teaspoon ground cinnamon
- 4 sheets frozen phyllo dough (14×9-inch rectangles), thawed
  Butter-flavor nonstick cooking spray
- 1 recipe Honey-Orange Dipping Sauce

1. Preheat oven to 350°F. Line a large baking sheet with parchment paper. In a small bowl combine plum, apricots, and cinnamon. Set aside.
2. Unroll phyllo dough. Place one sheet of phyllo dough on a flat surface, keeping the remaining sheets covered with plastic wrap. Lightly coat the phyllo sheet with cooking spray. Top with a second sheet; lightly coat with cooking spray. Using a pizza cutter or sharp knife, cut dough crosswise into six 2¼-inch strips. Place a well-rounded teaspoon of the plum mixture about ½ inch from the top of each strip. To fold into a triangle, bring a corner over filling so the short edge lines up with the side edge. Continue folding the triangular shape along the strip until it reaches the other end. Do not wrap too tightly. Repeat with remaining phyllo sheets and filling to make a total of 12 triangles.
3. Place triangles on prepared baking sheet. Bake for 20 to 22 minutes or until lightly browned. Serve warm or at room temperature with Honey-Orange Dipping Sauce.

HONEY-ORANGE DIPPING SAUCE: In a small bowl combine ⅓ cup plain fat-free yogurt, 1 tablespoon honey, and ½ teaspoon finely shredded orange peel.

PER SERVING: 104 cal., 1 g total fat (0 g sat. fat), 0 mg chol., 108 mg sodium, 21 g carb. (1 g fiber, 10 g sugars), 3 g pro. Exchanges: 1 starch, 0.5 carb. Carb choices: 1.5.

Nutty Chocolate Crunch

To keep from overdoing when you nibble this irresistible chocolate-and-cereal snack, pack individual servings in resealable plastic sandwich bags and tuck them in the refrigerator. Then when hunger hits, grab just one bag.

SERVINGS 7 (⅔ cup each)
CARB. PER SERVING 21 g

- Nonstick cooking spray
- ⅓ cup semisweet chocolate pieces
- 2 tablespoons sugar-free or reduced-calorie chocolate-flavor syrup
- 2½ cups bite-size rice square cereal
- 1 cup whole bran cereal (shreds)
- ⅓ cup unsalted dry-roasted peanuts

1. Lightly coat a large sheet of foil with cooking spray. In a medium saucepan combine chocolate pieces and chocolate syrup. Cook and stir over medium-low heat until chocolate pieces are melted. Remove from heat.
2. Add cereals and peanuts to melted chocolate; toss gently to coat. Spread onto prepared foil to cool. To store, place cereal mixture in an airtight container; cover. Store in the refrigerator for up to 3 days.

PER SERVING: 138 cal., 6 g total fat (2 g sat. fat), 0 mg chol., 108 mg sodium, 21 g carb. (3 g fiber, 6 g sugars), 4 g pro. Exchanges: 1.5 carb., 1 fat. Carb choices: 1.5.

Fruit Triangles

Thai Fruit Skewers

Yummy Yogurt

For a simple, satisfying, feel-full snack, start with 6 ounces plain fat-free Greek yogurt and add one of the following flavor and nutrition boosters.

1. **Halve, pit, and slice** a small fresh peach or nectarine and add a sprinkle of freshly grated nutmeg.

2. **Stir in a few** sliced fresh strawberries and a little finely shredded lemon peel.

3. **Peel and section** a small orange over the yogurt and then give it a stir.

4. **Grab a handful** of fresh blueberries and fold in with a few chopped walnuts.

5. **Try a few** fresh blackberries and a little finely shredded orange peel.

6. **Chop a couple slices** of fresh pear and stir in with a dash of cardamom.

7. **Fold in** a few dried cranberries and chopped pistachios.

8. **Go for some** fresh raspberries and a bit of snipped fresh lemon thyme.

Sweet and Spicy Wasabi Snack Mix

Stash a batch of this tasty combo in the freezer so it's handy when you crave something crunchy.

SERVINGS 14 (½ cup each)
CARB. PER SERVING 15 g

2½ cups crispy corn and rice cereal
2   cups pretzel sticks
1   cup wasabi-flavor dried peas
¾   cup whole almonds
¼   cup light butter
2   tablespoons rice vinegar
4   teaspoons sesame seeds
1   tablespoon reduced-sodium soy sauce
½   teaspoon ground ginger
¼   teaspoon cayenne pepper
½   cup snipped dried apricots

1. Preheat oven to 300°F. In a large bowl combine cereal, pretzel sticks, dried peas, and almonds. Set aside. In a small saucepan heat and stir butter, vinegar, sesame seeds, soy sauce, ginger, and cayenne over medium-low heat until butter melts. Drizzle butter mixture over cereal mixture; stir gently to coat. Transfer mixture to a 15×10×1-inch baking pan.

2. Bake about 30 minutes or until mixture is almost dry and almonds are lightly toasted, stirring twice. Stir in apricots. Spread mixture on a large piece of foil to cool. Store in an airtight container at room temperature for up to 3 days or in the freezer for up to 1 month.

PER SERVING: 127 cal., 7 g total fat (2 g sat. fat), 4 mg chol., 194 mg sodium, 15 g carb. (2 g fiber, 4 g sugars), 3 g pro. Exchanges: 1 starch, 1 fat. Carb choices: 1.

Kettle-Style Caramel Corn

The sweet-and-salty flavor of classic kettle corn comes through in this baked popcorn treat. Using brown sugar gives the coating a caramel flavor.

SERVINGS 11 (1 cup each)
CARB. PER SERVING 17 g or 11 g

- ½ cup packed brown sugar*
- 3 tablespoons tub-style vegetable oil spread
- ½ teaspoon salt
- 1 teaspoon vanilla
- 12 cups air-popped popcorn

1. Preheat oven to 300°F. In a small saucepan combine brown sugar, vegetable oil spread, and ¼ teaspoon of the salt; cook and stir over medium heat just until boiling and sugar is dissolved. Stir in vanilla.

2. Place popcorn in a shallow roasting pan. Drizzle brown sugar mixture over popcorn; toss to coat. Bake, uncovered, for 20 minutes, stirring once. Sprinkle with the remaining ¼ teaspoon salt. Transfer to a large piece of foil or a large roasting pan; let cool for 1 hour. Immediately place in an airtight container; cover and store at room temperature for up to 2 days.

*SUGAR SUBSTITUTE: Choose Splenda Brown Sugar Blend. Follow package directions to use product amount equivalent to ½ cup brown sugar.

PER SERVING: 95 cal., 3 g total fat (1 g sat. fat), 0 mg chol., 134 mg sodium, 17 g carb. (1 g fiber, 10 g sugars), 1 g pro. Exchanges: 1 starch, 0.5 fat. Carb choices: 1.

PER SERVING WITH SUBSTITUTE: Same as above, except 79 cal., 131 mg sodium, 11 g carb. (4 g sugars).

Fruity-Limeade Slushy

Fruity-Limeade Slushy

Fresh lime enhances the flavor of the cherry-limeade drink mix and complements the mixed berries in this icy treat.

SERVINGS 4 (1½ cups each)
CARB. PER SERVING 12 g

- 1 lime
- 3 cups water
- 4 2.2-gram packets low-calorie cherry-limeade drink mix
- 3 cups ice
- 2 cups frozen mixed berries
- 4 lime slices

1. Finely shred 1 teaspoon peel from the whole lime. Squeeze juice from the lime into a blender. Add lime peel, the water, and dry drink mix to lime juice in blender. Cover and blend until drink mix is dissolved. Add ice and mixed berries. Cover and blend until mixture is combined and ice is crushed. Pour into four glasses. Garnish with lime slices.

PER SERVING: 50 cal., 0 g total fat, 0 mg chol., 6 mg sodium, 12 g carb. (3 g fiber, 6 g sugars), 1 g pro. Exchanges: 0.5 fruit, 0.5 carb. Carb choices: 1.

delightful desserts

Celebrate! If you track your numbers and plan for a treat, you can indulge in one of these everyday-special desserts. Lightened up and made more healthful for you, each promises perfect sweetness. Try nutty blondies, fruity crisp, creamy cheesecake, and more.

Peanut Butter Swirl Chocolate Brownies

These two-tone brownies are so rich and luscious, no one will believe how low in fat and calories they are.

SERVINGS 20 (1 brownie each)
CARB. PER SERVING 17 g or 13 g

Nonstick cooking spray
¼ cup butter
¾ cup sugar*
⅓ cup cold water
¾ cup refrigerated or frozen egg product, thawed, or 3 eggs, lightly beaten
¼ cup canola oil
1 teaspoon vanilla
1¼ cups flour
1 teaspoon baking powder
¼ cup creamy peanut butter
½ cup unsweetened cocoa powder
¼ cup miniature semisweet chocolate pieces

1. Preheat oven to 350°F. Line a 9×9×2-inch baking pan with foil, extending foil up over the edges of the pan. Lightly coat foil with cooking spray. Set aside.
2. In a medium saucepan melt butter over low heat; remove from heat. Whisk in sugar and the water. Whisk in eggs, oil, and vanilla until combined. Stir in 1 cup of the flour and the baking powder until combined. (Batter will be thin at this point.) Place peanut butter in a small bowl; gradually whisk in ½ cup of the batter until smooth. Set aside. In another small bowl combine the remaining ¼ cup flour and the cocoa powder; stir into the plain batter. Stir chocolate pieces into chocolate batter; pour chocolate batter into prepared pan.
3. Drop peanut butter batter in small mounds over chocolate batter in pan. Using a thin metal spatula, swirl batters together. Bake for 20 to 25 minutes* or until top springs back when lightly touched and a toothpick inserted near the center comes out clean. Cool completely in pan on a wire rack. Cut into 20 bars.
*SUGAR SUBSTITUTES: Choose from Splenda Sugar Blend or Sun Crystals Granulated Blend. Follow package directions to use product amount equivalent to ¾ cup sugar. Decrease baking time to 15 to 18 minutes or until top springs back when lightly touched and a toothpick inserted near the center comes out clean.
PER SERVING: 151 cal., 8 g total fat (3 g sat. fat), 6 mg chol., 61 mg sodium, 17 g carb. (0 g fiber, 10 g sugars), 3 g pro. Exchanges: 1 carb., 1.5 fat. Carb choices: 1.
PER SERVING WITH SUBSTITUTE: Same as above, except 140 cal., 13 g carb. (6 g sugars).

Chocolate-Coconut
Macaroons

Caramel-Cashew Blondies

*Let the chocolate set before placing these caramelly squares
in a single layer in an airtight container to store.
They will keep at room temperature for up to three days.*

SERVINGS 16 (1 bar each)
CARB. PER SERVING 26 g or 18 g

Nonstick cooking spray
1 cup packed brown sugar*
½ cup light butter
½ cup refrigerated or frozen egg product, thawed, or
  2 eggs, lightly beaten
2 tablespoons fat-free milk
1½ teaspoons vanilla
1 cup all-purpose flour
½ cup whole wheat pastry flour or whole wheat flour
¾ teaspoon baking powder
¼ teaspoon ground cinnamon
⅛ teaspoon baking soda
½ cup lightly salted dry-roasted cashews, chopped
1 ounce semisweet chocolate, melted
2 tablespoons sugar-free caramel-flavor ice cream
  topping

1. Preheat oven to 350°F. Line a 9×9×2-inch baking pan
with foil, extending foil up over the edges of the pan.
Coat the foil with cooking spray; set aside.
2. In a medium saucepan heat brown sugar and butter
over medium heat until butter melts and mixture is
smooth, stirring constantly. Remove from heat. Cool
slightly. Stir in eggs until well combined. Stir in milk
and vanilla. Stir in all-purpose and whole wheat flours,
baking powder, cinnamon, and baking soda. Spread
batter in prepared baking pan. Sprinkle with cashews.
3. Bake for 18 to 20 minutes or until edges are browned
and a toothpick inserted near center comes out clean.
Cool in pan on a wire rack.
4. To serve, lift uncut bars from pan using foil. Drizzle
the top with melted chocolate. If necessary, stir to
soften caramel topping. Drizzle the top with caramel
topping. Cut into 16 bars to serve.
SUGAR SUBSTITUTES: Choose Splenda Brown Sugar Blend.
Follow package directions to use product amount
equivalent to 1 cup brown sugar.
PER SERVING: 167 cal., 6 g total fat (3 g sat. fat), 8 mg chol.,
110 mg sodium, 26 g carb. (1 g fiber, 15 g sugars), 3 g pro.
Exchanges: 1 starch, 1 carb., 1 fat. Carb choices: 2.
PER SERVING WITH SUBSTITUTE: Same as above, except
145 cal., 106 mg sodium, 18 g carb. (7 g sugars).
Exchanges: 0 carb. Carb choices: 1.

Chocolate-Coconut Macaroons

*Two great flavors meld together in these
heavenly, cloudlike puffs of yum.*

SERVINGS 18 (1 macaroon each)
CARB. PER SERVING 11 g

2 egg whites
½ teaspoon vanilla
⅛ teaspoon cream of tartar
  Dash salt
⅔ cup sugar*
¾ cup shredded coconut
2 ounces dark chocolate or semisweet chocolate,
  coarsely grated

1. Preheat oven to 325°F. Line two cookie sheets with
parchment paper; set aside. In a large mixing bowl beat
egg whites, vanilla, cream of tartar, and salt with an
electric mixer on high speed until soft peaks form (tips
curl). Gradually add sugar, about 1 tablespoon at a time,
beating until stiff peaks form (tips stand straight).
Gently fold in ½ cup of the coconut and the chocolate.
2. Drop mixture into a total of 18 mounds on the
prepared cookie sheets, using 2 tablespoons of the egg
white mixture for each mound and leaving about 1 inch
between the mounds. Sprinkle tops with remaining
¼ cup coconut. Place cookie sheets on separate oven
racks. Bake for 15 minutes. Rotate cookie sheets in oven
by putting cookie sheet that was on top rack on bottom
rack and bottom-rack cookie sheet on top rack. Turn off
oven; let macaroons dry in oven for 25 minutes. Transfer
macaroons to a wire rack and let cool.
* SUGAR SUBSTITUTES: We do not recommend using a sugar
substitute for this recipe.
PER SERVING: 72 cal., 3 g total fat (2 g sat. fat), 0 mg chol.,
28 mg sodium, 11 g carb. (1 g fiber, 11 g sugars), 1 g pro.
Exchanges: 1 carb., 0.5 fat. Carb choices: 1.

◗ QUICK TIP
For easy drizzling, place the melted chocolate and caramel topping in separate resealable plastic bags. Snip a hole in one corner of each and squeeze to drizzle.

Caramel-Cashew Blondies

Trail Mix Balls

Unsweetened large-flake coconut, often called desiccated coconut, adds chewiness without excess sweetness to these bite-size morsels. Look for this coconut at health food stores.

SERVINGS 30 (2 cookie balls each)

CARB. PER SERVING 17 g

⅓ cup honey
2 tablespoons water
⅓ cup peanut butter
½ teaspoon vanilla
¾ cup crisp rice cereal
¾ cup rolled oats, toasted*
⅓ cup dried fruit bits
¼ cup sunflower kernels
¼ cup lightly salted peanuts
¼ cup unsweetened large-flake coconut
1 tablespoon sesame seeds

1. In a small saucepan cook and stir honey and the water over low heat until the honey liquefies. Remove from heat. Add peanut butter and vanilla, whisking until peanut butter is melted and mixture is smooth.

2. Meanwhile, in a large bowl combine rice cereal, toasted oats, fruit bits, sunflower kernels, peanuts, coconut, and sesame seeds. Pour honey mixture over cereal mixture; stir to coat. Cover and chill for 1 to 2 hours or just until firm.

3. Using your damp hands, shape mixture into 30 balls, each about 1¼ inches in diameter. Chill balls until ready to serve. Store in a tightly covered container in the refrigerator for up to 1 week.

***TEST KITCHEN TIP:** To toast oats, place them in a dry medium skillet; cook over medium-high heat until lightly golden and fragrant, stirring frequently to prevent scorching.

PER SERVING: 153 cal., 8 g total fat (3 g sat. fat), 0 mg chol., 48 mg sodium, 17 g carb. (2 g fiber, 7 g sugars), 4 g pro. Exchanges: 1 starch, 1.5 fat. Carb choices: 1.

Trail Mix Balls

Almond Baklava

Flaky puff pastry takes the place of phyllo in this easy-to-make version of the classic Greek sweet.

SERVINGS 12 (2 triangles each)

CARB. PER SERVING 18 g

1	sheet frozen puff pastry (½ of a 17.3-ounce package)
¾	cup sliced or slivered almonds
5	tablespoons honey
¼	teaspoon vanilla
¼	teaspoon ground cinnamon

1. Thaw puff pastry according to package directions. Preheat oven to 400°F. Using a pizza cutter, cut pastry into six pieces (each about 5 inches long and 3 inches wide). Place pastry pieces on a baking sheet. Bake for 10 to 12 minutes or until golden. Using a wide metal spatula, transfer pastry pieces to a wire rack.

2. Meanwhile, place almonds in a large skillet; cook over medium heat about 8 minutes or until lightly browned, stirring frequently. Set aside 2 tablespoons of the almonds. In a small food processor combine the remaining almonds, 3 tablespoons of the honey, the vanilla, and cinnamon; cover and process until ground into a thick mixture.

3. Gently split each slightly warm pastry piece horizontally into two layers. Carefully spoon almond mixture in small dollops on bottoms of pastry layers. Replace top layers of pastry. Using a pizza cutter, cut each pastry in half crosswise and then cut diagonally in half to make four triangles per pastry.

4. Spoon the remaining 2 tablespoons honey into a glass measuring cup. Microwave on 100 percent power (high) about 10 seconds or until thinned and a pourable consistency. Drizzle the warm honey over the pastry triangles. Sprinkle with the reserved 2 tablespoons toasted almonds.

PER SERVING: 173 cal., 11 g total fat (2 g sat. fat), 0 mg chol., 51 mg sodium, 18 g carb. (1 g fiber, 8 g sugars), 3 g pro. Exchanges: 1 carb., 2.5 fat. Carb choices: 1.

Wonton Dessert Stacks

Apple-Nut Wedges

For softer apple chunks, use McIntosh apples.
For firmer chunks, use a variety such as Jonathan,
Braeburn, Cortland, or Empire.

SERVINGS 8 (1 wedge and about 1 tablespoon topping each)
CARB. PER SERVING 28 g or 18 g

Nonstick cooking spray
1 egg
2 egg whites
⅔ cup packed brown sugar*
1 teaspoon vanilla
⅓ cup flour
¾ teaspoon baking soda
⅛ teaspoon salt
2 large apples, cored and chopped (2 cups)
½ cup chopped walnuts or pecans, toasted
½ cup light sour cream
¼ cup vanilla low-fat yogurt sweetened with artificial sweetener
½ teaspoon vanilla

1. Preheat oven to 325°F. Coat a 9-inch pie plate with cooking spray; set aside.
2. In a large bowl combine egg, egg whites, brown sugar, and the 1 teaspoon vanilla. Beat with an electric mixer on medium speed about 1 minute or until smooth. In a small bowl stir together flour, baking soda, and salt. Add flour mixture to egg mixture; stir just until combined. Fold in apples and nuts. Spread batter evenly in the prepared pie plate.
3. Bake for 25 to 30 minutes or until center is set. Cool slightly on a wire rack. Meanwhile, for topping, in a small bowl whisk together sour cream, yogurt, and the ½ teaspoon vanilla.
4. To serve, cut dessert into eight wedges. Serve warm. Spoon about 1 rounded tablespoon of the topping over each serving.
***SUGAR SUBSTITUTES:** Choose Splenda Brown Sugar Blend. Follow package directions to use product amount equivalent to ⅔ cup brown sugar.
PER SERVING: 186 cal., 7 g total fat (1 g sat. fat), 31 mg chol., 195 mg sodium, 28 g carb. (1 g fiber, 22 g sugars), 4 g pro. Exchanges: 2 carb., 1 fat. Carb choices: 2.
PER SERVING WITH SUBSTITUTE: Same as above, except 155 cal., 190 mg sodium, 18 g carb. (12 g sugars). Exchanges: 1 carb. Carb choices: 1.

Wonton Dessert Stacks

When baked, wonton wrappers become crispy,
pastrylike sheets.

SERVINGS 4 (1 stack each)
CARB. PER SERVING 26 g

Nonstick cooking spray
8 wonton wrappers
Sugar
½ cup sliced fresh strawberries
2 kiwifruits, peeled and sliced
1 6-ounce carton low-fat lemon yogurt
2 fresh strawberries, cut in half

1. Preheat oven to 350°F. Line a large baking sheet with foil; lightly coat with cooking spray. Place wonton wrappers flat on the baking sheet; lightly coat with additional cooking spray. Sprinkle lightly with sugar. Bake for 6 to 8 minutes or until golden brown and crisp. Remove from oven; cool slightly.
2. Meanwhile, in a medium bowl combine the ½ cup sliced strawberries and the kiwifruit slices.
3. To assemble, place one baked wonton wrapper on each of four dessert plates. Top the wrappers with half of the yogurt. Divide the fruit mixture evenly among the stacks. Add another baked wonton to each stack. Top with remaining yogurt. Top each stack with a strawberry half.
PER SERVING: 127 cal., 1 g total fat (0 g sat. fat), 4 mg chol., 118 mg sodium, 26 g carb. (2 g fiber, 14 g sugars), 4 g pro. Exchanges: 0.5 fruit, 1.5 carb. Carb choices: 2.

Apple-Nut Wedges

Upside-Down Orange Carrot Cake

Refreshing orange slices and a yummy carrot cake give this upside-down dessert a delectable flavor twist.

SERVINGS 10 (1 wedge each)
CARB. PER SERVING 26 g or 21 g

- 1 tablespoon canola oil or cooking oil
- 2 tablespoons packed brown sugar
- ¼ cup coarsely chopped pecans, lightly toasted
- 1 orange, peeled, thinly sliced, and seeded
- ¾ cup all-purpose flour*
- ¼ cup yellow cornmeal
- ½ cup granulated sugar**
- 1½ teaspoons pumpkin pie spice
- 1 teaspoon baking powder
- ⅛ teaspoon salt
- 1 cup finely shredded carrots
- ⅓ cup refrigerated or frozen egg product, thawed, or 3 egg whites, lightly beaten
- ¼ cup canola oil
- ¼ cup fat-free milk
- Orange peel twists (optional)

Upside-Down
Orange Carrot Cake

1. Preheat oven to 350°F. Pour the 1 tablespoon oil into an 8×1½-inch round cake pan; tilt pan to coat bottom evenly with oil. Sprinkle brown sugar evenly in pan. Top with pecans. Arrange orange slices on pecans. Set aside.

2. In a medium bowl combine flour, cornmeal, granulated sugar, pumpkin pie spice, baking powder, and salt. Add carrots, eggs, the ¼ cup oil, and the milk. Stir just until combined. Spread mixture evenly over orange slices in pan.

3. Bake for 30 to 35 minutes or until a toothpick inserted near center comes out clean. Cool in pan on a wire rack for 5 minutes. Loosen sides of cake from pan; invert cake onto a serving plate. Serve warm. If desired, garnish with orange peel twists.

*TEST KITCHEN TIP: You can substitute whole wheat pastry flour or white whole wheat flour for up to half of the total all-purpose flour used.

**SUGAR SUBSTITUTES: We do not recommend sugar substitute for the brown sugar. Choose Splenda Sugar Blend for Baking to substitute for the granulated sugar. Follow package directions to use product amount equivalent to ½ cup granulated sugar.

PER SERVING: 191 cal., 9 g total fat (1 g sat. fat), 0 mg chol., 81 mg sodium, 26 g carb. (1 g fiber, 15 g sugars), 3 g pro. Exchanges: 1.5 carb., 1.5 fat. Carb choices: 2.

PER SERVING WITH SUBSTITUTE: Same as above, except 176 cal., 21 g carb. (10 g sugars). Carb choices: 1.5.

Apple-Spice Cake

Apple-Spice Cake

Subtly spiced with cinnamon, ginger, and cloves, each cake square is chock-full of chopped apple.

SERVINGS 9 (1 cake square and about 1 tablespoon topping each)

CARB. PER SERVING 29 g or 23 g

Nonstick cooking spray
¾ cup all-purpose flour
½ cup white whole wheat flour
¼ cup flaxseed meal
1 teaspoon baking powder
¾ teaspoon ground cinnamon
½ teaspoon baking soda
½ teaspoon ground ginger
¼ teaspoon salt
⅛ teaspoon ground cloves
1 egg, lightly beaten
1 6-ounce carton plain low-fat yogurt
⅓ cup packed brown sugar*
¼ cup unsweetened applesauce

3 tablespoons vegetable oil
1 tablespoon molasses
1 large apple (such as Granny Smith, Braeburn, or Gala), cored and finely chopped (1 cup)
⅔ cup frozen light whipped dessert topping, thawed
Ground cinnamon

1. Preheat oven to 350°F. Lightly coat an 8×8×2-inch baking pan with cooking spray; set aside.

2. In a large bowl stir together all-purpose flour, white whole wheat flour, flaxseed meal, baking powder, cinnamon, baking soda, ginger, salt, and cloves. In a medium bowl combine egg, yogurt, brown sugar, applesauce, oil, and molasses. Add egg mixture to flour mixture; stir just until combined. Fold in apple. Spread batter evenly in the prepared baking pan.

3. Bake about 35 minutes or until a toothpick inserted near center comes out clean. Cool slightly on a wire rack.

4. To serve, cut cake into nine squares. Serve warm. Top each serving with whipped topping and sprinkle with additional cinnamon.

*SUGAR SUBSTITUTES: Choose from Sweet'N Low Brown or Sugar Twin Granulated Brown. Follow package directions to use product amount equivalent to ⅓ cup brown sugar.

PER SERVING: 193 cal., 7 g total fat (1 g sat. fat), 25 mg chol., 186 mg sodium, 29 g carb. (2 g fiber, 13 g sugars), 4 g pro. Exchanges: 2 carb., 1 fat. Carb choices: 2.

PER SERVING WITH SUBSTITUTE: Same as above, except 170 cal., 184 mg sodium, 23 g carb. (7 g sugars). Exchanges: 1.5 carb. Carb choices: 1.5.

QUICK TIP

If you wish, use a thin metal blade to loosen the cheesecake from the bottom of the springform pan and then carefully remove it using a large pancake turner.

Orange Swirled Cheesecake
recipe on page 144

Black Forest Cupcakes

If greasing and flouring muffin cups is too fussy for you, line them with paper bake cups that have been coated with nonstick cooking spray. Remove paper bake cups before assembling desserts.

SERVINGS 12 (1 cupcake, scant 2 tablespoons sauce, and 2 tablespoons whipped topping each)
CARB. PER SERVING 28 g

- 1 cup flour
- ½ cup unsweetened cocoa powder
- ¾ teaspoon baking powder
- ¾ teaspoon baking soda
- ¼ teaspoon salt
- ¾ cup buttermilk
- ¼ cup granulated sugar*
- ¼ cup packed brown sugar*
- ¼ cup canola oil
- ¼ cup refrigerated or frozen egg product, thawed, or 1 egg
- 1 tablespoon cherry liqueur (optional)
- 1 recipe Simple Cherry Sauce
- 1½ cups fat-free or light frozen whipped dessert topping, thawed

1. Preheat oven to 350°F. Grease and lightly flour twelve 2½-inch muffin cups; set aside. In a medium bowl combine flour, cocoa powder, baking powder, baking soda, and salt; set aside.

2. In a small bowl whisk together buttermilk, granulated sugar, brown sugar, oil, egg, and, if desired, liqueur. Add milk mixture to flour mixture. Beat with a wire whisk just until combined.

3. Spoon batter evenly into prepared muffin cups, filling each two-thirds to three-fourths full. Bake about 14 minutes or until a toothpick inserted near centers comes out clean. Cool in muffin cups on a wire rack for 5 minutes. Remove cupcakes from muffin cups. Cool completely on wire rack.

4. To serve, pool a scant 1 tablespoon Simple Cherry Sauce on each dessert plate. Cut cupcakes in half. Place the bottom halves on top of sauce on plates; top each with another scant tablespoon sauce and cake tops. Add a spoonful of whipped topping to each dessert.

SIMPLE CHERRY SAUCE: Place 1½ cups fresh or frozen (thawed) unsweetened pitted tart red cherries in a blender or food processor. Cover and blend or process until smooth. Transfer pureed cherries to a small saucepan. Stir in ¾ cup halved fresh or frozen (thawed) unsweetened pitted tart red cherries and 2 tablespoons sugar.* Heat and stir just until boiling. Cool slightly before serving.

Black Forest Cupcakes

*SUGAR SUBSTITUTES: Choose Splenda Sugar Blend to substitute for the granulated sugar in the cupcakes. Choose Splenda Brown Sugar Blend to substitute for the brown sugar in the cupcakes. Choose from Splenda Granular or Sweet'N Low bulk or packets to substitute for the sugar in the Simple Cherry Sauce. Follow package directions to use product amount equivalent to sugar amount called for.

PER SERVING: 166 cal., 5 g total fat (1 g sat. fat), 1 mg chol., 184 mg sodium, 28 g carb. (2 g fiber, 14 g sugars), 3 g pro. Exchanges: 1 starch, 1 carb., 1 fat. Carb choices: 2.
PER SERVING WITH SUBSTITUTE: Same as above, except 145 cal., 182 mg sodium, 21 g carb. (8 g sugars). Exchanges: 0.5 carb. Carb choices: 1.5.

Orange Swirled Cheesecake

Use a hot knife to cut this creamy delight into perfect wedges. Pictured on page 142.

SERVINGS 12 (1 wedge each)

CARB. PER SERVING 13 g or 6 g

3¾ teaspoons unflavored gelatin
1 teaspoon finely shredded orange peel (set aside)
½ cup orange juice
⅓ cup fat-free milk
1 8-ounce package reduced-fat cream cheese (Neufchâtel), softened
2½ cups plain low-fat or fat-free Greek yogurt
½ cup sugar*
1 teaspoon vanilla
Orange paste food coloring**
Fresh raspberries and/or orange peel curls (optional)

1. In a small saucepan sprinkle 2½ teaspoons of the gelatin over the orange juice; let stand for 5 minutes. Heat and stir orange juice mixture over low heat just until gelatin is dissolved. Remove from heat and cool for 5 minutes.

2. In another small saucepan sprinkle remaining 1¼ teaspoons gelatin over the milk; let stand for 5 minutes. Heat and stir over low heat just until gelatin is dissolved. Remove from heat; cool for 5 minutes.

3. In a large bowl beat cream cheese with an electric mixer on medium speed until smooth. Beat in yogurt, sugar, and vanilla until smooth. Remove ½ cup of the cream cheese mixture and add it to the milk mixture, whisking until smooth. Gradually beat orange juice mixture into the remaining cream cheese mixture until smooth. Tint to a light orange color with the orange food coloring. Stir in the 1 teaspoon orange peel.

4. Spoon half of the orange cream cheese mixture into a 7- to 8-inch springform pan. Spoon half of the white cream cheese mixture into mounds over orange cream cheese mixture. Using a narrow, thin-blade metal spatula or a table knife, swirl white mixture into orange mixture. Repeat layering and swirling remaining orange mixture and white mixture. Cover and chill for 4 to 24 hours or until set.

5. To serve, using a small sharp knife, loosen cheesecake from sides of springform pan; remove sides of pan. If desired, garnish with fresh raspberries and/or orange peel curls. To serve, cut cheesecake into 12 wedges.

*SUGAR SUBSTITUTES:** Choose from Splenda Granular or Equal Spoonful or packets. Follow package directions to use product amount equivalent to ½ cup sugar.

TEST KITCHEN TIP: If you don't have paste food coloring, you can use 4 drops yellow and 1 drop red liquid food colorings to get an orange color.

PER SERVING: 126 cal., 5 g total fat (3 g sat. fat), 17 mg chol., 85 mg sodium, 13 g carb. (0 g fiber, 13 g sugars), 7 g pro. Exchanges: 1 carb., 1 lean meat, 0.5 fat. Carb choices: 1.

PER SERVING WITH SUBSTITUTE: Same as above, except 97 cal., 6 g carb. (5 g sugars). Exchanges: 0.5 carb. Carb choices: 0.5.

Lemon-Blueberry Angel Cake Dessert

Looking for a company-special dessert? This one will delight your guests, yet suit your diabetes meal plan.

SERVINGS 12 (about ½ cup each)

CARB. PER SERVING 14 g

½ of a 7- to 8-inch purchased angel food cake (5 ounces)
1 8-ounce tub light cream cheese
1½ teaspoons finely shredded lemon peel
2 tablespoons lemon juice
1½ cups frozen light whipped dessert topping, thawed
2 cups fresh blueberries
Lemon peel strips (optional)

1. Cut cake into ½-inch cubes. (You should have about 4½ cups cubes.) Place half of the cubes in a 2-quart soufflé dish.

2. In a medium bowl beat cream cheese with an electric mixer on medium speed until smooth. Add lemon juice, beating until smooth. Stir in finely shredded lemon peel. Fold in about ¼ cup of the dessert topping until combined. Fold in the remaining dessert topping. Divide the mixture in half; stir 1½ cups of the blueberries into one portion of the cream cheese mixture. Spoon over cake cubes in dish. Top with the remaining cake cubes and the remaining plain cream cheese mixture. Cover and freeze about 4 hours or until firm.

3. Sprinkle with the remaining blueberries before serving. If desired, garnish with lemon peel strips.

PER SERVING: 100 cal., 4 g total fat (3 g sat. fat), 9 mg chol., 177 mg sodium, 14 g carb. (1 g fiber, 8 g sugars), 3 g pro. Exchanges: 1 carb., 0.5 fat. Carb choices: 1.

Lemon-Blueberry
Angel Cake Dessert

Key Lime Pie

Raspberry Tiramisu

*SUGAR SUBSTITUTES: Choose from Splenda Granular or Equal Spoonful or packets. Follow package directions to use product amount equivalent to 2 tablespoons sugar.
PER SERVING: 170 cal., 7 g total fat (4 g sat. fat), 42 mg chol., 81 mg sodium, 23 g carb. (1 g fiber, 17 g sugars), 3 g pro. Exchanges: 1.5 carb., 1.5 fat. Carb choices: 1.5.
PER SERVING WITH SUBSTITUTE: Same as above, except 127 cal., 12 g carb. (6 g sugars). Exchanges: 1 carb. Carb choices: 1

Key Lime Pie

For a decorative top, garnish with small spoonfuls of light whipped dessert topping and small lime wedges.
SERVINGS 8 (1 wedge each)
CARB. PER SERVING 17 g

- 1½ cups small pretzel twists (2 ounces; about 34)
- 2 tablespoons sliced almonds, toasted
- 3 tablespoons butter, melted
- 1 4-serving-size package sugar-free, low-calorie lime-flavor gelatin or regular lime-flavor gelatin
- 1 cup boiling water
- 2 6-ounce cartons low-fat Key lime pie-flavor yogurt
- ½ of an 8-ounce container frozen light whipped dessert topping, thawed
- 1 teaspoon finely shredded lime peel

1. Preheat oven to 350°F. For crust, in a food processor combine pretzels and sliced almonds; cover and process until finely crushed. Add butter; cover and process until combined. Press pretzel mixture onto the bottom and up the sides of a 9-inch pie plate. Bake for 8 to 10 minutes or until lightly browned. Cool on a wire rack.
2. Place gelatin in a medium bowl. Add the boiling water and stir until gelatin is dissolved (about 2 minutes). Cover and chill about 30 minutes or until mixture is partially set (the consistency of unbeaten egg whites). Fold in yogurt, whipped topping, and lime peel. Pour into cooled crust. Chill for at least 4 hours.
3. To serve, cut into eight wedges.
PER SERVING: 153 cal., 7 g total fat (5 g sat. fat), 13 mg chol., 180 mg sodium, 17 g carb. (0 g fiber, 10 g sugars), 3 g pro. Exchanges: 0.5 starch, 0.5 carb., 1.5 fat. Carb choices: 1.

Raspberry Tiramisu

These pretty parfaits are perfect to assemble one day and pull out for a fabulous treat to eat the next.
SERVINGS 2 (1 dessert each)
CARB. PER SERVING 23 g or 12 g

- ¼ of a 3-ounce package ladyfingers, cubed (6 halves)
- 2 tablespoons espresso or strong coffee
- ¼ cup reduced-fat cream cheese (Neufchâtel)
- ¼ cup light sour cream
- 2 tablespoons sugar*
- 1 teaspoon vanilla
- ¼ cup raspberries
  Fresh mint sprigs and/or raspberries (optional)

1. Divide half of the ladyfinger cubes between two 5- to 6-ounce dessert dishes. Drizzle ladyfinger cubes with half of the espresso. Set aside.
2. In a medium bowl stir cream cheese to soften. Stir in sour cream, sugar, and vanilla. (Beat smooth with a wire whisk if necessary.) Stir in the ¼ cup raspberries with a wooden spoon, mashing slightly.
3. Spoon half of the cream cheese mixture over ladyfinger cubes. Add remaining ladyfingers and drizzle with remaining espresso. Top with remaining cream cheese mixture. Cover and chill for 1 to 24 hours. If desired, garnish with fresh mint sprigs and/or additional raspberries.

Banana Cream
Pie Tartlets

Country-Style Peach-Plum Tart

*If you have a patch of mint growing in your yard,
grab a few small leaves to sprinkle over the top.*

SERVINGS 10 (1 wedge tart and 1 tablespoon topping
each)

CARB. PER SERVING 23 g

Flour
1 recipe Cornmeal Pastry
1 tablespoon cornstarch
1 teaspoon finely shredded lemon peel
¼ teaspoon ground cinnamon or ground nutmeg
4 medium plums, halved, pitted, and sliced
3 medium peaches, halved, pitted, and sliced
¼ cup honey
   Fat-free milk
10 tablespoons frozen fat-free whipped dessert topping,
   thawed

1. Preheat oven to 375°F. Line a baking sheet with foil;
sprinkle lightly with flour. Place Cornmeal Pastry on foil.
Slightly flatten dough ball. Using a rolling pin, roll dough
from center to edges into a 12-inch circle. Set aside.
2. In a large bowl stir together cornstarch, lemon peel,
and cinnamon. Add plum slices and peach slices. Toss
to coat. Drizzle with honey; toss gently to coat. Mound
fruit mixture in center of pastry circle, leaving a 2-inch
border around the edges. Fold border up over fruit
slices, pleating dough as needed. Brush pastry lightly
with milk.
3. Bake for 30 to 40 minutes or until fruit slices are
tender and pastry is lightly browned. If necessary to
prevent fruit from drying out, cover tart with foil for the
last 10 to 15 minutes of baking. Cool for 30 minutes and
serve warm. (Or cool completely.) Cut into 10 wedges and
serve with whipped topping.
CORNMEAL PASTRY: In a medium bowl stir together 1 cup
flour, ⅓ cup yellow cornmeal, and ¼ teaspoon salt. Using
a pastry blender, cut in ⅓ cup chilled tub-style vegetable
oil spread until pieces are pea-size. Sprinkle 1 tablespoon
cold water over part of the flour mixture; gently toss with
a fork. Push moistened dough to the side of the bowl.
Repeat moistening flour mixture, using 1 tablespoon cold
water at a time, until all flour mixture is moistened (3 to
4 tablespoons cold water total). Shape dough into a ball.
PER SERVING: 150 cal., 5 g total fat (1 g sat. fat), 0 mg chol.,
102 mg sodium, 23 g carb. (2 g fiber, 7 g sugars), 2 g pro.
Exchanges: 0.5 fruit, 1 starch, 1 fat. Carb choices: 1.5.

Banana Cream Pie Tartlets

*Purchased tart shells and instant pudding make these
banana-topped individual tarts a cinch to prepare.
Plus, they are delicious and diabetes-friendly.*

SERVINGS 6 (1 tartlet each)

CARB. PER SERVING 31 g

1 4-serving-size package fat-free sugar-free
   reduced-calorie vanilla instant pudding mix
2 cups fat-free milk
1 medium banana, cut into 18 slices
1 tablespoon lemon juice
6 purchased graham cracker crumb tart shells
2 tablespoons bittersweet chocolate curls and/or
   coarsely chopped unsalted dry-roasted peanuts

1. Prepare pudding mix according to package directions,
using the 2 cups fat-free milk. Cover and chill.
2. Meanwhile, in a small bowl combine banana slices
and lemon juice; toss to coat.
3. Divide pudding among six tart shells. Top with
banana slices. Cover and chill for up to 1 hour before
serving. Sprinkle with chocolate and/or peanuts just
before serving.
PER SERVING: 201 cal., 7 g total fat (2 g sat. fat), 2 mg chol.,
381 mg sodium, 31 g carb. (1 g fiber, 14 g sugars), 4 g pro.
Exchanges: 1 starch, 1 carb., 1.5 fat. Carb choices: 2.

Country-Style
Peach-Plum Tart

▶ QUICK TIP
If you don't have six to serve, chill the extra fruit and topping mixtures separately. Another day, assemble and microwave to warm before serving.

Peach-Blackberry Crisp with Oatmeal-Coconut Topping

Peach-Blackberry Crisp with Oatmeal-Coconut Topping

What's the secret to this no-bake delight? It's cooking the topping and then the fruit mixture in a skillet.

SERVINGS 6 (about ⅔ cup fruit mixture and 2 tablespoons topping each)
CARB. PER SERVING 25 g or 18 g

- 2 tablespoons butter
- ¼ cup chopped pecans
- ¼ cup regular rolled oats
- 3 tablespoons packed brown sugar*
- 2 tablespoons sweetened shredded coconut
- ⅛ teaspoon ground cinnamon
- 4 firm, ripe peaches, pitted and sliced
- 1 tablespoon lemon juice
- 1 cup fresh blackberries
- 1½ cups low-fat or light vanilla ice cream or frozen yogurt (optional)

1. For topping, in a large nonstick skillet melt 1 tablespoon of the butter over medium heat. Stir in pecans, oats, 1 tablespoon of the brown sugar, the coconut, and cinnamon. Cook and stir for 6 to 8 minutes or until mixture begins to brown. Spread topping evenly on a baking sheet; set aside. Wipe out the skillet with a paper towel.

2. In the same skillet melt the remaining 1 tablespoon butter over medium-high heat. Add peaches, the remaining 2 tablespoons brown sugar, and the lemon juice. Bring to boiling; reduce heat. Simmer, uncovered, about 5 minutes or until juices are slightly thickened. Fold in blackberries.

3. To serve, spoon about ⅔ cup of the peach mixture into each of six serving dishes. Sprinkle the topping over fruit. If desired, serve with ice cream.

***SUGAR SUBSTITUTES:** Choose from Sugar Twin Granulated Brown or Sweet'N Low Brown. Follow package directions to use product amount equivalent to 3 tablespoons brown sugar.

PER SERVING: 179 cal., 9 g total fat (4 g sat. fat), 10 mg chol., 36 mg sodium, 25 g carb. (4 g fiber, 17 g sugars), 3 g pro. Exchanges: 1 fruit, 0.5 carb., 2 fat. Carb choices: 1.5.
PER SERVING WITH SUBSTITUTE: Same as above, except 152 cal., 18 g carb. (11 g sugars). Exchanges: 0 carb. Carb choices: 1.

Double Berry Pie Squares

The duo of strawberries and raspberries accounts for the fresh flavor and ruby red color of this refreshing dessert.

SERVINGS 9 (1 square and ½ tablespoon dessert topping each)
CARB. PER SERVING 25 g or 16 g

- ⅓ cup sugar*
- 1 envelope unflavored gelatin
- 1 pound fresh strawberries, hulled and diced
- 1 12-ounce package frozen raspberries, thawed
  Nonstick cooking spray
- ⅔ cup finely crushed graham crackers
- 2 tablespoons sugar*
- 2 tablespoons butter, melted
- ⅓ cup frozen sugar-free whipped dessert topping, thawed

1. For filling, in a large saucepan combine the ⅓ cup sugar and the gelatin; add strawberries and raspberries. Cook and stir over medium-high heat until gelatin is dissolved and mixture is simmering.

2. Transfer berry mixture to a shallow bowl. Chill about 1 hour or until mixture begins to set up around the edges, stirring occasionally.

3. For crust, lightly coat a 2-quart square baking dish with cooking spray. In a medium bowl stir together finely crushed graham crackers, the 2 tablespoons sugar, and the melted butter. Press graham cracker mixture evenly over the bottom of the prepared baking dish. Place in freezer while filling chills.

4. Carefully pour filling over the crust. Chill about 3 hours or until filling is completely set. To serve, cut into nine squares. Top with whipped dessert topping.

***SUGAR SUBSTITUTES:** Choose from Splenda Granular or Sweet'N Low bulk or packets. Follow package directions to use product amounts equivalent to ⅓ cup and 2 tablespoons sugar.

PER SERVING: 138 cal., 4 g total fat (2 g sat. fat), 7 mg chol., 80 mg sodium, 25 g carb. (4 g fiber, 15 g sugars), 2 g pro. Exchanges: 1 fruit, 0.5 carb., 1 fat. Carb choices: 1.5.
PER SERVING WITH SUBSTITUTE: Same as above, except 103 cal., 16 g carb. (6 g sugars). Exchanges: 0 carb. Carb choices: 1.

Ice Cream Finger Sandwiches

*TEST KITCHEN TIP: To prevent the ice cream from getting too soft during assembly, prepare half of the sandwiches at a time.

PER SERVING: 118 cal., 6 g total fat (4 g sat. fat), 26 mg chol., 37 mg sodium, 15 g carb. (1 g fiber, 10 g sugars), 2 g pro. Exchanges: 1 carb., 1 fat. Carb choices: 1.

Milk Chocolate-Strawberry Ice Cream

Treat guests to this homemade chocolate ice cream enhanced with bits of milk chocolate and fresh strawberries.

SERVINGS 10 (about ½ cup each)
CARB. PER SERVING 24 g or 15 g

- 6 ounces milk chocolate, chopped
- 2½ cups reduced-fat milk (2%)
- ½ cup sugar*
- 2 eggs, lightly beaten
- 1 teaspoon vanilla
- 1 cup chopped fresh strawberries
- Halved strawberries (optional)

1. Reserve ¼ cup of the chopped chocolate; cover and set aside. In a medium saucepan stir together the remaining chopped chocolate, the milk, and sugar. Cook over medium heat just until boiling, whisking constantly. Whisk about ½ cup of the milk mixture into the eggs. Return egg mixture to the remaining milk mixture in saucepan. Cook and stir for 1 minute (do not boil). Remove from heat and place saucepan in a large bowl half-filled with ice water; stir constantly for 2 minutes. Strain through a fine-mesh sieve into a bowl; stir in vanilla. Cover and chill for 8 to 24 hours.
2. Pour chilled mixture into a 1½-quart ice cream freezer. Freeze according to manufacturer's directions. Stir reserved ¼ cup chopped chocolate and the 1 cup strawberries into frozen ice cream. Transfer mixture to a 2-quart freezer container. Cover and freeze for 4 hours before serving. To serve, scoop into small dessert dishes. If desired, serve with a few strawberry halves.
*SUGAR SUBSTITUTES:** Choose Splenda Granular. Follow package directions to use product amount equivalent to ½ cup sugar.
PER SERVING: 181 cal., 7 g total fat (5 g sat. fat), 51 mg chol., 55 mg sodium, 24 g carb. (1 g fiber, 23 g sugars), 5 g pro. Exchanges: 1.5 carb., 1.5 fat. Carb choices: 1.5.
PER SERVING WITH SUBSTITUTE: Same as above, except 146 cal., 15 g carb. (14 g sugars). Exchanges: 1 carb. Carb choices: 1.

Ice Cream Finger Sandwiches

This yummy warm-weather treat works best with soft-texture ladyfingers rather than those that are firm and crunchy.

SERVINGS 12 (1 sandwich each)
CARB. PER SERVING 15 g

- 1 cup low-fat or light strawberry ice cream or no-sugar-added reduced-fat cherry-vanilla ice cream
- 12 ladyfingers, split
- 3 ounces bittersweet, semisweet, or milk chocolate, melted
- ½ cup flaked coconut, toasted

1. Line a large baking sheet with waxed paper; set aside. Spoon ice cream into a small chilled bowl; stir just until ice cream is slightly softened. Working quickly,* spread ice cream on the cut sides of half of the ladyfinger halves. Top with the remaining ladyfinger halves, cut sides down. Gently press together.
2. Dip one end of each sandwich in melted chocolate, using a thin metal spatula or butter knife to spread chocolate over the ice cream. Sprinkle with coconut. Place on prepared baking sheet. Freeze for 30 minutes before serving.

Milk Chocolate-
Strawberry Ice Cream

recipe index

A

Almonds
Almond Baklava 137
Cinnamon-Almond-
Topped Carrots 91

Apples
Apple-Nut Wedges 138
Apple-Spice Cake........................... 141
Grilled Salmon with
Apple-Onion Relish 29
Asian Pork Quesadillas..................... 78
Asian-Style Tuna Kabobs 30

Asparagus
Dilled Salmon and
Asparagus Soup........................ 74
Lemon Couscous with Asparagus . 97
Quick Sautéed Vegetables 94
Roasted Tomato and Asparagus
Crustless Quiche 115

Avocados
Avocado BLT Sandwiches 78
Avocado Cream................................ 112
Citrus Salad with Avocado 106
Mini Grilled Tomato
Sandwiches 127

B

Bacon
Avocado BLT Sandwiches 78
Bacon and Egg Breakfast Wraps ... 116
BLT Cups.. 122
Broccolini with Bacon and Feta 92
Baked Corn Dogs 13
Baked Eggs with Tomato Topper 112

Bananas
Banana Cream Pie Tartlets............ 148
Oatmeal Pancakes with
Maple Fruit 105
Barbecue Glazed Turkey 26

Barley
Barley-Vegetable Pilaf...................... 95
Pork Barley Salad 50
BBQ Bean Chili 62
BBQ Chicken Bites 124

Beans
BBQ Bean Chili 62
Carne Asada Salad 53
Chicken Salad with Creamy
Tarragon-Shallot Dressing....... 46
Chipotle Quinoa with Beans 95

Easy Pasta and Pepper Primavera.. 37
Edamame and Cabbage Salad
with Peanut Dressing................ 56
Green Beans with
Caramelized Mushrooms......... 93
Italian Beef and Polenta 12
Lamb and Chickpea Stew 66
Lentil and Veggie Shepherd's Pie ... 38
Miso Soup with Pork and
Edamame.................................. 64
Moroccan-Style Simmered Beans.. 94
Pasta e Fagioli................................... 59
Pork Barley Salad 50
Pumpkin, Bean, and
Chicken Enchiladas 20
Red Beans and Rice with Chicken.. 23
Spicy Broccoli and Bean Soup......... 72
Spicy Pork Tenderloin Green Chili. 63
Stuffed Zucchini with Black Beans,
Corn, and Poblano Peppers 39
Tangy Tomato and
Goat Cheese Dip 126
Tex-Mex Bean Tostadas 36
Turkey Chipotle Chili....................... 62

Beef
Beef with Mushrooms and Pearl
Onions in Red Wine Reduction . 7
Carne Asada Salad 53
Cheeseburger Soup 66
Cheesesteaks with Sweet Peppers
and Mushrooms 82
Chicken-Fried Steak 10
Classic Diner Meat Loaf................... 13
Easy Taco Salad................................. 53
Greek Feta Burgers 80
Grilled Flank Steak Salad................ 50
Italian Beef and Polenta 12
Jerk-Seasoned Beef Skewers 9
Pepper-Stuffed Burgers.................... 81
Spiced Bulgur with
Beef and Mango 10
Sweet Asian Beef Stir-Fry 8
Beer Pork Soup.................................. 65
Beets, Turkey Spinach Salad with 42
Berries. *See specific berries*
Blackberry-Peach Crisp with
Oatmeal-Coconut Topping..... 151
Black Forest Cupcakes........................ 143
BLT Cups.. 122

Blueberries
Lemon-Blueberry
Angel Cake Dessert................144
Oatmeal Pancakes with
Maple Fruit 105
Peach-Blueberry Parfaits 107
Breads. *See also* **Tortillas**
Panzanella Salad with a Twist...... 100
Peachy Granola Muffins 108
Snickerdoodle Crescent Rolls 109
Breakfast Bars to Go 111
Breakfast Lasagna Rolls.................... 115
Breakfast Pita Pizza 119

Broccoli
Broccoli Slaw 80
Chicken-Peanut Stir-Fry 23
Spicy Broccoli and Bean Soup......... 72
Sweet Asian Beef Stir-Fry 8
Broccolini with Bacon and Feta........... 92
Bruschetta Planks 123

Bulgur
Chilled Salmon and Tabbouleh........... 54
Spiced Bulgur with Beef and Mango ... 10

Burgers
Greek Feta Burgers 80
Peppered Pork Burgers 77
Pepper-Stuffed Burgers.................... 81

C

Cabbage
Asian Pork Quesadillas 78
Edamame and Cabbage Salad
with Peanut Dressing................ 56
Sweet Asian Beef Stir-Fry 8

Cakes
Apple-Spice Cake........................... 141
Black Forest Cupcakes.................... 143
Lemon-Blueberry
Angel Cake Dessert................ 144
Mocha Coffeecake 111
Upside-Down Orange
Carrot Cake.............................. 140
Caramel-Cashew Blondies 134
Carne Asada Salad 53

Carrots
Carrot-Radish Salad......................... 24
Cinnamon-Almond-
Topped Carrots 91

Shrimp with Curried
  Lime Carrots.............................33
Upside-Down Orange
  Carrot Cake...............................140
Cashew-Caramel Blondies.................134
Cauliflower, Roasted, Salad.................92

Cereal
Nutty Chocolate Crunch...............128
Sweet and Spicy Wasabi
  Snack Mix..............................130
Trail Mix Balls..........................136

Cheese
Broccolini with Bacon and Feta......92
Cheeseburger Soup.....................66
Cheesesteaks with Sweet Peppers
  and Mushrooms........................82
Chile Rellenos...........................36
Feta-Yogurt Spread......................89
Fruit Skewers with
  Goat Cheese Dip......................103
Greek Feta Burgers.....................80
Homemade Walking Tacos.............26
Hot Ham and Pear Melts................79
Huevos Rancheros
  Breakfast Nachos....................116
Italian Meatball Rolls.....................84
Lobster Mac and
  Cheese Casserole.....................34
Mediterranean Stuffed Chicken....20
Mini Grilled Tomato
  Sandwiches............................127
Orange Swirled Cheesecake.........144
Pepper-Stuffed Burgers.................81
Pizza Lettuce Cups......................124
Prosciutto Salad with
  Blue Cheese...........................48
Salmon Melts............................89
Tangy Tomato and
  Goat Cheese Dip......................126
Cherry Sauce, Simple.....................143

Chicken
BBQ Chicken Bites........................124
Chicken Cacciatore.........................17
Chicken Parmesan Soup.................69
Chicken-Peanut Stir-Fry.................23
Chicken Salad with Creamy
  Tarragon-Shallot Dressing.......46
Cream of Chicken and
  Rice Florentine.........................68
Curried Chicken Sandwiches.........85
Grilled Chicken and Peach Wraps.87
Indonesian Chicken and Soba
  Noodle Soup..........................69
Jerk Braised Chicken Thighs with
  Sweet Potatoes.......................19
Mediterranean Stuffed Chicken....20
Mushroom and Chicken
  Stroganoff.............................24
Orange and Fennel Chicken Salad.44
Orzo Chicken Salad with
  Avocado-Lime Dressing...........44
Pumpkin, Bean, and
  Chicken Enchiladas.................20

Red Beans and Rice with Chicken..23
Sautéed Chicken Breasts with
  Simple Chive Sauce.................19
Warm Chicken and
  New Potato Salad.....................43
Chicken-Fried Steak........................10

Chile peppers
Chile Rellenos..............................36
Roasted Corn and
  Poblano Chowder.....................73
Spicy Pork Tenderloin
  Green Chili.............................63
Stuffed Zucchini with Black Beans,
  Corn, and Poblano Pepper........39

Chili
BBQ Bean Chili............................62
Spicy Pork Tenderloin
  Green Chili.............................63
Turkey Chipotle Chili.....................62
Chilled Salmon and Tabbouleh...........54
Chipotle Quinoa with Beans.............95

Chocolate
Black Forest Cupcakes...................143
Chocolate-Coconut Macaroons....134
Ice Cream Finger Sandwiches......152
Milk Chocolate-Strawberry
  Ice Cream.............................152
Mocha Coffeecake......................111
Nutty Chocolate Crunch...............128
Peanut Butter Swirl
  Chocolate Brownies.................133
Cinnamon-Almond-Topped Carrots...91
Citrus Salad with Avocado.................106
Classic Diner Meat Loaf.....................13

Coconut
Chocolate-Coconut Macaroons....134
Ice Cream Finger Sandwiches......152
Peach-Blackberry Crisp with
  Oatmeal-Coconut Topping.....151
Trail Mix Balls..........................136

Cookies and bars
Breakfast Bars to Go....................111
Caramel-Cashew Blondies............134
Chocolate-Coconut Macaroons....134
Peanut Butter Swirl
  Chocolate Brownies.................133

Corn
Corn on the Cob with
  Cilantro-Lime Butter................93
Pork with Fresh Corn Salad............48
Roasted Corn and
  Poblano Chowder.....................73
Stuffed Zucchini with Black Beans,
  Corn, and Poblano Peppers......39
Turkey Chopped Salad with
  Orange-Poppy Seed Dressing..42

Cornmeal
Baked Corn Dogs.........................13
Cornmeal Pastry.........................148
Mole-Style Pork and Tamale Pie.....14
Country-Style Peach-Plum Tart........148
Couscous, Lemon, with Asparagus.....97
Crab and Pasta Salad, Gazpacho..........56

Cream of Chicken and
  Rice Florentine.........................68
Crunchy Egg Salad Sandwiches..........89

Cucumbers
Cucumber Sauce.........................80
Cucumber-Yogurt Sauce................83
Layered Salad with
  Spicy Buttermilk Dressing.....100
Pickled Red Onion and Cucumber.85
Vegetable Sandwiches with
  Feta-Yogurt Spread.................89
Cupcakes, Black Forest....................143
Curried Chicken Sandwiches.............85

D
Desserts. *See also* **Cakes**
Almond Baklava.........................137
Apple-Nut Wedges......................138
Banana Cream Pie Tartlets............148
Caramel-Cashew Blondies............134
Chocolate-Coconut Macaroons....134
Country-Style Peach-Plum Tart...148
Double Berry Pie Squares.............151
Ice Cream Finger Sandwiches......152
Key Lime Pie.............................147
Milk Chocolate-Strawberry
  Ice Cream.............................152
Orange Swirled Cheesecake.........144
Peach-Blackberry Crisp with
  Oatmeal-Coconut Topping.....151
Peanut Butter Swirl
  Chocolate Brownies.................133
Raspberry Tiramisu......................147
Trail Mix Balls..........................136
Wonton Dessert Stacks.................138
Dilled Salmon and Asparagus Soup....74

Dips and spreads
Feta-Yogurt Spread......................89
Granola-Topped Caramel
  Fruit Dip..............................127
Honey-Mustard Spread.................77
Honey-Orange Dipping Sauce.......128
Mediterranean Salmon Spread....126
Spicy Tomato Salsa.....................123
Tangy Tomato and
  Goat Cheese Dip......................126
Double Berry Pie Squares..................151

Drinks
Fruity-Limeade Slushy.................131

E
Easy Pasta and Pepper Primavera........37
Easy Taco Salad.............................53

Edamame
Edamame and Cabbage Salad with
  Peanut Dressing......................56
Miso Soup with Pork
  and Edamame..........................64
Pork Barley Salad........................50

Eggplant
Ratatouille Stew.........................71

Eggs
Bacon and Egg Breakfast Wraps... 116
Baked Eggs with Tomato Topper.. 112
Breakfast Lasagna Rolls 115
Chile Rellenos................................36
Crunchy Egg Salad Sandwiches 89
Eggs Benedict with
    Avocado Cream 112
Huevos Rancheros
    Breakfast Nachos 116
Mushroom-Olive Frittata.............. 119
Roasted Tomato and Asparagus
    Crustless Quiche 115
scrambled egg additions.............. 117
Enchiladas, Pumpkin, Bean, and
    Chicken 20

F

Fennel
Orange and Fennel
    Chicken Salad 44
Seared Tuna with Fennel Salad......56
Feta-Yogurt Spread 89
Fish. See also Salmon
Asian-Style Tuna Kabobs.................30
Fish and Chips-Style Cod.................28
Fish and Sugar Snap Peas
    en Papillote 27
Seafood Stew with
    Toasted Baguette Slices 74
Seared Tuna with Fennel Salad......56
Tuna and Noodles 30
Frankfurters
Baked Corn Dogs 13
Fresh Macaroni Salad...........................98
Frittata, Mushroom-Olive 119
Frozen-meal tips 18
Fruit. See also specific fruits
Breakfast Bars to Go...................... 111
Citrus Salad with Avocado 106
Fruit and Nut Quinoa..................... 106
Fruit Salad with a Crunch 103
Fruit Skewers with
    Goat Cheese Dip 103
Fruit Triangles 128
Granola-Topped Caramel
    Fruit Dip 127
Thai Fruit Skewers 128
Thin and Crispy Fruit Pizza...........127
Trail Mix Balls 136
Fruity-Limeade Slushy 131

G

Gazpacho Crab and Pasta Salad......... 56
Ginger-Sesame Scallop Soup 75
Grains. See also Cornmeal; Oats
Barley-Vegetable Pilaf.....................95
Chilled Salmon and Tabbouleh.....54
Chipotle Quinoa with Beans...........95
Cream of Chicken and Rice
    Florentine................................68
Fruit and Nut Quinoa.....................106

Italian Beef and Polenta 12
Pork Barley Salad 50
Red Beans and Rice with Chicken..23
Spanish-Style Rice 97
Spiced Bulgur with
    Beef and Mango 10
Granola-Topped Caramel Fruit Dip . 127
Grapes
Fruit Skewers with
    Goat Cheese Dip 103
Panzanella Salad with a Twist......100
Greek Feta Burgers............................. 80
Green beans
Chicken Salad with Creamy
    Tarragon-Shallot Dressing.......46
Green Beans with
    Caramelized Mushrooms.........93
Italian Beef and Polenta 12
Greens. See also Lettuce; Spinach
Grilled Shrimp Salad with
    Creamy Garlic Dressing...........54
Prosciutto Salad with
    Blue Cheese 48
Seared Tuna with Fennel Salad......56
Grilled Chicken and Peach Wraps 87
Grilled Flank Steak Salad 50
Grilled Pork and Peach Salad 47
Grilled Salmon with
    Apple-Onion Relish...................29
Grilled Shrimp Salad with
    Creamy Garlic Dressing 54
Grilled Turkey Gyros 82

H

Ham
Breakfast Lasagna Rolls 115
Hot Ham and Pear Melts 79
Prosciutto Salad with
    Blue Cheese 48
Herbed Pasta with Pine Nuts 97
Herbed Potatoes and Peas 95
Homemade Walking Tacos 26
Honey-Mustard Spread.......................77
Honey-Orange Dipping Sauce 128
Hot Ham and Pear Melts 79
Huevos Rancheros
    Breakfast Nachos 116

I–J

Ice cream
Ice Cream Finger Sandwiches 152
Milk Chocolate-Strawberry
    Ice Cream 152
Indonesian Chicken and
    Soba Noodle Soup 69
Italian Beef and Polenta......................12
Italian Meatball Rolls 84
Jerk Braised Chicken Thighs with
    Sweet Potatoes 19
Jerk-Seasoned Beef Skewers 9
Jicama Radish Slaw 103

K–L

Kettle-Style Caramel Corn 131
Key Lime Pie...................................... 147
Kiwifruit
Fruit Salad with a Crunch 103
Thai Fruit Skewers 128
Wonton Dessert Stacks 138
Lamb and Chickpea Stew   66
Layered Salad with
    Spicy Buttermilk Dressing.... 100
Lemon-Blueberry Angel Cake
    Dessert 144
Lemon Couscous with Asparagus 97
Lentil and Veggie Shepherd's Pie 38
Lettuce
Avocado BLT Sandwiches 78
BLT Cups....................................... 122
Carne Asada Salad 53
Chicken Salad with Creamy
    Tarragon-Shallot Dressing.......46
Easy Taco Salad................................53
Grilled Flank Steak Salad 50
Grilled Pork and Peach Salad 47
Layered Salad with
    Spicy Buttermilk Dressing 100
Orange and Fennel Chicken Salad.44
Pizza Lettuce Cups 124
Pork Barley Salad 50
Turkey Chopped Salad with
    Orange-Poppy Seed Dressing..42
Limes
Fruity-Limeade Slushy 131
Key Lime Pie.................................. 147
Lobster Mac and Cheese Casserole.... 34

M

Mango
Spiced Bulgur with
    Beef and Mango 10
Thai Fruit Skewers 128
Turkey and Mango Salad with
    Chutney Vinaigrette 41
Turkey Mango Sandwiches 85
Meat. See Beef; Lamb; Pork
Meatballs
Italian Meatball Rolls......................84
Turkey Meatball Soup......................61
Meat Loaf, Classic Diner 13
Mediterranean Salmon Spread 126
Mediterranean Stuffed Chicken 20
Milk Chocolate-Strawberry
    Ice Cream 152
Mini Grilled Tomato Sandwiches 127
Miso Soup with Pork and Edamame.. 64
Mocha Coffeecake 111
Mole-Style Pork and Tamale Pie......... 14
Moroccan-Style Simmered Beans......94
Muffins, Peachy Granola................... 108

Mushrooms
Beef with Mushrooms and Pearl
Onions in Red Wine Reduction . 7
Breakfast Pita Pizza 119
Bruschetta Planks 123
Cheeseburger Soup 66
Cheesesteaks with Sweet Peppers
and Mushrooms 82
Green Beans with Caramelized
Mushrooms 93
Italian Meatball Rolls 84
Mushroom and
Chicken Stroganoff 24
Mushroom-Olive Frittata 119
Mushroom-Tomato Stuffed-
Pork Loin 16
Roasted Tomato and Mushroom
Pasta Salad 57
Wild Mushroom and Leek Soup 72

N–O

Nachos, Huevos Rancheros
Breakfast 116
Noodles
Chicken-Peanut Stir-Fry 23
Indonesian Chicken and
Soba Noodle Soup 69
Mushroom and
Chicken Stroganoff 24
Tuna and Noodles 30
Nuts. *See also specific nuts*
Apple-Nut Wedges 138
Fruit and Nut Quinoa 106
Nutty Chocolate Crunch 128
Oats
Breakfast Bars to Go 111
Oatmeal Pancakes with
Maple Fruit 105
Peach-Blackberry Crisp with
Oatmeal-Coconut Topping 151
Trail Mix Balls 136
Onion, Red, and Cucumber, Pickled 85
Oranges
Citrus Salad with Avocado 106
Jerk-Seasoned Beef Skewers 9
Orange and Fennel Chicken Salad . 44
Orange Swirled Cheesecake 144
Upside-Down Orange
Carrot Cake 140
Orzo Chicken Salad with Avocado-
Lime Dressing 44

P

Pancakes, Oatmeal, with
Maple Fruit 105
Pan-Seared Scallops with Tomato,
Olives, and Fresh Basil 34
Panzanella Salad with a Twist 100
Pasta. *See also* **Noodles**
Breakfast Lasagna Rolls 115
Chicken Parmesan Soup 69
Easy Pasta and Pepper Primavera .. 37

Fresh Macaroni Salad 98
Gazpacho Crab and Pasta Salad 56
Herbed Pasta with Pine Nuts 97
Lemon Couscous with Asparagus . 97
Lobster Mac and Cheese
Casserole 34
Orzo Chicken Salad with
Avocado-Lime Dressing 44
Pan-Seared Scallops with Tomato,
Olives, and Fresh Basil 34
Pasta e Fagioli 59
Roasted Tomato and
Mushroom Pasta Salad 57
Sweet Asian Beef Stir-Fry 8
Peaches
Country-Style Peach-Plum Tart ... 148
Grilled Chicken and Peach Wraps . 87
Grilled Pork and Peach Salad 47
Peach and Spinach Salad
with Feta 103
Peach-Blackberry Crisp with
Oatmeal-Coconut Topping 151
Peach-Blueberry Parfaits 107
Peachy Granola Muffins 108
Peanut butter
Breakfast Bars to Go 111
Chicken-Peanut Stir-Fry 23
Peanut Butter Swirl Chocolate
Brownies 133
Trail Mix Balls 136
Peanuts
Breakfast Bars to Go 111
Nutty Chocolate Crunch 128
Trail Mix Balls 136
Pears
Fruit Salad with a Crunch 103
Hot Ham and Pear Melts 79
Peas
Fish and Sugar Snap Peas
en Papillote 27
Ginger-Sesame Scallop Soup 75
Herbed Potatoes and Peas 95
Peppers. *See also* **Chile peppers**
BBQ Chicken Bites 124
Breakfast Pita Pizza 119
Bruschetta Planks 123
Cheesesteaks with Sweet Peppers
and Mushrooms 82
Easy Pasta and Pepper Primavera .. 37
Grilled Flank Steak Salad 50
Italian Beef and Polenta 12
Jerk-Seasoned Beef Skewers 9
Layered Salad with
Spicy Buttermilk Dressing 100
Peppered Pork Burgers 77
Pepper-Stuffed Burgers 81
Quick Sautéed Vegetables 94
Ratatouille Stew 71
Pickled Red Onion and Cucumber 85
Pies
Key Lime Pie 147
Lentil and Veggie Shepherd's Pie ... 38
Mole-Style Pork and Tamale Pie 14

Pineapple
Fruit Salad with a Crunch 103
Fruit Skewers with
Goat Cheese Dip 103
Thai Fruit Skewers 128
Pizza
Breakfast Pita Pizza 119
Thin and Crispy Fruit Pizza 127
Pizza Lettuce Cups 124
Plums
Country-Style Peach-Plum Tart ... 148
Fruit Triangles 128
Polenta, Italian Beef and 12
Popcorn
Kettle-Style Caramel Corn 131
Pork
Asian Pork Quesadillas 78
Avocado BLT Sandwiches 78
Bacon and Egg Breakfast Wraps ... 116
Beer Pork Soup 65
Breakfast Lasagna Rolls 115
Grilled Pork and Peach Salad 47
Hot Ham and Pear Melts 79
Miso Soup with Pork
and Edamame 64
Mole-Style Pork and Tamale Pie 14
Mushroom-Tomato-Stuffed
Pork Loin 16
Peppered Pork Burgers 77
Pork Barley Salad 50
Pork Picadillo Soup 65
Pork Scaloppini in
White Wine Sauce 14
Pork Tenderloin Sandwiches 80
Pork with Fresh Corn Salad 48
Prosciutto Salad with
Blue Cheese 48
Spicy Pork Tenderloin Green Chili . 63
Potatoes
Herbed Potatoes and Peas 95
Jerk Braised Chicken Thighs
with Sweet Potatoes 19
Lentil and Veggie Shepherd's Pie ... 38
Sausage Skillet 118
Two-Tone Potato Salad 98
Warm Chicken and
New Potato Salad 43
Poultry. *See* **Chicken; Turkey**
Prosciutto Salad with Blue Cheese 48
Pumpkin, Bean, and
Chicken Enchiladas 20

Q

Quesadillas, Asian Pork 78
Quiche, Crustless, Roasted Tomato
and Asparagus 115
Quick Sautéed Vegetables 94
Quinoa
Chipotle Quinoa with Beans 95
Fruit and Nut Quinoa 106

R

Radishes
Carrot-Radish Salad 24
Jicama Radish Slaw 103

Raspberries
Double Berry Pie Squares 151
Fruit and Nut Quinoa.....................106
Raspberry Tiramisu.......................147
Ratatouille Stew 71
Red Beans and Rice with Chicken 23

Rice
Cream of Chicken and
Rice Florentine.......................68
Red Beans and Rice with Chicken..23
Spanish-Style Rice 97
Roasted Cauliflower Salad 92
Roasted Corn and Poblano Chowder...73
Roasted Tomato and Asparagus
Crustless Quiche 115
Roasted Tomato and Mushroom
Pasta Salad...............................57

S

Salad Dressings)
Avocado-Lime Dressing...................44
Chutney Vinaigrette 41
Cilantro Dressing 51
Creamy Garlic Dressing 54
Creamy Tarragon-Shallot
Dressing 47
Dijon Vinaigrette 50
Garlic-Lime Aïoli Dressing 56
Honey-Mustard Vinaigrette 103
Honey-Rosemary Vinaigrette.........48
Lemon Vinaigrette 48
Lime-Honey Dressing....................103
Orange Dressing..............................44
Orange-Poppy Seed Dressing 42
Peanut Dressing..............................57
Spicy Buttermilk Dressing.............100
Spicy Tomato Dressing....................56

Salads (main-dish)
Carne Asada Salad 53
Chicken Salad with Creamy
Tarragon-Shallot Dressing.......46
Chilled Salmon and Tabbouleh......54
Citrus Salad with Shrimp 106
Easy Taco Salad...............................53
Edamame and Cabbage Salad with
Peanut Dressing..........................56
Gazpacho Crab and Pasta Salad 56
Grilled Flank Steak Salad.................50
Grilled Pork and Peach Salad 47
Grilled Shrimp Salad with
Creamy Garlic Dressing............54
ideas for personalizing....................52
Orange and Fennel Chicken Salad .44
Orzo Chicken Salad with
Avocado-Lime Dressing............44
Pork Barley Salad 50
Pork with Fresh Corn Salad............48

Prosciutto Salad with
Blue Cheese 48
Roasted Tomato and
Mushroom Pasta Salad 57
Seared Tuna with Fennel Salad......56
Turkey and Mango Salad with
Chutney Vinaigrette.................41
Turkey Chopped Salad with
Orange-Poppy Seed Dressing ..42
Turkey Spinach Salad with Beets...42
Warm Chicken and
New Potato Salad.....................43

Salads (side-dish)
BLT Cups......................................122
Broccoli Slaw 80
Carrot-Radish Salad........................24
Citrus Salad with Avocado 106
Fresh Macaroni Salad......................98
Fruit Salad with a Crunch 103
Fruit Skewers with
Goat Cheese Dip 103
Jicama Radish Slaw 103
Layered Salad with
Spicy Buttermilk Dressing 100
Panzanella Salad with a Twist......100
Peach and Spinach Salad
with Feta 103
Roasted Cauliflower Salad..............92
Two-Tone Potato Salad 98

Salmon
Chilled Salmon and Tabbouleh......54
Dilled Salmon and
Asparagus Soup.........................74
Grilled Salmon with
Apple-Onion Relish 29
Mediterranean Salmon Spread 126
Salmon Melts..................................89
Salsa, Spicy Tomato 123

Sandwiches. *See also* **Burgers**
Avocado BLT Sandwiches 78
Bacon and Egg Breakfast Wraps ...116
Cheesesteaks with Sweet Peppers
and Mushrooms 82
Crunchy Egg Salad Sandwiches 89
Curried Chicken Sandwiches 85
egg salad sandwich
flavoring ideas 86
Grilled Chicken and Peach Wraps .87
Grilled Turkey Gyros.......................82
Hot Ham and Pear Melts 79
Italian Meatball Rolls......................84
Mini Grilled
Tomato Sandwiches 127
Pork Tenderloin Sandwiches 80
Salmon Melts..................................89
Shrimp Po'Boys..............................87
Turkey Mango Sandwiches 85
Vegetable Sandwich with
Feta-Yogurt Spread 89

Sauces
Cucumber Sauce...............................80
Cucumber-Yogurt Sauce 83
Simple Cherry Sauce 143

Sausages
BBQ Bean Chili 62
Sausage Skillet 118
Sautéed Chicken Breasts with
Simple Chive Sauce................. 19

Scallops
Ginger-Sesame Scallop Soup 75
Pan-Seared Scallops with Tomato,
Olives, and Fresh Basil 34
Seafood Stew with
Toasted Baguette Slices 74
Seafood Stew with
Toasted Baguette Slices 74
Seared Tuna with Fennel Salad.........56

Shellfish. *See also* **Shrimp**
Gazpacho Crab and Pasta Salad 56
Ginger-Sesame Scallop Soup 75
Lobster Mac and Cheese Casserole34
Pan-Seared Scallops with Tomato,
Olives, and Fresh Basil 34
Seafood Stew with
Toasted Baguette Slices 74

Shrimp
Citrus Salad with Shrimp 106
Grilled Shrimp Salad with
Creamy Garlic Dressing............54
Seafood Stew with
Toasted Baguette Slices 74
Shrimp Kabobs with
Lemon Marinade 33
Shrimp Po'Boys..............................87
Shrimp with
Curried Lime Carrots 33

Slaws
Broccoli Slaw 80
Jicama Radish Slaw 103
Snickerdoodle Crescent Rolls 109

Soups. *See also* **Chili; Stews**
Beer Pork Soup 65
Cheeseburger Soup.........................66
Chicken Parmesan Soup.................69
Cream of Chicken and Rice
Florentine..................................68
Dilled Salmon and
Asparagus Soup.........................74
Ginger-Sesame Scallop Soup 75
Indonesian Chicken and Soba
Noodle Soup 69
Miso Soup with Pork
and Edamame............................64
Pasta e Fagioli.................................59
Pork Picadillo Soup.........................65
Roasted Corn and
Poblano Chowder 73
Spicy Broccoli and Bean Soup.........72
Strawberry-Lemon Thyme Soup ...71
tips for freezing...............................67
Turkey Meatball Soup......................61
Vegetable Garden Soup
with Turkey 61
Wild Mushroom and Leek Soup 72

Spanish-Style Rice.................................97
Spiced Bulgur with Beef and Mango . 10
Spicy Broccoli and Bean Soup............72
Spicy Pork Tenderloin Green Chili.....63
Spicy Tomato Salsa 123

Spinach
Breakfast Lasagna Rolls 115
Cream of Chicken and
Rice Florentine 68
Grilled Pork and Peach Salad 47
Orange and Fennel Chicken Salad.44
Panzanella Salad with a Twist......100
Peach and Spinach Salad
with Feta 103
Pork with Fresh Corn Salad............48
Turkey and Mango Salad with
Chutney Vinaigrette.................41
Turkey Spinach Salad with Beets...42
Vegetable Sandwiches with
Feta-Yogurt Spread 89

Squash. *See* Pumpkin; Zucchini
Stews. *See also* Chili
Lamb and Chickpea Stew 66
Ratatouille Stew................................71
Seafood Stew with
Toasted Baguette Slices 74

Strawberries
Double Berry Pie Squares 151
Fruit Skewers with
Goat Cheese Dip 103
Milk Chocolate-Strawberry
Ice Cream 152
Strawberry-Lemon Thyme Soup ...71
Wonton Dessert Stacks.................138
Stuffed Zucchini with Black Beans,
Corn, and Poblano Peppers.....39
Sweet and Spicy Wasabi
Snack Mix 130
Sweet Asian Beef Stir-Fry.....................8

Sweet potatoes
Jerk Braised Chicken Thighs with
Sweet Potatoes...........................19
Two-Tone Potato Salad 98

T
Tacos, Homemade Walking................26
Taco Salad, Easy....................................53
Tandoori-Style Chicken Kabobs 24
Tangy Tomato and
Goat Cheese Dip 126

Tarts
Banana Cream Pie Tartlets............148
Country-Style Peach-Plum Tart ...148
Tex-Mex Bean Tostadas......................36
Thai Fruit Skewers 128
Thin and Crispy Fruit Pizza 127

Tofu
Breakfast Pita Pizza.........................119
Spicy Broccoli and Bean Soup.........72

Tomatillos
Roasted Corn and
Poblano Chowder 73
Spicy Pork Tenderloin Green Chili.63

Tomatoes
Avocado BLT Sandwiches 78
Baked Eggs with Tomato Topper..112
BLT Cups...122
Mini Grilled Tomato Sandwiches 127
Pan-Seared Scallops with Tomato,
Olives, and Fresh Basil..............34
Pizza Lettuce Cups 124
Roasted Tomato and Asparagus
Crustless Quiche 115
Roasted Tomato and
Mushroom Pasta Salad 57
Spicy Tomato Salsa 123
Tangy Tomato and
Goat Cheese Dip 126

Tortillas
Asian Pork Quesadillas 78
Bacon and Egg Breakfast Wraps ...116
Easy Taco Salad..................................53
Grilled Chicken and Peach Wraps .87
Homemade Walking Tacos 26
Huevos Rancheros
Breakfast Nachos 116
Pumpkin, Bean, and
Chicken Enchiladas 20
Tex-Mex Bean Tostadas 36
Turkey Chopped Salad with
Orange-Poppy Seed Dressing..42
Tostadas, Tex-Mex Bean 36
Trail Mix Balls 136

Tuna
Asian-Style Tuna Kabobs.................30
Seared Tuna with Fennel Salad......56
Tuna and Noodles 30

Turkey. *See also* Sausages; Turkey bacon
Barbecue Glazed Turkey 26
Grilled Turkey Gyros.........................82
Homemade Walking Tacos 26
Italian Meatball Rolls.......................84
Tandoori-Style Chicken Kabobs.....24
Turkey and Mango Salad with
Chutney Vinaigrette.................41
Turkey Chipotle Chili.......................62
Turkey Chopped Salad with
Orange-Poppy Seed Dressing..42
Turkey Mango Sandwiches 85
Turkey Meatball Soup.......................61
Turkey Spinach Salad with Beets...42
Vegetable Garden Soup
with Turkey 61

Turkey bacon
BLT Cups..122
Broccolini with Bacon and Feta......92
Two-Tone Potato Salad.........................98

U–V
Upside-Down Orange Carrot Cake 140
Vegetables. *See also specific* vegetables
Barley-Vegetable Pilaf......................95
Lentil and Veggie Shepherd's Pie ...38
Quick Sautéed Vegetables 94
simple side dish ideas 35
Vegetable Garden Soup
with Turkey 61
Vegetable Sandwiches with Feta-
Yogurt Spread 89
Veggie-Topped Rye Crisps.............121

W–Z
Warm Chicken and New Potato Salad 43
Wild Mushroom and Leek Soup..........72
Wonton Dessert Stacks.......................138

Yogurt
Cucumber-Yogurt Sauce 83
Feta-Yogurt Spread............................89
Granola-Topped Caramel Fruit
Dip 127
Honey-Orange Dipping Sauce.......128
Key Lime Pie 147
Orange Swirled Cheesecake 144
Peach-Blueberry Parfaits 107
stir-ins...128
Wonton Dessert Stacks 138

Zucchini
Mole-Style Pork and Tamale Pie.....14
Pork Picadillo Soup..........................65
Quick Sautéed Vegetables 94
Ratatouille Stew................................71
Stuffed Zucchini with Black Beans,
Corn, and Poblano Peppers 39

metric information

The charts on this page provide a guide for converting measurements from the U.S. customary system, which is used throughout this book, to the metric system.

Product Differences

Most of the ingredients called for in the recipes in this book are available in most countries. However, some are known by different names. Here are some common American ingredients and their possible counterparts:

* All-purpose flour is enriched, bleached or unbleached white household flour. When self-rising flour is used in place of all-purpose flour in a recipe that calls for leavening, omit the leavening agent (baking soda or baking powder) and salt.
* Baking soda is bicarbonate of soda.
* Cornstarch is cornflour.
* Golden raisins are sultanas.
* Light-colored corn syrup is golden syrup.
* Powdered sugar is icing sugar.
* Sugar (white) is granulated, fine granulated, or castor sugar.
* Vanilla or vanilla extract is vanilla essence.

Volume and Weight

The United States traditionally uses cup measures for liquid and solid ingredients. The chart below shows the approximate imperial and metric equivalents. If you are accustomed to weighing solid ingredients, the following approximate equivalents will be helpful.

* 1 cup butter, castor sugar, or rice = 8 ounces = 1/2 pound = 250 grams
* 1 cup flour = 4 ounces = 1/4 pound = 125 grams
* 1 cup icing sugar = 5 ounces = 150 grams

Canadian and U.S. volume for a cup measure is 8 fluid ounces (237 ml), but the standard metric equivalent is 250 ml.

1 British imperial cup is 10 fluid ounces.

In Australia, 1 tablespoon equals 20 ml, and there are 4 teaspoons in the Australian tablespoon.

Spoon measures are used for smaller amounts of ingredients. Although the size of the tablespoon varies slightly in different countries, for practical purposes and for recipes in this book, a straight substitution is all that's necessary. Measurements made using cups or spoons always should be level unless stated otherwise.

Common Weight Range Replacements

Imperial/U.S.	Metric
1/2 ounce	15 g
1 ounce	25 g or 30 g
4 ounces (1/4 pound)	115 g or 125 g
8 ounces (1/2 pound)	225 g or 250 g
16 ounces (1 pound)	450 g or 500 g
1 1/4 pounds	625 g
1 1/2 pounds	750 g
2 pounds or 2 1/4 pounds	1,000 g or 1 Kg

Oven Temperature Equivalents

Fahrenheit Setting	Celsius Setting*	Gas Setting
300°F	150°C	Gas Mark 2 (very low)
325°F	160°C	Gas Mark 3 (low)
350°F	180°C	Gas Mark 4 (moderate)
375°F	190°C	Gas Mark 5 (moderate)
400°F	200°C	Gas Mark 6 (hot)
425°F	220°C	Gas Mark 7 (hot)
450°F	230°C	Gas Mark 8 (very hot)
475°F	240°C	Gas Mark 9 (very hot)
500°F	260°C	Gas Mark 10 (extremely hot)
Broil	Broil	Grill

*Electric and gas ovens may be calibrated using celsius. However, for an electric oven, increase celsius setting 10 to 20 degrees when cooking above 160°C. For convection or forced air ovens (gas or electric), lower the temperature setting 25°F/10°C when cooking at all heat levels.

Baking Pan Sizes

Imperial/U.S.	Metric
9×1 1/2-inch round cake pan	22- or 23×4-cm (1.5 L)
9×1 1/2-inch pie plate	22- or 23×4-cm (1 L)
8×8×2-inch square cake pan	20×5-cm (2 L)
9×9×2-inch square cake pan	22- or 23×4.5-cm (2.5 L)
11×7×1 1/2-inch baking pan	28×17×4-cm (2 L)
2-quart rectangular baking pan	30×19×4.5-cm (3 L)
13×9×2-inch baking pan	34×22×4.5-cm (3.5 L)
15×10×1-inch jelly roll pan	40×25×2-cm
9×5×3-inch loaf pan	23×13×8-cm (2 L)
2-quart casserole	2 L

U.S. / Standard Metric Equivalents

1/8 teaspoon = 0.5 ml	
1/4 teaspoon = 1 ml	
1/2 teaspoon = 2 ml	
1 teaspoon = 5 ml	
1 tablespoon = 15 ml	
2 tablespoons = 25 ml	
1/4 cup = 2 fluid ounces = 50 ml	
1/3 cup = 3 fluid ounces = 75 ml	
1/2 cup = 4 fluid ounces = 125 ml	
2/3 cup = 5 fluid ounces = 150 ml	
3/4 cup = 6 fluid ounces = 175 ml	
1 cup = 8 fluid ounces = 250 ml	
2 cups = 1 pint = 500 ml	
1 quart = 1 litre	